GRILLED

Also available in the Bloomsbury Sigma series:

GRILLED

Turning Adversaries into Allies to Change the Chicken Industry

Leah Garcés

BLOOMSBURY SIGMA
LONDON · OXFORD · NEW YORK · NEW DELHI · SYDNEY

BLOOMSBURY SIGMA
Bloomsbury Publishing Plc
50 Bedford Square, London, WC1B 3DP, UK

BLOOMSBURY, BLOOMSBURY SIGMA and the Bloomsbury Sigma logo
are trademarks of Bloomsbury Publishing Plc

First published in the United Kingdom in 2019

A catalogue record for this book is available from the British Library

Library of Congress Cataloguing-in-Publication data has been applied for

ISBN: HB: 978-1-4729-6258-4; TPB: 978-1-4729-6260-7;
eBook: 978-1-4729-6259-1

2 4 6 8 10 9 7 5 3 1

Typeset by Deanta Global Publishing Services, Chennai, India
Printed and bound in Great Britain by CPI Group (UK) Ltd,
Croydon CR0 4YY

Bloomsbury Sigma, Book Forty-seven

To find out more about our authors and books visit www.bloomsbury.com
and sign up for our newsletter

Contents

Prologue

M ae Jemison was a NASA astronaut. On September 12, 1992, on board the Space Shuttle *Endeavour*, she became the first African-American woman to travel into space. She said of her achievement, "It's your place in the world; it's your life. Go on and do all you can with it, and make it the life you want to live."

I sometimes take Mae Jemison's words and turn them over in my head, kneading them like dough. As a mother of three, and someone passionate about ending factory farming, I keep them close by to shake off the doubt that comes from time to time.

People who work in social-justice issues often recall a moment when they found their calling. They can pinpoint an event or a person that catapulted them into an irreversible journey. They identify the moment that shoulders got heavy and they couldn't unknow what they had learned. For me, that moment was when I became a mother in 2007.

That day was not just about Ruben being born, but also about me becoming someone different—a mother—and the whole world shifting as a result. The world I lived in, what it offered, how I impacted it, and—especially—my time, meant something very different to me after him. Suddenly, there were very definite limits to time. Not only did working for a cause now mean sacrificing time with my son; I was also thinking of the world I wanted him to grow up in.

By the time I was 30, I had traveled to more than 30 countries, working in animal protection. I had been working for 10 years in the European animal protection movement, first at the nonprofit Compassion in World Farming and then as the Director of Campaigns and Programs at the World Society for the Protection of Animals. From bullfighting in Spain to stray dogs in Thailand, zoos in parts of Asia, working horses in Colombia, dolphins captured in Fiji and shipped alive to dolphinariums in Mexico, bear-bile farming in South

Korea and Vietnam, factory farming in China and Brazil, and whaling in Norway, I had seen it all. Every horrific way in which human beings abuse animals.

So. Much. Suffering.

Having been all over the world and having seen every abuse imaginable to animals, one struck me as the worst. It affects the greatest number of animals, and causes the most suffering and destruction—and almost every person on the planet is involved with it on a daily basis: factory farming. From the European Union to the United States, from Brazil to China, animals are locked in cages, stuffed in barns, commoditized and treated like sacks of potatoes, never to see the light of day until they are sent to their deaths so they can end up on our plates. I wanted it to stop. I didn't want to do anything else with my time anymore, especially now that I was a mother.

It may not be obvious how someone could feel fulfilled by dedicating a life to changing the world for chickens. For me, it is ultimately about the way we relate to animals and to each other—which turned out to be exactly the life I needed to live in order to pursue my dreams for the future world in which my children would grow up.

So, when the lightbulb went off after the birth of my son, I made the decision to move from London, England, to the heart of the factory-farming industry: Georgia, in the southeastern corner of the United States. Georgia produces more chicken than any other state in the country—1.4 billion every year[1]—and is arguably the birthplace of factory farming. If Georgia were a country, it would be right up there with China and Brazil in terms of chicken production. The state nestles among what is known as the "broiler belt"—a row of states that among them raise the majority of the country's meat chickens. "Broiler" is the industry word for a chicken raised for meat. Broilers are usually slaughtered at around just six weeks old.

Shortly after moving to Georgia, I experienced my first sight—the first of many—of the realities of chicken farming in America. It was mid-July, a time of year in Atlanta when the world becomes slow like molasses with the heat. That day my family went to the Braves Stadium to get our fill of summer baseball. We used water-mist fans to cool off, to no avail. My heavily pregnant sister was so hot we had to leave. The heat was dizzying. As we walked through the parking lot, the black tarmac below us sunk and molded under our steps, melted from the 100°+ temperature.

The next day we headed to the mountains northeast of Atlanta to escape the heat. One week each year, my family heads up to Standing Indian campground with a group of my beloved friends to make peace with the world and ourselves. We unplug, unwind, and recharge.

Only about an hour into our journey, the smell hit us like a punch to the gut. We were approaching the pulsing heart of the industry that keeps me up at night, and makes me leap out of bed in the morning. The towns and signs show just how deep rooted is the chicken industry in the region. For example, Jessie Jewell Parkway is named for the man who started the first fully vertically integrated chicken company in the world. Gainesville, Georgia, arguably the birthplace of factory farming, is one of the counties that raises and slaughters most chickens in the country.

Ahead we saw an industrial truck. My then six-year-old asked if there was snow falling off the back of the truck. It was not snow of course, not in that heat, but something fluffy and white was falling out the back of the truck, and that smell was getting stronger as we grew near. Heatwaves were rising off the pavement, creating a mirage effect.

I knew what we were about to see: a truck stacked with cages of chickens headed to slaughter, full from top to bottom, back to front. I didn't know whether to ask my children to cover their eyes or not. It is a question I imagine many residents of Georgia have asked themselves before—do I look away or not? Trucks like these are all too common on the roads of Georgia.

We pulled alongside the truck, and I tried to take in the individual chickens and what they were going through. It was 100°F (37°C) outside. They had never seen sunlight before this day; they had never felt the wind or heard the noise of the road. Now they were stuffed with 10 other birds in crates stacked 8 high and 15 wide. Some were panting; some were contorted, their legs, wings, necks, squeezed or trapped in corners of the crates. The feathers my son had innocently taken for snow were whipping off the truck, littering the road, leaving a trail softly floating in the air, as if in slow motion. The birds were exhausted. Even from the car, you could see they were done with this life. They could not live another day even if they were allowed to. Their bodies were like balloons with toothpicks for legs sticking out beneath. Most had large patches of feathers missing from their chests or bottoms. They were babies, just six weeks old despite their oversized bodies, but they couldn't have survived much longer. This is likely the only time most Americans can see these birds alive: the rest of the time they live behind closed doors, deliberately kept out of sight and out of mind.

As I scanned the truck, one bird caught my eye. She had somehow found a steady position in the crate. She looked straight ahead. This was her last day, but I thought she might be thinking, "At least it's over now."

My younger son broke the spell, saying something about how sad the chickens looked. At that moment, I couldn't think of what to say to him to explain why they were there or why they looked like that. We drove alongside as the truck slowed down for an exit which inevitably brought the chickens to their end, along with hundreds of thousands of other birds that day at just a single plant. Across the country, 287 chickens are killed every second: 287 killed, in the time it takes to read the figure "287."[2]

Whether fried, rotisserie, or roasted; whether as wings, tenders, or nuggets; chicken is America's favorite protein. As individuals, chickens now vastly outnumber people: nine billion are raised and slaughtered every year within our borders alone.[3]

When you check beneath the hood of chicken packages boasting labels like "all-natural," all too often you'll find a uniform factory-produced product: the chicken in our supermarkets, restaurants, and cafeterias is nearly always all the same. Raised in massive warehouses mostly situated in lower-income rural areas, these billions of birds are hidden out of sight from most Americans. The birds are virtually all one of two specific genetic breeds, selected to grow very large very fast; they are virtually all the exact same number of days old when slaughtered; and they are virtually all killed in the same way.

On Super Bowl Sunday, Americans eat 1.3 billion chicken wings[4], enough for every man, woman, and child in the country to have four wings (from two birds). The National Chicken Council proudly reports,[5] "If the wings were laid end-to-end they would circle the circumference of the Earth—more than twice—a distance that would reach approximately a quarter of the way to the moon." That is on a single day. Americans' consumption of pork and beef has been steadily declining[6], but our chicken consumption has risen almost every year since 1965. In 2017, more chickens were raised in the United States than ever before: more than 9 billion animals in total.[7] When it comes to chicken, we are on autopilot, incorporating it as our number-one protein source into our daily meals. Animal products account for more than half of the value of all U.S. agricultural products[8], but chicken is at the top of the pile. Americans eat more chicken than any other protein—more than 90 pounds (40kg) per capita per year[9]. That means each person is eating about 25 individual chickens per year. In terms of money, chicken is the cheapest source of protein in the country—but in other terms, it comes at a steep cost: diseased meat, farmers treated like indentured servants, and cruelty to animals, to name a few of its side effects.

It is impossible to grasp the scale of this abuse, given that most Americans will never see a chicken on a factory farm, where the majority of the animals are raised behind closed doors, out of sight, out of mind. In fact, more than 90 per cent of all factory-farmed animals are chickens. Egg-laying hens, beef cattle, dairy cattle, and pigs combined don't even come close to the number of chickens raised and slaughtered each year in the United States.

I know most people do not love and respect poultry the way I do. I am the odd duck. I had the great and rare privilege in my childhood of watching wild ducks hatch eggs in my backyard over many years. This gave me an empathy for poultry that most people do not have. I had a front-row seat to their private lives, their struggles, their motivations and desires. Chickens, like fish and crustaceans, are often harder to empathize with than other animals because they do not share our facial expressions or vocalizations. But, like us, ducks, chickens, and turkeys experience joy, fear, sadness, curiosity, and even pride. Day-old chicks are capable[10] of abstract thought and can count. Yet their needs and wants are completely disregarded in the massive factory-farming system that profits off their deaths.

I started writing this book because I wanted people to care more about chickens. I wanted people to consider the sentient creatures that ended up at the end of their forks. But I completed this book also wanting people to consider the sentient being across the table from them—the human being staring them in the eyes. I learned that solving difficult problems is always about connecting with people. I went from being someone who hated chicken farmers to someone who was finding a way to stand shoulder to shoulder with them. Connection requires vulnerability and risks. Connecting with these people pushed me to my limits of comfort. It requires getting comfortable with being uncomfortable.

In the years after my move to Georgia, I would meet individuals both inside and outside of agricultural companies who would work to radically transform the chicken industry. Jointly, they would create a tidal wave in the market and do what many people said many times was impossible—improve the lives of these animals.

In working on this issue, I have inevitably become a character in the story of the enormous shift taking place in the chicken industry. Along the way, I spoke with food scientists creating plant-based meat that tastes just like chicken. I shared the stage with the CEO of one of the world's largest chicken producers. And most surprisingly, I befriended and partnered with whistleblowing factory farmers who risked everything to tell the truth about how consumers were being lied to about the realities of factory farming. As an animal activist, trying to befriend and gain the trust of factory farmers put me in unfamiliar territory. I realized that some farmers hated factory farming every bit as much as I did, but were trapped by debt, unable to escape. A few strong individuals with nothing to gain and everything to lose were brave enough to speak up and allow cameras into their houses and farms to bring the truth to Americans. The videos they made were seen by millions. As awareness grew, the entire animal protection movement came to focus on overhauling the very worst of America's innovations: chicken factory farming.

We began to find ourselves sitting across the table from the biggest industry players in the world, the Goliaths to our David. Many times I felt conflicted and uncomfortable as I sat with the biggest companies in the world and worked cooperatively for incremental, though meaningful, improvements. The idealist in me wanted more. I wanted bigger changes, and ideally someday a world without slaughterhouses at all. But I know that progress is made one step at a time. Every step forward was one step closer to the world I wanted my children to grow up in. While it was out of my comfort zone, the policies achieved in partnership with these companies had the potential to improve the lives of hundreds of millions of animals every year.

The scale of the problem is massive—it reaches into the homes and onto the plates of nearly every American. I set out to shine a light onto one of America's darkest food secrets, and to work for a better way. But instead of just exposing injustice, I bore witness to something I never expected—that I would be working with once sworn enemies toward a common goal.

When the meat industry, in particular the chicken industry, found itself in an existential crisis—exposed for what it was,

an inefficient, unsafe, cruel protein-production machine—
the most remarkable innovations started to emerge. This
is the story of how protein production is shifting from
destroying the planet to saving it, from raising animals in
dark and dirty warehouses to creating meat in sterile labs in
Silicon Valley and from plants. This is the surprising story of
how it is happening.

Today, the same inventive spirit that created the cruel and
destructive system of factory farming is helping to unmake it.
Everyday we get a step closer to changing the way animals are
treated in our food and farming system in the United States.

The problems are not black and white. The solutions and
the heroes will not be the ones we expected.

We are seeing the very first signs that major meat companies
are remaking themselves by investing in plant-based protein
companies and "clean meat" technology—growing real meat
using only the cells of animals. The companies that produce
the factory-farmed meat most of us eat are betting that factory
farming may be going the way of the gaslight and the horse
and buggy, transformed by innovation that could change our
futures forever. The massive chicken industry, and the wider
meat industry, are on the brink of radical change. This change
will affect every single one of us, no matter what we like to
eat for dinner.

This is the story of what happens when we cross enemy lines
to look for solutions. It's the story of giving in to discomfort
for the sake of progress. It's the story of the power of human
connection, and what happens when we practice empathy
toward our enemies.

CHAPTER ONE

The Determined Mother Duck

I spent my early childhood in the swamps of central Florida. My neighborhood backed up into Wekiva Springs, a state park lined with turtles and alligators sunning themselves. To this day, it remains one of the only places I know I can always find peace.

When I looked out from the glass sliding doors of my home, my heart would ache with a need to be inside that world. Cypress trees dipped their branches. Spanish moss hung like drapes. The place hummed with the wild. My mother could not keep me from exploring the backyard canal, catching tadpoles, baby turtles, and lizards, chasing dragonflies, picking flowers, eating terribly sour wild oranges. I was deeply curious about everything that swam, crept, crawled, and flew through this world. I collected tadpoles whose legs had started to grow and wondered exactly *when did they know* it was the right time to emerge, to change, to move from water to land. The hummingbirds and falcons, the white ibis and blue herons, they all made for a prehistoric, magical childhood landscape.

After a heavy downpour, the tiniest of frogs would emerge from what would seem to me like thin air and hop around inside our screened-in porch. I would put them in a bucket and try to catch gnats (known as "no-see-ems" because, well, you can't see them) to feed them, letting the frogs back into the swamp after a while. Once I caught a larger frog, convinced she was the mother of all the small frogs. I was so pleased with myself, uniting mother and babies. I was horrified when within seconds she started to snap up the little ones into her mouth. I had inadvertently provided dinner and death in one poor decision! My mother said I came in screaming that the mama frog was eating her babies. I was inconsolable for hours.

It was their mothering instincts that first drew me to the ducks. They were my great love and fascination of these years. Some of my earliest memories are of these ducks, who were mighty characters. They had drama, relationships, humor, even pride. I believed all animals had their own secret complex language; we just weren't smart enough or on the right frequency to understand them. When my dog Buster whined, I'd squint my eyes and push my neck forward and concentrate. I imagined myself the Nobel prize-winning genius who would break the code.

My mother was very proud of her flower beds, which lined the screened porch with impatiens of fuchsia, orange, purple, and white that grew as high as a five year's old chest. Dense and vibrant mini-forests of color, they proved a favorite place for a nest for the Muscovy ducks in our backyard and canals. A few times a year, a mother duck would work her way through the flowers. My mother would allow only one thing to disturb her flowers—the drive of another mother, looking for the safest place to lay her eggs. The mother duck would work and work and work on a nest, flattening parts of the flowers to make a soft floor, collecting materials from our backyard or the swamp. I would lie on my belly watching her from inside the screen, holding my breath, hoping she would not mind my intrusion. She paid me no mind. She was focused, relentless, determined. Years later, when I became a mother, I would discover the same qualities.

By the time I was seven, I knew the pattern well. The nest building was just the beginning. The laying of eggs was labored activity. And like a tadpole knowing when to emerge from the swamp as a frog, the mother duck just knew when it was time to lay her eggs.

It's no wonder that ducks and chickens are depicted in children's literature as strong maternal characters. A study by Dr Joanne Edgar of the University of Bristol College of Veterinary Science found that chickens are capable of empathy—"the ability to know another's pain"—a characteristic once thought to be human alone. Edgar blew puffs of air at the baby chicks, and measured the response of the mother. The puffs of air caused distress in the chicks—and also in their mothers. The mothers were easily able to anticipate and mirror the distress of their chicks.

The Telegraph[1] summarized the results: "The hens' heart rate increased, their eye temperature lowered—a recognized stress sign—and they became increasingly alert. Levels of preening were reduced, and the hens made more clucking noises directed at their chicks." Edgar was clear about the implications of her research: "We found that adult female birds possess at least one of the essential underpinning attributes of 'empathy', the ability to be affected by, and share, the emotional state of another."

When the study came out in 2015, I excitedly told my mother about it. She thought it was blatantly obvious that a mother duck or chicken could be empathetic. "Of course they are. Aren't they all mothers?" she said.

Of course, chickens raised for meat in commercial settings encounter others in distress on a regular basis. In chicken factory farms, it is not uncommon to find a chicken that can no longer walk (at 40 days of age, 26.7 per cent of chickens have difficulty walking and 3.3 per cent cannot walk at all[2]), having collapsed under the weight of her own overly large body due to unnaturally rapid growth. Given that chickens are empathetic, one can only imagine the distress not just for that collapsed bird, but also for her flockmates.

For some reason, most people believe chickens are stupid. I loved Disney's Moana for its depiction of an empowered young girl following her dreams, persevering, and being brave beyond her years. My husband Ben and I have always tried to teach our daughter Andrea that a princess is powerful, intelligent, and not afraid of anything. I loved seeing Disney create a princess who was more than just a damsel in distress.

But the character of Hei Hei the chicken, Moana's accidental companion throughout her journey, was a perfect example of popular beliefs about chickens' intelligence. Hei Hei is cross-eyed and simple-minded. He pecks at anything and struts in any direction, even right off a boat. Moana still loves him, and he survives in spite of the series of calamities he gets himself into. But I can't help but be disappointed that chickens remain a subject of mockery for their perceived stupidity. This is factually incorrect.

Dr Lori Marino is the founder and executive director of The Kimmela Center for Animal Advocacy. She was formerly a senior lecturer at Emory University for 19 years and faculty affiliate at the Emory Center for Ethics. After a thorough review of literature regarding cognition in chickens, Marino said: "My overall conclusion is that chickens are just as cognitively, emotionally, and socially complex as most other birds and mammals in many areas, and that there is a need for further noninvasive comparative behavioral research with chickens as well as a re-framing of current views about their intelligence."[3] In other words, chickens are smarter than we think—and it's time we realized it.

Chickens, in fact, are amazing. They can see colors we cannot see.[4] They can hear sounds at frequencies we cannot hear.[5] They have visual perception that we will never have, and perhaps will never be able to conceive of. They have the ability to see both far away and up close at the same time.[6]

Studies with day-old chicks have shown they are capable of understanding basic math concepts such as ordinality, or putting groups of things in order of highest to lowest or vice versa.[7] This is certainly more than my children were capable of in their first years of life, let alone the first days. A pivotal paper published in Science in 2015 concluded that "number-space mapping in the newborn chick resembles humans' mental number line."[8] This means a newborn can essentially count, can understand that two comes before three and three before four in terms of size. They can understand that four is less than six and six is more than five. As with so many species, our perception of chickens is only as good as our scientific tests of them—and we may not even be using the right tools to understand exactly how smart they are.

Frans de Waal is a Dutch primatologist and ethologist, and a longtime resident of Atlanta. He is the Charles Howard Candler Professor of Primate Behavior in the Emory

University psychology department in Atlanta, Georgia; director of the Living Links Center at the Yerkes National Primate Research Center; and author of some fascinating books, including *Chimpanzee Politics* and the *Bonobo and the Atheist*. De Waal has used behavioral and psychological animal science to challenge our rather limited and egotistical view of ourselves as the only truly intelligent species.

I took my eldest son Ruben to see de Waal at the Decatur Book Festival in August 2016, speaking about his book *Are We Smart Enough to Know How Smart Animals Are?* Between his Dutch accent and his comical animal videos, his presentation was enthralling to Ruben—full of colorful stories about animals' intelligence, morality, and complex political relationships.

De Waal argues that we might not know how to really understand another animal's intelligence. The only way to do that would be to try to understand a species' intelligence within its own context, or *umwelt*: the animal's "self-centered subjective world, which represents only a small tranche of all available worlds."[9] To understand other species—their cognitive abilities and their sentience—we have to see the world through their eyes.

I've tried to imagine what it would be like to see out of the eyes of a chicken, to feel like a chicken. To joyously shovel my feathers in the dirt and puff up my back as I bathe in a cloud of dust. To be able to see the smallest bug from far away, barely detectable in the blades of grass, and to move so quickly that the bug doesn't stand a chance. The sharpness and depth of that sort of vision baffles me; I can't even find my keys most mornings. Perhaps most astounding of all is that chickens have a whole other sensory capacity we lack: they can orient themselves by using Earth's magnetic fields.[10] This seems supernatural to me.

Sometimes as a small child I would catch the mother duck laying her eggs in my backyard—the quiet and steadfast pushing from under the tail feather. Sometimes I would miss it altogether and find her one day, just sitting on a clutch of eggs ... her eggs.

My own mother was very admiring of the determined activities of the mother duck. She'd go on long monologues about how the duck was selfless, determined, and patient; how "mother nature" made animals natural caregivers, better than most humans. The duck would sit and sit and sit, doing nothing all day but sitting and caring for those eggs, warming them under her belly, waiting.

I would catch my mother sipping her tea—always on a saucer, the only proper way to drink tea she'd say—stirring it, clicking her spoon against the cup, quietly admiring the mother duck and her sacrifice. I thought my mother was contemplating her own choices, taking comfort in knowing that the mother duck—driven by her nature, her genetics, her core being—was doing the only thing she knew to do: laying eggs in a nest and focusing relentlessly on ensuring the wellbeing of her babies. Perhaps the duck's example helped my mother feel that her own choices were only right and natural.

Of course, occasionally the mother duck would have to get up from the nest to eat and stretch her legs, amongst other business. Ducks are clean and careful creatures. They preen, and they won't defecate in the nest. But when it came time to watch her eggs, that was the sole purpose of the mother duck's being.

Occasionally a mother duck would lay her eggs outside the warmer season, in the winter. Florida is mostly mild, but there are the occasional cold snaps when temperatures can get down into the 30s and 40s (0–10°C). When that happened, my mother took it upon herself be an extra caregiver in the nest. It was almost as if my mother and the ducks had an agreement. In winter, the ducks would place their nest directly under the dryer vent, where warm air would gently blow on it whenever the dryer was on. My mother worried when the mother duck went out into the canal. When the mother duck left the nest, my mom would be watching, and she'd turn on the dryer, wet clothes or not, to keep those eggs warm while the mother was away. I can remember at least one occasion when my dad was reviewing the heating and electricity bill, mystified as to why in the world it was so high. My mom revealed nothing of her duck-egg-warming activities.

Mind you, my dad had his own soft spot for the ducks. He took it upon himself to watch over the ducklings after they'd hatched, when they went for their first journey to the canal. It was an anxious day when the mother duck decided it was time for the ducklings to go out into the world for the first time. Always at dawn, she'd give a call and off they'd go, following her in a line to the canal waterfront—a canal full of alligators and otters and turtles, to whom a duckling makes a very tasty snack. This caused no end of distress for my dad, who would jump up from the breakfast table upon seeing the determined mother head out. In his suit and tie, with a small hand-net in one hand, he'd get into our metal canoe and follow the mother and ducklings at a safe distance. If he felt one of the ducklings had fallen too far behind, he would scoop the baby up in a net, careful not to taint her with his smell, and place her in the bottom of the canoe. The chick would confusedly peep around. Dad would continue following until the baby was safely returned to her brothers and sisters, sometimes not satisfied until they were all back on land, back in the nest.

The day the eggs hatched was always a family occasion for us. Someone would see the first crack on the first egg, and it would be breaking news in my household. We'd see a beak, then wet feathers, then a small, weak, and floppy chick would emerge. Sometimes a leg would come out before the rest of the body, which my brother and I found hilarious. The mother would sit, get up, check, sit again, anxiously watching her babies emerge. So would we. We'd have dinner on the porch on those days, to keep up with the events, to count how many were out, how many we thought were boys or girls. Sometimes there'd be an egg that didn't hatch. The mother would study this last egg. She wouldn't remove it. She'd still sit, holding onto hope, well after the others were waddling out of the nest.

The swamps of Florida are a dangerous place to be a duck, and more than once I found this out the hard way. Once a mother duck was confronted by a hungry raccoon who wanted to eat her eggs. My mother talks about a gallant battle: the mother drew the raccoon out and sacrificed her life when it broke her neck. At the side of our house, my mother found a mess of feathers and blood. My mother talks about this event to this day as deeply traumatic, crinkles her nose when I mention the word raccoon. She remained practical: raccoons are predators, and they need to eat. She just didn't have to like it.

When that mother duck died, we were presented with a serious responsibility—the now-abandoned eggs. Left alone, not only would they not receive the constant incubating heat of their mother, but they'd be easy prey for raccoons or snakes. We decided there was only one answer: we'd have to hatch them ourselves. This was before the days ot the internet and Google search, and our local library left much to be desired. Still, we felt it was something we could take on—hadn't we watched dozens upon dozens of eggs hatch over the years?

My dad set up what we thought was a workable artificial incubator on his workbench in the garage. We wrapped the eggs in newspaper, and used the workbench light above the eggs to produce a warm heat. We'd turn the eggs a few times a day, but otherwise we just waited and waited. I'd pick them up and hold them to the light to see if I could make out anything alive inside, moving. I'd hold my ear to the shells. Never had I had such access. I'd try to think what did the mother do. How could we replicate her constant, instinctive care?

The eggs never hatched. It's impossible to know why, but several days after the point when they should have hatched, they started to smell rotten. Despite our efforts, we could not replicate the mother duck. Her death had meant the end of her eggs, too. This was a hard lesson for me, but one that prepared me to be more sympathetic to those I would later try to convince to change in the poultry industry. Anyone can end up on the wrong path, despite the best of intentions.

That early empathetic connection with the ducks created a foundation of compassion for animals that led me to my current career. When I saw animals in distress, I felt called to do something. Any animals. Many people have a hard time being empathetic with non-mammalian species. Birds are so different from us, but they are every bit as curious, driven, and capable of joy, fear, and sadness as the dogs and cats who share our homes.

For a long time, the study of animal emotions was only based on measuring negative emotions: fear, pain, and suffering. We now know, thanks to the works of scientists like Jonathan Balcombe, a renowned ethologist and the author of *Pleasurable Kingdom*, that all animals, including chickens, can experience pleasure.[11] They can be happy. That's easy to see when a dog bounds toward us when we get home from work, but it is more difficult to accept that a chicken can feel happiness, too.

The domestic chicken (*Gallus gallus domesticus*) evolved from the red jungle fowl (*Gallus gallus*). Today's domestic chickens retain the needs and wants they and their ancestors had for millennia. They want and need to do chicken things: scratch, peck, forage, perch, and nest.

A recent paper stresses that it is necessary not only to minimize negative experiences for animals on farms, but also "to provide the animals with opportunities to have positive experiences." Such experiences can arise "when animals are kept with congenial others in spacious, stimulus-rich and safe environments which provide opportunities for them to engage in behaviors they find rewarding. These behaviors may include environment-focused exploration and food acquisition activities as well as animal-to-animal interactive activities, all of which can generate various forms of comfort, pleasure, interest, confidence and a sense of control."[12]

That may seem like a tall order for a working farm, but Richie Hardy doesn't find it difficult at all to imagine that chickens can be joyful. He is a long-time friend and fellow animal advocate, and he and his partner Pru rescue chickens. Although we live 5,000 miles apart, thanks to Instagram I'm a regular visitor to his backyard gals. In one video, they are bounding around after him, excited he's arrived, no different from frolicking puppies. In fact, when I first watched the video, I thought that is what they were—happy, energetic puppies. It's impossible to see these chickens and argue they aren't feeling joy. I can't "heart" this video enough.[13]

For most people, chickens' difference from us makes it easy to disregard their emotional needs. The birds don't voice their fear or excitement, and nor are their faces capable of expressing what they are feeling. It is easier for us to look away.

In my childhood, I had the great privilege of being inside those ducks' lives, seeing their secret struggles. Having spent so much time with them, I feel instinctively that ducks deserve a good life, just as much as my pet dog does. I know the private life of the mother duck. And because of this, I know there is also a private life behind the eyes of every chicken.

When I was 11, the family moved from Florida to Madrid, Spain. We moved back when I was 17—and there were no more ducks. Not one. It took me a few weeks to realize this. One day, when we were settled back into the house where I'd grown up, I was walking barefoot through the thick blades of St. Augustine grass, looking around expectantly. I realized that I was looking for the ducks. I panicked when I realized they weren't there. The canal that had once flowed clear now looked like pea soup. The surface was covered with a thick layer of algae. It smelled rotten.

In the years we had been gone, landscaped lawns had become far more popular, and maintaining them meant regular spraying with chemicals to keep out the weeds. These chemicals ran down the lawns and into the canal, which ran into Wekiva State Park. In addition, a water-treatment plant had opened upstream. The result was a toxic amount of nitrogen and phosphorous, which led to an explosion of algae. The algae choked out oxygen, and the possibility for a whole chain of life—fish, plants, and birds.

The ducks must have fled this toxic disaster.

It took more than a decade for the county to get the balance back again and clear the water of that green muck, but the ducks never came back. While I deeply missed seeing them every day, I'm glad they had the option to escape. They left when their home had become too dirty and inhospitable. They chose to go because it was no longer tolerable or safe for them and their families—the families I had watched grow up, that had filled me with a deep appreciation for animals as sentient beings with needs and wants.

I would remember my ducks the first time I stepped into a chicken factory farm nearly two decades later. They had fled something as simple as an algal bloom in my backyard. But these chickens, stuffed wall to wall, lying in their own feces, panting through the ammonia-laden air, could not make such a choice. They could not escape.

When I was an adult, my mother made a confession. She told me that after my brother, my sister, and I were asleep, she would tiptoe into our bedroom, and whisper in our ears. To each of us, she would say one phrase: "You can do anything you want if you work hard enough."

Perhaps because of my early years with the ducks, I had some extra thought for their *umwelt*, their unique experience of the world. Perhaps because I spent so many days of my childhood on my belly, inches away from a mother duck, staring into her eyes, I can imagine more easily than most what experiencing a factory farm would be like, not for me, but for the birds. I feel deeply what it would be like to be inside those barns, breathing ammonia, sitting on feces, no place to go. I think it would be awful.

But thanks to my mom's subliminal programming, I'm also an incurable optimist. As awful as those farms are, I believed change was possible.

CHAPTER TWO

The Belly of the Beast

I have never been someone who tolerates wasting time. I rush. I leave drawers open and caps half screwed on (much to the annoyance of my husband). I was born three weeks early. I finished school early. Whenever I can get away with it, I go faster. I have the moving violations* to prove it. Some would say I am impatient and reckless. But as my friend Will Harris once told me, "Patience ain't no goddamn virtue."

I've always been in a rush. But when I became a mother, wasting time became especially intolerable. It put everything into sharp, even excruciating, focus. The day Ruben was born, I looked at my newborn son and knew, without a doubt, that 18 years from that moment he would leave. If he was anything like me, he would go to another continent to fully express his freedom. This beautiful, precious boy I grew inside my own body would go. It was natural, inevitable—I couldn't keep him with me any more than I could stop time.

At the end of my first day back at work after his birth, I ran home in my pointy shoes and pencil skirt. I sprinted across puddled streets, down a crowded escalator, and onto the too-slow tube. I fumbled with my keys, pushed open the door, and barged into my north London flat until I had scooped Ruben up into my arms and felt whole again.

When I became pregnant with Asher, time moved even faster. The days shortened and were gobbled up by tasks. Every single moment was accounted for. Each minute needed to be meaningful either for work or for my baby.

---

* Moving violations in the US occurs whenever a traffic law is violated by a vehicle in motion. A fine or warning is issued by the police.

It's no surprise that, by the time I got the call telling me I could start a Compassion in World Farming (CIWF) office in Georgia, I was already living there. I've never been good at waiting for permission. Still, when Philip Lymbery, CEO of CIWF, called me one day in spring 2010 to say he'd found the money for me to start a small US office, I jumped for joy—literally. Baby strapped to me in an Ergo carrier, toddler at my knees, I jumped for joy. All Philip could give me was two days of pay and a laptop, but I didn't care. I would have worked for less. It had been a hard year, moving countries with a baby and toddler. I was more than ready to dig in.

In 2009, I had left my globe-trotting job and gritty London. I'd moved to Georgia seven months pregnant, with a toddler in tow. My husband had been headhunted for a job at the Center for Disease Control, and we decided to take the leap.

I had no job. I did not know a soul. All I knew was that Georgia was in the Deep South—and it was the birthplace of factory farming. Coming from cosmopolitan, liberal London, that was plain scary. It was truly the belly of the beast. But once I got that call from Philip, I realized it was actually a perfect base from which to start fighting this horrific system.

I thought uncovering the realities of chicken farming would be straightforward. I thought there would be transparency. It's our food, for goodness' sake. But the business was far from transparent. Indeed, the truth about what happened on factory farms was well hidden. The first task became not educating people about the facts, but finding out what those facts actually were.

Where Factory Farming Was Born

As I struggled to settle in to my new mission, I could see the scale of the problem all around me—literally. Chicken farming was everywhere in my new home state. Arguably, the model that modern-day chicken farming uses to this day originated in north Georgia in the first half of the 20th century, thanks largely to a man named Jesse Jewell, a feed salesman from Gainesville, Georgia.[1]

During the Great Depression of the 1930s, farmers across the country had become desperate to survive. They had little extra income to spend on purchasing feed or chicks, and no hope of expanding their farming operations. Jewell was running a small family feed business and looking at ways to increase sales when he came up with a novel idea: he started selling baby chicks to Georgia farmers on credit. The farmers raised the chicks and, when they were fully grown, sold them back to Jewell.

Jewell soon had enough farmers producing chickens for him that he was able to invest in his own processing plant and hatchery. He essentially came up with the first form of vertical integration, in which he owned every aspect of the business, from chick to feed to slaughter. The only part he did not own was the infrastructure in which the chickens were raised, which he contracted out. This system—it came to be known as "contract farming"—proved an essential model for the rapid growth of the poultry industry.[2]

In 1939, there were fewer than 60 chicken farms in Hall County, where Gainesville is located, in north Georgia.[3] With the onset of World War II in 1939, the poultry industry in Georgia expanded rapidly. All the chicken processed in north Georgia was reserved by the War Food Administration, creating a guaranteed buyer for the chickens Jewell and others produced. While red meat was rationed, chicken was not, which gave chicken farmers the opportunity to expand and fill the void on American plates.[4] After the war's end in 1945, Jewell's model only became more and more popular. By 1950, Hall County alone had more than 1,000 farms.[5] Jewell's business continued to grow and, by 1954, he had expanded to owning a feed mill and a rendering plant.*

Broiler production in the region increased dramatically between 1947 and 1960, and continued to grow through the

---

* A feed mill is where crops are brought and processed to produce food for farmed animals. Meat **rendering plants** process animal byproduct materials for the production of tallow, grease, and high-protein meat and bone meal.

following decades. Consumer demand kept rising, and production kept pace. These factory farms also became more and more efficient, and competition in the industry resulted in low prices[6]—which in turn kept demand strong. Economists call this a virtuous circle; for the chickens, of course, it was an entirely vicious cycle.

During the 1990s, the number of chicken-producing companies kept decreasing and consolidating. If you wanted to survive, you had to be able to supply large markets with a high volume of birds. Through widespread use of vertical integration and contract farmers, a few companies were able to process a great deal more chickens than had previously been possible. In less than a decade, the number of Georgia chicken farms was reduced by approximately one-half.[7] Today, only a few companies dominate the industry.[8] In 2006, Gold Kist, an Atlanta-based company founded during the Great Depression, merged with Pilgrim's Pride Corporation, which was then bought by JBS to form one of the world's largest meat companies.[9] Other companies in the industry based in Georgia include Cagle's, Fieldale Farms, Claxton, and Mar-Jac. Tyson, Con-Agra, Continental Grain, and Perdue are based in other states.

All of these companies, without exception, use the model Jesse Jewell dreamed up. They are all vertically integrated and continue Jewell's practice of contracting with poultry farms to raise chickens. Contract farming has now been an integral component of the poultry industry for more than 50 years.

The poultry industry makes up the largest segment of Georgia's agriculture. The state's broiler business alone is valued at over $4.25 billion annually, making up nearly half of all of Georgia's $9 billion agriculture cash receipts.[10] Poultry is big business in Georgia.

Along with Jesse Jewell's contract farming model, another defining moment for the chicken industry was the Chicken of Tomorrow contest.[11] In 1948, the Great Atlantic & Pacific Tea Company (A&P), then the largest supermarket chain in the country (and until 1965 the largest retailer of any kind),[12] held a contest to find a breed of chicken that matched a certain profile: bigger breast meat, faster and cheaper to raise. At the time, A&P was every bit as much of an icon as Walmart or Amazon are today.[13] And this was the company that changed the pathway of the American chicken industry forever.

The United States Department of Agriculture (USDA) became an official partner in the contest, in an effort to grow the industry and America's chicken consumption. As Alexis Coe wrote in *Modern Farmer*: "It was an alliance with a specific goal: The 'development of superior meat-type chickens.' The winning chicken would have broader breasts, bigger drumsticks, plumper thighs, and above all, more white meat. And they would grow faster, too, so that the consumer would eventually come to depend on the bird as a reliable kitchen staple."[14]

In 1946, the competition initially included hundreds of farmers from 31-state regional contests. It was so successful that, in 1948, the contest went national, complete with a blonde Chicken of Tomorrow Queen (Nancy McGee of Maryland) and a $10,000 cash prize.[15]

The contest changed the industry forever. Previously, birds had been dual-purposed, grown both for eggs and for meat. The contest marked the moment in which a breed better suited for egg laying and one better suited for meat production became separate concerns. The contest also began the specific selection of chickens for large breast meat.

The breeds that "outperformed" all others—those that gained weight the fastest—came from brothers Kenneth and Charles Vantress from Vantress Hatchery, a company that's still around today. Their company is now called Cobb Vantress. Tyson, the largest chicken company in the world, acquired Vantress in 1974. By 1986, Tyson further consolidated the breeding industry by joining Vantress and Cobb as a Tyson joint venture.[16] The main breed this modern company uses, the Cobb 500, is the dominant breed of bird used globally. It is known as the world's "most efficient" chicken.[17]

The Chicken of Tomorrow contest began a decades-long arms race for a faster-growing, bigger chicken. Over the last 50 years, chicken growth rates have quadrupled in the pursuit of cheaper and cheaper meat.[18] Where once it took a bird 112 days to get to a slaughter weight of 2.5lb (1.1kg), today's birds take only 47 days to get to a slaughter weight of more than double that (6.2lb/2.8kg).[19] But forcing a bird to its genetic maximum, as farmers would later find out, was not without its unintended consequences—and not just for the birds.

The modern chicken

About 10 years before I moved to Georgia in 2003, the animal rights group Compassion Over Killing had produced a video exposé of the biggest farm-animal industry in the country— the factory farming of chickens raised for meat. Until 2014, that remained the last time the public saw in any detail the life of a factory-farmed broiler chicken in the United States.

It is remarkable that an industry so big had managed to remain so secretive. Globally, the world raises and slaughters some 40 billion chickens for meat every year, 9 billion of which live and die in the United States. And 99 per cent of US broiler chickens are raised in barren, windowless, enclosed warehouses

Unfortunately, it is no different for the majority of the 31 million chickens in other parts of the world. From Brazil and China to the United Kingdom, Thailand, South Africa, and Australia, you will find the same fast-growing breed of chicken in the same long warehouses, crammed in, living on litter that is not changed during their entire lives, with little or no enrichments. It is a nightmarish cookie-cutter model of farming that has erupted around the world.

In Brazil, for example, between 1970 and 1991 the poultry industry grew from small backyard farmers to become a multinational mechanized industry that was almost entirely vertically integrated. Originally, major companies gave small family farmers day-old chicks and paid them to raise them. Sadia was one example. The family-owned company employed 14,000 smallholder farmers to raise chickens on their mixed farms, with a clear benefit to those farming families. The chickens were brought back to Sadia, which processed and distributed them to consumers.

This system began to change in early 2000, when I was beginning my career. These family-owned entities were taken over by financial interest groups and foreign companies. Sadia now raised, provided feed for, and processed its own chickens in large production units. Most of the 14,000 mixed farmers who had previously raised chickens for Sadia did not benefit.[20] In 2009, Sadia merged with Perdigão and gave rise to BRF, now one of the largest food companies in the world, further consolidating control over the farms in the hands on one company.

The same model is used from the United States to India. What started as an entrepreneur's effort to make more money in the middle of Georgia during the Depression has spread like an infectious disease around the world.

In the early years of my career, the United Nations predicted that factory farming would become global and first began expressing concerns about the unintended consequences on the environment and local communities and business. The United Nations Food and Agriculture Organization referred to this as "Livestock's Long Shadow," describing the impact "livestock production" would have around the world. I wrote a report called the *Detrimental Impact of Industrial Animal Agriculture* in early 2000 which I presented at the UN Rio +10 conference in South Africa. We held a side event with other nonprofits to express our concern that factory farming was spreading. This terrible idea, this terrible food model, was coming to town and its consequences would be difficult to control.

As I write this book, nearly two decades later, it pains me to see that our prediction was correct—and that so little has been done to stop the industry's spread. Today, more animals are in factory farms than ever before in history. Our work to reverse the impact of this detrimental food system has never been more urgent.

There are international variations—some better and some worse—when it comes to the broiler factory farms. In China and Russia, companies have begun creating multi-story broiler warehouses. Broiler cages are stacked on top of the other to the ceiling, further attempting to maximize the system. In warmer climates with less reliable electricity to guarantee air circulation, such as Brazil, the majority of the chicken warehouses still have natural light and open sides for fresh air. But the birds remain overcrowded and the breeds fast-growing, and there is an active effort to enclose birds in darkened houses.

In the European Union, minimal legislation has been provided for broiler chicken welfare, but there are loopholes. For example, while there are minimum space requirements, farmers can crowd the birds even more if they can justify it and show they have good management practices. Regardless of the legislation, the majority of birds around the EU are raised in windowless houses, with no access to the outdoors or the light of day, using fast-growth breeds that result in many birds having trouble walking.

During my time at World Animal Protection, I saw at first hand how these farms started to take hold around the world in Thailand, Mexico, Brazil, and China. By then, they were already (and remain) the norm in the United Kingdom and Australia. I desperately tried to think of how we could stop the spread of factory farming. I worked to create programs to promote alternatives in Brazil and China, where it was predicted that factory farming would dominate the decades ahead in what was called the "livestock revolution." As such countries rose out of poverty, the theory went, so would their populations demand cheap protein in the form of meat, dairy, and eggs. Factory farming would be there to meet that demand. Under the surface, however, factory farming would also be working to destroy small independent farmers, dump toxins into the environment, and keep animals in increasingly more torturous conditions.

As difficult as it was to watch this happening, to see how factory farming was being welcomed with open arms around the world, my time at World Animal Protection would later give me the perspective I needed to understand the enormity of the task and the urgency of the problem.

In those first months living in Georgia, I took a trip to the north of the state, where the factory farms remained inaccessible to anyone outside the industry. I drove past row upon row of uniform metal warehouses—500 feet (150m) long, 40 feet (12m) wide, and windowless—on otherwise barren properties. What hid behind the walls? All I saw were signs reading "No trespassing" and "No visitors" and warnings about "biosecurity." It was the type of signage you might expect to see at a nuclear-waste site—not at a farm.

In the years ahead, I'd be granted access to these warehouses, but not in the ways I expected. I would see for myself the realities not just for the chickens, but also for the farmers and the companies behind the farms.

As I came to learn, chickens are put into long, windowless structures soon after hatching. What starts off as a seemingly spacious and clean environment—though barren and dimly lit—soon changes. A full 30,000 individual animals defecate in the same enclosed space for 35 to 50 days, depending on the birds' target weight. The chickens get a lot bigger, rapidly growing from the size of your fist to the size of a soccer ball. As they grow, they crowd the space, with each individual only having room equivalent to less than a piece of 8 by 11 inch (20 x 27cm) paper. I learned that inside each of those mysterious warehouses is a sea of chickens from wall to wall, sitting in their own feces, struggling to move, in large part because of genetics that drive them to grow very big, very fast.

Ever since the Chicken of Tomorrow contest, the modern broiler chicken has been unnaturally large and bred to grow at a fast rate. This selective breeding produces serious consequences for the animals' health, including painful leg disorders; skeletal, developmental, and degenerative diseases; heart and lung problems; breathing difficulties; and premature death. The University of Arkansas Division of Agriculture explains the unnaturally fast growth rate as follows: "If you grew as fast as a chicken, you'd weigh 349 pounds [158kg] at age 2."[21] These unnatural, rapidly growing birds are forced to breathe ammonia- and dust-filled air, and have no natural lighting.

While trying to raise a family in Georgia, this became my sole obsession: to shine a light on the darkness within these farms, to bring the truth to the American people and my own friends and family, and to work for a better way. I wanted to see the inside of those warehouses with my own eyes. I wanted to understand the industry that had such a massive presence in my new home state, and in the country as a whole.

The United States still raises the largest number of broiler chickens in the world, followed in descending order by Brazil, the European Union, and China.[22] Almost all farmed animals raised in the United States are in what the government calls "confined animal feeding operations." I call them factory farms. Georgia, where I was now raising my three children, is at the heart of the broiler chicken industry in the United States. About 1.7 billion of these birds are slaughtered every year[23] in Georgia, making up 18 per cent of the nation's production of around 9.2 billion[24] birds. It is the largest chicken-producing state, and nearly all of the chickens raised for meat in Georgia are raised in factory farms.

At any one time, some counties in Georgia, such as Franklin, are home to as many as 20 million chickens being raised solely to end up on people's plates[25], outnumbering people in the county 906 to 1.[26] The public, concentrated around cities such as Atlanta and Savannah, remains largely unaware not only of the industry's prominence, but also of its impact on animal welfare, the environment, communities, and health. It is an industry that intentionally hides itself from plain view.

The number of broiler operations continues to increase in the United States. According to the USDA,[27] from 1997 to 2012 the number of broiler operations increased from 35,500 to 42,200, while the number of broilers housed at any one moment increased from 1.2 billion to 1.5 billion. And that growth is not slowing down. The number of animals kept on one farm keeps getting larger year after year, and the number of actual farms keeps getting smaller.[28] Thanks to Jesse Jewell, the chicken industry is vertically integrated, so that a single company owns everything from the feed to the chicks to the processing plant, and the broiler chicken industry is the most consolidated. The top five largest corporations control

75 per cent of the chicken raised for meat in the US, and the top three companies control 60 per cent of chicken production in the country.[29]

Taking on this massive industry wouldn't be easy—and the law was not on my side. Whereas Europe recognized in law that animals, including farmed animals, are sentient beings back in 1997,* farmed animals are written out of America's Animal Welfare Act (AWA). They are regulated under AWA only when used in biomedical research, testing, teaching, and exhibition. The USDA interprets the act to exclude birds, all cold-blooded animals (such as reptiles and fish), rats and mice bred for research, as well as farmed animals used or intended for use as food or fiber. Few federal-level regulations, apart from those related to food safety, apply to farmed animals.

Attempts to increase federal-level regulations have, for the most part, failed, but there is some federal regulation for farmed animals when it is time for them to die. In 2002, improvements were passed in the Farm Bill to the Humane Method of Slaughter Act (originally created in 1958 and amended in 1978), stating that the act should be fully enforced so that animals are rendered "fully insensible to pain before they are harvested." But there is one catch—the act excludes chickens, fish, rabbits, and a few other animals slaughtered for food. So the large majority of farmed animals remain without protection. It is a challenge to think of how to protect these animals when the law does not apply to them.

Another significant challenge in the United States is figuring out how one would even push for new laws. Government and agribusiness often have close relationships, making it hard to push legislation that would limit the

---

* In 1997 the concept of animal sentience was written into the basic law of the European Union. The legally-binding Protocol annexed to the Treaty of Amsterdam recognizes that animals are "sentient beings," and requires the EU and its Member States to "pay full regard to the welfare requirements of animals."

business of industrial farming. The real problem is money—lobbying and campaign contributions, to be precise.

When Americans think of corporate influence in Washington, DC, their minds usually go to Big Tobacco, Big Pharma, and gun manufacturers. But the food industry also wields outsized influence on Congress and federal agencies. The "food processing and sales industry" makes up one of the largest sectors contributing financially to candidates and their campaigns during elections. That industry includes food retailers and grocery store chains such as Safeway, Kroger, and Publix, as well as meat-processing companies such as Tyson, Hormel, and Smithfield.[30]

Individuals and political action committees associated with the industry gave around $13.9 million in political contributions at the federal level during the 2014 election cycle.[31] The number-three contributor during the 2015/6 cycle was the grocery-store chain Publix, with $957,000 in contributions.[32]

These companies spend even more money on lobbying, especially leading up to major elections. The Grocery Manufacturers Association (GMA) is a trade association that represents the world's largest branded food, beverage, and consumer-product companies. GMA's lobbying expenditures jumped from about $7.3 million in 2011/2 to more than $13 million in 2015/6, the year running up to the presidential election. Tyson Foods, one of the largest producers of poultry in the world, had a lobbying expenditure of around $2 million from 2015/6. The Shineway Group (parent company of Smithfield), the largest producer of pigs in the world, spent $2.8 million in 2015/6. Nestle, the largest purchaser of dairy in the world, spent $5.6 million in the same period.[33]

Among the most notorious lobby groups is the National Chicken Council (NCC), which spent $1.5 million on federal lobbying in 2015. For example, in September of 2017, it petitioned the USDA to make slaughter-line speeds even faster. The line speeds are already too fast—up to 140 birds per minute, which contributes to rough handling by workers trying to grab and shackle birds as quickly as possible, causing countless birds to suffer from botched slaughter as well as increased risks for workers who already have problems with carpal tunnel syndrome. The NCC lobbied to speed the lines even more, which would result in even less time to inspect the birds for signs of contamination. Its petition was just the latest in a long series of attempts by the NCC to minimize regulation of the chicken industry—and will no doubt not be the last.

In October 2016, the administration of President Donald Trump, praised by the NCC, decided to ignore the objections and permit faster line speeds. Plants only needed to receive a government waiver in order to speed up lines up to 175 birds per minute.[34] It was a move that puts the animals, workers, and food safety all at risk in one fell swoop.

In addition to campaign contributions and lobbying, industry and government are also linked by a "revolving door." For example, some 56 per cent of current lobbyists used by the poultry and egg industries have held government positions at one time or another.[35] Needless to say, this level of intimacy between agribusiness and government makes it hard to make progress on farmed-animal welfare legislation when the industry itself is not onboard.

For the most part, the market remains a difficult place for a small independent farmer to compete. As Food and Water Watch have explained:

A few large companies dominate the meat and poultry industries. Their control over these markets allows them to use oppressive contracts to squeeze both small producers and consumers. Chicken processing companies regularly require growers to make costly equipment upgrades, sometimes for little or no reason and often pay growers less for the chickens than what they cost to raise. Companies have retaliated against growers that complain. Growers put up with it because in many parts of the country, there is only one processing company for chickens.[36]

In other words, the chicken industry is massive, secretive, and protected by a host of legal and political obstacles that prevent change. Even if individual farmers did want to make change, the system ensure that they would be almost as powerless as the chickens they're raising. The size and power of the industry essentially means that legislation on farmed animals does not come unless the companies want it.

The Rebel Alliance

I was about to take on one of the most powerful industries on this planet, and all I had on my side was the conviction that I was doing the right thing. For Compassion in World Farming, however, this kind of David-and-Goliath battle was nothing new.

CIWF was started in 1967 by a British dairy farmer named Peter Roberts. Farmers have grit: they work hard, they overcome odds, they are opportunistic yet calculated risk-takers. They are fiercely loyal to their families, neighbors, land, and history. And they keep the rest of us alive—that's useful, too. I have my own garden with five boxes, and year after year I fail miserably to grow much more than a handful of beets, tomatoes, or kale. If I had to grow our food, we would all starve to death. Needless to say, Peter Roberts knew a lot about perseverance.

Peter and his wife, Anna, were unhappy about the way the animal farming industry was consolidating in the 1960s. Farmers like them were being told to get big or get out. But as John Lewis—my formidable Congressman who marched alongside Martin Luther King, Jr—said: "Sometimes you have to do something out of the ordinary. Sometime you have to make a way out of no way." And that's what Peter Roberts did.

Roberts's new way was CIWF. He started making leaflets at his kitchen table, with Anna and their three daughters. He got to know Ruth Harrison, the author of *Animal Machines*, and Peter Singer, the author of *Animal Liberation*, and arguably the most influential living philosopher. Together, they protested against battery cages for hens and veal crates for calves.

Ruth Harrison had published *Animal Machines* in 1964. It was a shocking wake-up call to the United Kingdom, and one that Peter Roberts took to heart. Peter Singer still says her book was one of the reasons he became vegetarian. The book depicted for the first time the dark innards of intensive animal farming, and is largely credited with inspiring the European Convention for the Protection of Animals Kept for Farming Purposes.[4] Inspired by these great thinkers, Roberts's vision was to end factory farming everywhere. That mission still drives CIWF today.

Today, CIWF's team comes from all walks of life, but we are all drawn to that same mission. In 2001, when I first met Philip Lymbery, the man who would eventually approve my request to open a CIWF office in Georgia, he had his own company, Turnstone Consultancy. He created novel campaigns to advocate for better treatment of animals. Most animal activists at the time were talking about the welfare of pigs and calves, but Philip was thinking about an animal not many considered: fish. He was researching the welfare of farmed salmon and trout kept by the thousands in sea cages and pens. In 2002, he released a report titled "In Too Deep," which exposed the need for reform on fish farms. He promoted his report with a stunt at the Scottish Parliament, when he put a celebrity in a bathtub to illustrate how little room salmon—migratory animals that naturally swim as much as 1,000 miles to spawn—get in sea cages. I was greatly impressed by Philip's ability to take something incomprehensible like the space a salmon gets and turn it into something tangible and pressworthy.

Philip grew up more interested in the birds in his back garden than the books in his backpack. He hated school. Every second he got, he was skipping out to explore the woodlands and fields, looking for more interesting ways to learn about the world. When he finished school at 18, he had no interest in college. Why put himself through more schooling, he thought, when he could be out exploring the world?

After a year spent watching wildlife and volunteering on nature reserves, Philip ran out of money and took a design job at a packaging company. In 1990, his opportunity came to find his true calling, when he became Peter's assistant at

CIWF. He'd work in the campaigns team for a decade, quickly being given the title of campaigns director and even marrying Peter's daughter, Helen. Philip developed strategies to ban barren battery cages for laying hens, veal crates for calves, and sow stalls for mother pigs. He'd leave CIWF only briefly, to run his consultancy company and to give bird watching tours a try, and to work for World Animal Protection (previously known as the World Society for the Protection of Animals).

On one of those digressions, while he was heading up campaigns at World Animal Protection, Philip took a gamble and gave me my first campaigning job, as his deputy. Three years later, he returned to CIWF to become the CEO, and I took over his job at World Animal Protection. We continued like that for years, me following slightly behind him, benefiting from the path he cleared ahead.

Once at the helm of CIWF, even though he was no longer my boss, Philip continued to coach me. In the summer of 2009, we met in a coffee shop in Godalming, the small village in southeast England where CIWF is headquartered. I was running a big global team of nearly 80 staff at World Animal Protection. I was also pregnant for the second time, just starting to show.

That day, I showed up with a proposal: CIWF should open a US office. Now that I had kids, I didn't want to waste any time doing anything else except helping farmed animals. As an organization with a mission to end factory farming, I believed CIWF should be where factory farming was born, where more than 9 billion animals are raised and slaughtered every year.

I didn't get an answer for about nine months. There were lots of reasons Philip could say no. There was no money, for one thing. But he was intrigued. And eventually he decided to take a chance and let me try to tackle factory farming from inside the belly of the beast.

Finding the Courage to Leap

Starting that office was a leap of faith both for CIWF and for me. We were both driven by our desire to build a better world. But I know that I couldn't have taken such a leap without the courage and determination I learned from my dad.

In Colombia, my father was constantly getting suspended from school. The nuns regularly called my grandmother to come and collect him. "Mrs. Garces, your son has been naughty again," they'd say.

Maybe he rebelled there because he was privileged, and the road was easy. But when he immigrated to the United States with his four sisters and single mother, he fell from wealth to poverty. The move meant he had to struggle—and it turned out that struggle was what he needed to thrive.

Dad arrived in Miami in summer 1962. As an immigrant, he had to prove himself. He took to walking the streets in search of new friends. Back home, a soccer ball would have done the trick. He kicked a ball down the street, hoping to pick up a game, but he was laughed at. So he put the soccer ball away. He turned to baseball and never looked back.

He graduated from high school early and went to the University of Miami with a fierce determination to succeed. He worked two jobs to pay his way through school. He secured a job as a sales engineer and stayed with the same company for 45 years, climbing his way from the bottom to the top.

I enjoyed all the benefits of Dad's hard work in America, and never lacked for anything I needed. But I still craved struggle. I felt flat without it. Like my father, I could not resist the buzz and purity of hard work once I found it. He used that drive to secure a multimillion-dollar contract. I would use mine to chase the end of factory farming.

Five days a week, my dad was intensely focused on work. But he had one great distraction—sailing. My mom used to call Memories, our 17ft (5.1m) sailboat, his "mistress." The waterways of Florida were his playground. We spent almost every weekend out on the water.

The intercoastal waters gave us access to a world not many could reach, backing up to Cape Canaveral National Seashore and Mosquito Lagoon. These were protected areas, because they surrounded NASA. I had the privilege of watching a dozen or so space shuttle launches from the boat's bow. I explored islands with horseshoe crabs and gopher tortoises. I watched pods of dolphins glide alongside our boat, peering up at us through their curious glass eyes.

Our favorite places to explore were the spoil islands—artificial islands created when earth and sand is dredged up to create a shipping channel and deposited in a heap that becomes an island. There was only one way to get to the spoil islands. If the boat got too close, we'd run aground, so my dad would make us swim. My brother and I would stand on the bow of the boat, the island in sight. The dark and murky waters evoked nightmarish images for me. I was terrified to throw myself to the monsters that lay beneath: bull sharks, jellyfish, crabs, and unknown creatures I imagined lurked there, waiting to pull me down. We never wanted to touch the bottom, even when the water was shallow enough. It was marshy, and you'd sink into the mud, no doubt to touch some sharp, menacing monster hiding there.

My dad's message was clear. He'd quote Roosevelt to us: "The only thing we have to fear is fear itself." He wouldn't even go first. He would give us the opportunity to overcome our fear on our own. He would give us a grand speech about not letting our minds or fears take over our actions, not letting fear stop us from doing what we wanted.

Each time I stood on the edge of the boat, trying to overcome my fears, my mind would run down all the terrible ways my life might end. My brother was particularly terrified of the horseshoe crabs—prehistoric creatures, from the age of the dinosaurs. If your feet mistakenly brushed the bottom, you might be met by the knifelike lance of the horseshoe crab. They were as big as an adult's head. We couldn't think of anything scarier. The mushy sea bottom was hiding these menacing swords, ready to pierce our feet.

I still don't know how I managed to throw myself over the edge—but I always did. I would always jump and swim hard. And when I got to the shore, I would always think, that was not nearly as bad as I had imagined. The things we are afraid of, that make our hearts race, are never as scary as we thought they'd be. In fact, they're usually the things that are most worth the effort. My brother and I explored those islands with a sense of entitlement— we had earned arriving there.

Shonda Rhimes, the titan producer of award-winning series *Scandal, How to get Away with Murder,* and *Grey's Anatomy,* talks in her book *Year of Yes* about a whole year in which she decided to say yes to doing things that made her uncomfortable, that she was afraid of. Each time she'd do a new thing, the next one would get easier, until she became more and more comfortable facing challenges and unknowns.

I've thought about those moments on the boat many times as an adult. Those moments on the edge of the boat trained me to take risks and do things that scare me—like crossing the battle lines to befriend chicken factory farmers.

When I moved to Georgia, I took another leap into the unknown. I found myself in the place that had created a system of cruel efficiency and domination. I was raising my children surrounded in every direction by confined chickens. I did not have to go far to start unpicking the system and meeting its victims, villains, and heroes. Driving to the mountains, to the beach, or to the west, I'd smell or see a chicken farm or truck every time. Chickens were everywhere—but always behind closed doors. This was a place that had kept its dark secrets for far too long.

What surprised me most was that I found that people were ready to talk. They were ready for change. I just had to ask the right questions—and not even too many of them. The people I met were overflowing with deep emotions. They needed to tell their stories of all that had gone wrong. They spilled their stories to me—and so began the great unravelling of the long-held secrets of America's chicken factory farms.

CHAPTER THREE

No Good Choices

"In a time of deceit, telling the truth is a revolutionary act."

— *George Orwell*

It started out as an ordinary shopping trip. It was fall 2012, and I wasn't thinking about animal rights—I was focused on getting the kids out of the car and shuffling them through the parking lot. They were still small enough to fit into the shopping cart. I never shopped with a list or plan. I just rushed down the aisles, letting them remind me of what I didn't have. In went cereal, apples, the usual stuff. As we passed the meat counter, my eyes cruised over the labels. I'm not sure what I was searching for, but I slowed down to see what was on offer.

Glistening packages of pink and brown meats sat under cool air and bright lights. They were tightly wrapped. I could not resist the urge to push on the nearest package with my finger. It was cold and mushy, and when I touched it, clear and red juices moved ever so slightly from one spot to another and back again. I bet if I had turned to see my children, I would have found them staring at me in disbelief, the vegan poking at meat packages. But I was lost in my own world.

This was where America met its meat. Right here, at counters like these across the country. This was as close as most any Americans got to a farm, unless they were a farmer.

I trailed my fingers over the cool packages, scanning the labels, until one made me stop. It looked attractive and trustworthy. It was green, with modern, inviting branding. I leaned in closer. The label said "Simple Truth" and in smaller letters "all natural," "humanely raised," and "cage-free." I wrinkled my brow. "Cage-free?" All broiler chickens in the United States are cage-free. Only egg-laying chickens—hens—are kept in cages. I picked up the package.

I turned it over. I searched and searched for an explanation. I looked at the surrounding, similarly packaged, chicken parts. They all read the same. There was no further explanation of what this meant.

I walked over to the deli counter and asked to speak to the meat manager. "Yes, ma'am, how can I help you?" asked a man wearing an all-white apron with brown stains. Arms crossed, he seemed to be expecting a complaint.

"Well, I saw this label—see here?" I pointed to the curious wording. "Do you know what it means? Do you know where this chicken comes from?"

He did not know. He could not answer. No matter how I asked, he didn't know what it meant. Were the birds kept in a barn, or did they have access to pasture? Did they have more space than other chickens raised for meat? Did they have perches? He thought so, but couldn't say for sure.

The man got so exasperated by my questions that he ended up dragging out the box the meat had been shipped in. Then we got somewhere. It was from Perdue Farms. It was Perdue chicken. That was all he could tell me. He advised me to call customer service.

I stood there for a while and watched the meat counter as people quickly moved over it, picking up that green-labelled package. Did they question the label? Did they just trust it was true? What were they imagining in their heads when they read the words "humanely raised?" I suspect they pictured chickens in green fields shaded by trees, kicking their legs in leaves and dirt, finding an escaping beetle and snatching it up to eat. They might imagine birds perching and pecking and dustbathing and basking in the sunshine.

It took a long time to uncover the truth behind that label— and the truth was nothing like the bucolic picture conjured up by the words "humanely raised."

Caring About Chicken

I got my crash course in Georgia chicken farming 101 from the Sierra Club's Georgia state director, Colleen Kiernan.

I first met with her in 2011 at her office, a converted warehouse in Decatur, Georgia. I'd just moved to the state. All I knew was that chicken farming was big here. Colleen was my guide, helping me understand what was already being done about factory farming in the number one poultry-producing state in the country. She was approachable and ready to reach into her contact list to help get some activity going around chicken factory farming.

Colleen was also clear about what was at stake. "I think the sheer amount of chickens and the sheer amount of waste that chickens produce in Georgia is a threat to our environment," she said.[1] "They produce nine times as much waste as the human population in Georgia, and we're not really sure where that waste goes. It likely gets in our waterways, which are already burdened with other sources of pollution … Anyone who cares about the environment should be caring about chicken factory farming in Georgia."

Colleen introduced me to Juliet Cohen, an attorney for Upper Chattahoochee Riverkeeper, an environmental organization focused on protecting the Chattahoochee River, which runs through Georgia and along the Georgia–Alabama border. Cohen explained that a lot of chicken farms and processing plants in Georgia are in the Lake Lanier watershed.

"Lake Lanier is the most highly recreationally used lake in the nation," she told me. She was concerned that chicken production and processing can release pollutants like nitrate, phosphorous, and harmful bacteria. "When we have an overload of bacteria in our public waterways, then what is supposed to be a public resource is no longer accessible to families to play in, to explore with their children and their pets, because it's unsafe," she said. "When an industrial business like a chicken-processing facility dumps large quantities of bacteria into what is supposed to be a public waterway, they are essentially hijacking that public waterway from the public good."

I thought about the weekend I had joined my husband's work event on Lake Lanier, letting our kids muck around in the water. I thought of the time I had met my aunt and uncle camping there, and had swung off of a rope into the very water Cohen was describing. Once you know, you can never unknow. I could never go into that water again.[2]

Colleen had already helped orient me to chicken farming in Georgia. But she was keen to get me out there digging deeper. Next, she wanted me to meet someone named Will Harris.

In the heat of the summer of 2011, I drove 170 miles (275km) south of Decatur to meet Will, the owner of White Oak Pastures. Will is a fifth-generation farmer who in the late 1990s decided to give up conventional farming and go all out for pasture-raised. Today, Will has been written about and featured everywhere from *The New York Times* to *Vice* magazine and feature-length documentaries, but back in 2011 he was just beginning to make his voice heard.

That voice speaks in a Southern drawl like no other I've heard before, smooth like molasses. Will always wears boots, a belt buckle, and a wide-brimmed hat. He has a wicked sense of humor. He once told me that monks make wine bottles the size they do because they intend that to be a single serving—an entire bottle. Possum, his three-legged dog, came everywhere with Will, and jumped into the open-top Jeep with us the first time we toured the farm.

You can drive alongside Harris's farm in Bluffton, Georgia, any time of the day or night and see exactly how the chickens are living—in the fields, in the trees, in the shrubs. Will and his daughters, Jenni and Jodi, will greet you with pride and eagerness to share their farm. They'll encourage you to take photos of the birds.

The typical factory farm never allows visitors, and some states have even outlawed undercover investigators from documenting factory-farm conditions. But White Oak Pasture operates with an open-door policy because the Harris family know the way their farm looks is their greatest asset. These are the images we think of when we think of "farm"— green pastures and animals roaming.

Late into the afternoon on that first visit, Will and I walked around with the chickens, just chatting about our kids, our families, our ambitions, even daring to delve into religion. We sat in the amber grasses, now seeding and gently swishing with the breeze. The pastures were green and lush. Will, ever the iconic cowboy, was chewing on grass. I don't have any idea why people do that, but it looked like a good idea, so I did it too. He definitely noticed, but he just smirked and we kept chatting.

Will told me that modern chickens aren't even chickens anymore. He tried to explain animal welfare in its most common-sense form: "Animals were born with certain predetermined instinctive behaviors. So often, through the industrialized meat production system, we don't allow that. We believe the way we raise our animals is much better in terms of animal welfare, environmental sustainability, and economic impact. I believe good animal welfare means me as the stockman creating an environment that allows the animals to express their instinctive behavior."

Each time I see Will, I wonder if he can sense my discomfort about any business involved in animal slaughter. But in contrast to almost every other chicken farm I was aware of, this was one of the few where the animals seemed to truly have a decent life before they were killed.

It was also one of the first farms I had been to that considered the environment. Will had adopted the Serengeti model of farming: rotating cattle, followed by sheep, followed by chickens, on the same pasture. Rotation meant that a variety of grasses were eaten at different times, the ground was turned up continually, and a variety of manures hit the soil. The result was a rich pasture where, instead of carbon being taken out of the land, it was being put back in.

I long for the day we swap meat for plants, wholesale. But that's not going to happen overnight. Until then, if people are going to eat chickens, I would much rather the chickens come from a place like Will's farm than a crowded, dark, barren warehouse. So, that summer, I had an idea. With Will's help, I met with other Georgia farmers who shared his outlook, as well as some great thinkers and activists, and we resolved to air our state's dirty laundry. We decided to expose the impact chicken factory farming was having on our state and show that a better way was possible.

It was a diverse group: a chef, a farmer, a workers' justice lawyer, an environmental lawyer, an environmental activist, a supermarket, and me, the vegan animal activist. We wrote an in-depth report called *Out of Sight, Out of Mind: the impact of chicken meat farming on the state of Georgia*. We wanted to make it clear that we were not just focused on the problem, but on a path forward. Janice Ray, the celebrated Southern author of *Ecology of a Cracker Childhood*, wrote a moving forward to that report:

In the neighbor's field are two industrial broiler houses, lit night and day, where the chickens are fed all sorts of atrocities, including their own feces, I hear, and where the farmer is a slave to a contract written not in his or her best interest, but in the interest of profitmaking by a corporation. Sometimes the smell of burning chicken corpses fills the air. Sometimes the air is putrid with the smell of chicken litter being spread on nearby fields, because something has to be done with it.

Any one of us middle-aged Americans could be the poster child for the story of agriculture in the United States, one that began with working farms, farm animals, seed saving, a land-based, subsistence economy, farming children. And, poof, all that was gone, brushed aside so casually. Many people still alive today have seen the entire process of American ag: the function, the falling apart, the rise of big chemical and factory farming, and now the coming back. We are witnessing in agriculture a revolution, a full circle. Except it's not a circle.

We are not returning to where we were. With some of the old knowledge intact and armed with fresh knowledge, we are looping forward to a new place. And we're coming there different. We are coming better prepared. We're coming educated. We understand this, our food is killing us. Food raised on small, organic, sustainable farms by conscientious farmers is healthier, tastier, and better for the environment.

Our group aimed high. Armed with our report, we wanted to rework America's—or at least Atlanta's—menu and shelf options when it came to chicken. We asked chefs in Atlanta restaurants to swap out their conventional chicken for pasture-raised chicken for just a week, just to try it, in the hope that they might keep going and become a part of the solution to ending the worst factory-farming practices. Who could say no to that?

Will Harris and White Oak Pastures offered discounts to participants. Pastured-poultry farmers like Brandon Chonko and Daniel Dover called restaurants and sold them on the idea. Chef Shaun Doty got out his cellphone and called everyone he knew, getting them to sign up. Compassion in World Farming volunteers lobbied restaurants to participate. The Sierra Club rallied their members. Journalists Maryn McKenna at *Wired* and John Kessler at *The Atlanta Journal-Constitution* wrote pieces on the need for the change. In that first year, more than 50 restaurants participated. The event felt wildly successful.

By the second year, we had 100 restaurants participating, and by the third the week had expanded to Charleston and New York. In theory, the expansion could keep going until the campaign was national. But we soon hit roadblocks.

Finding local farms in new areas that met our criteria proved difficult. In New York, the warm season for outdoor access for the birds is very short. Pasture-raised chicken can only be supplied for about four or five months of the year. Because the chicken was a slower-growing breed, the birds took longer to get to market weight. That meant they were more expensive. In Charleston, the chefs didn't want to pay more for slower-growing, pasture-raised birds. Even when restaurants were keen, the supply from local farms was low and inconsistent. So few farmers across the country were farming like this. It would appear Georgia was uniquely positioned, not just for understanding the problem of factory farming, but for moving away from it.

At the end of the third year of the program, Compassion in World Farming conducted a survey to try to understand how many conventional chickens were being displaced for pasture-raised among participating restaurants. How many of the restaurants had made a permanent commitment to never go back to conventional chicken?

I remember the day the I opened up the survey. I thought there was a zero missing. We found that 20,000 chickens had been replaced thanks to the program—compared with the 9 billion chickens slaughtered in the United States every year. Those 20,000 pasture-raised chickens wouldn't even come close to changing the enormous total market. Worse, only two restaurants had committed to going 100 per cent pasture-raised going forward. No retailer except Whole Foods Market committed to even having meat from pasture-raised birds permanently on the shelf. It had taken so much work to pull this program together, and we were nowhere near affecting 1 per cent of America's chickens; we were nowhere near affecting even .001 per cent of America's chickens.

Supporters called us and asked where they could buy pasture-raised chicken and which restaurants had it on the menu all year. The answer was virtually none. All but a few places carried on with business as usual. They took the positive publicity from the event and then went back to buying factory-farmed birds. Conventional chicken remained the norm even at farm-to-table restaurants that otherwise sold grass-fed beef and pasture-raised eggs.

I felt defeated. There was no way we could change the lives of 9 billion chickens this way—restaurant by restaurant, phone call by phone call. The problem was too big.

Why? Why, when so many consumers were clearly interested in ending their support for factory farming, was it so difficult to make better options available? Why was it so easy for even crunchy, organic, farm-to-table restaurants to buy factory-farmed chicken? Why were supermarkets so reluctant to stock a better option that consumers said they wanted?

When I asked Will Harris what was the number one thing stopping pasture-raised chicken from being more successful in the market, he answered without a pause: "Greenwashing." Chicken that presented itself with a "green," "humane" label, with the same kind of marketing and labelling as his, but for half the price. How could he compete? To the uninformed consumer, chicken from Will's farm, next to a greenwashed factory-farmed chicken that sold far cheaper, looked like a rip-off.

When I walked into that Kroger with my kids in 2012, I knew I was seeing that greenwashing in action. I stood and watched consumers fall for it. I knew I was looking at people who wanted a better choice. The tragedy was, they thought they were getting it.

Through the Looking Glass

My conversation with that meat manager at my local Kroger sent me down a rabbit hole, trying to find out what "all natural," "humanely raised," "cage free" chicken really meant. I spent the following week, late into the evenings, researching and calling both Kroger and Perdue customer service lines, trying to get specifics on what these phrases meant. Simple Truth was a new brand and product line, and the teams seemed unprepared for such detailed questions. My local store was actually part of the soft launch before the product's official debut, which came in fall 2012.[3]

As I started researching this new product, I learned that Walmart also had a brand, Harvestland, that was remarkably similar in its marketing. It turned out this, too, was being produced by Perdue, to be sold with the labels "cage free" and "humanely raised." I had seen how shoppers reacted to this branding. Now I wanted to document how meat managers and store managers were explaining such labels to questioning customers.

In October 2012, my coworker Richie Hardy, CIWF's Head of Investigations, and I posed as a couple grocery shopping. We recorded store managers responding to our questions around labels from the two brands, Harvestland and

Simple Truth. We went to Walmarts and Krogers in Kentucky, Alabama, and Georgia, where again and again, we asked the same question. What did the package mean by "raised in a humane environment," "cage-free," and "all natural?"

One evening, as the day was getting cooler, Richie and I walked through a brightly-lit Walmart in Alabama, busy with shoppers. We found the meat manager and told him we wanted to know what the difference was between the brand touting words like "cage free" and "raised in a humane environment" and other brands with no such wording. I asked him why the one cost more than the other.

The meat manager, with tattooed arms and a tired look on his face, took a second or two to look at the one brand before reaching in and picking up a Harvestland package.

"Humanely raised and cage free," he said, thinking it over. "A lot of the big manufacturing, they are trying to produce as much chicken as possible. You've read about the process?"

I played dumb. "The what?"

"The process, like how they raise the chickens," he said. "There's some nasty stuff done to them. The difference is, well, my mom raises chickens, so I know. It says humanely raised and cage free because a lot of the manufacturers put them in the smallest place possible to get the most meat for the money."

"So you think these chickens have more space?" I asked.

"I think it means they don't get drugs, and they weren't fed their own feces," he said. "I'm guessing that's why it costs more."

We weren't expecting him to go there. Chickens aren't fed their own feces. It's cattle, not chicken, that can be fed chicken litter, which of course contains chicken poop.[4] We knew that answer couldn't be right.

I continued to push for answers. "Do you think that they are outside?"

"Yeah," he said. "If it's raised cage free then it's free range."

Wrong again—factory farms can and do pack thousands of chickens into a massively overcrowded space, but they're not technically in cages, so they're "cage free."

We moved on, but in store after store the managers told us that the Simple Truth and Harvestland brands that claimed to be "cage free" and "raised in a humane environment" were free-range chickens. They said the other brands raised birds in cages and gave them hormones—neither of which is true. All meat chickens are cage free in the United States (it's laying hens that are kept in cages), and it is prohibited by federal law to give hormones to any pigs or poultry.

One particular manager really got to me. She clearly wanted very much for there to be another option on the shelf. And when she looked at the label, you could tell she was imagining an idyllic vision of how these birds lived their lives.

"Why does this one cost more?" I asked.

This manager—we'll call her Katy—had a heavy Southern accent, blonde hair, and a fuchsia shirt. She offered me a friendly smile. Katy was confident and pleasant. She told me how her brother lived out in California and only ate whole foods. She said that if he shopped at anything but farmers' markets, he'd buy this chicken.

"This is more organic, it's cage free, it's humanely raised," she said. "It's only fed certain things, no hormones. It's more of a high end, better value, better for your body. People say if you smoke, you get cancer, if you are in the sun, you get cancer. Well, you are going to have hormones in regular chicken." Katy shrugged, alluding to the unknown risks of hormones. "That's what they do to make the chickens bigger and give them larger breasts, larger thighs. But this is all natural."

I couldn't believe how far Katy's imagination had taken her, but I kept pushing. "So when it says raised in a humane environment, that means it's cage free?"

"Right, so if you've ever driven past a chicken truck you'd know it, you'd smell it," Katy offered eagerly. "I lived in Rushville and Golden Poultry is there. You see the big 18-wheeler full of chicken cages going down the road. It's all open to be able to keep them alive. They go to the chicken plant that way, but they are kept in a large coop. In this case," she said, pointing to the Simple Truth package, "it's like they are almost on a farm, running around."

"Almost" on a farm. I wondered if Katy knew, deep down, that what she was saying couldn't be true. "So when it says humane environment, what does that look like?" I asked.

"They are raised in a way that they aren't tortured," she said. "The way that they are killed is better. It's more of an outdoor farm." She told me that other chicken brands would keep as many as 10 chickens in a cage the size of her meat counter. But these birds, she said, were kept in pastures and fed whole grains. "They aren't fed junk."

I wanted to sit down and tell Katy everything I knew, how misleading the label was—that no chickens raised for meat are kept in cages, so calling it "cage-free" was deceptive. Her heart was in the right place. That "humanely raised" is an unregulated term that any company can slap on its packages. But she had been led astray by the gap these companies were pretending to bridge—the gap between how people wish farmed animals are treated, and how they're really treated.

I knew Katy's picture of these chickens' lives was wishful thinking. I was sure these chickens weren't pasture-raised—thanks to my previous work, I knew how expensive pasture-raised chicken was. But proving my hunch right would be a whole other thing.

Getting to the Truth

I was not the only one who had noticed these misleading labels. Across the country, two different organizations—the Humane Society of the United States and Compassion Over Killing—were separately in the middle of major legal battles to find out exactly what "humanely raised" meant. It would seem that everyone was a little suspicious of such a bold claim.

One of those suspicious people was Erica Meier. Growing up in the 1970s, Erica idolized the TV character Wonder Woman. When she got older, she got a W tattoo on her left upper arm. To Erica, Wonder Woman was who she wanted to be: someone willing to fight for justice and truth. She believed in transparency and honesty. She thought everyone deserved that. And she thought that, if people got that, the world would be better. Like, all better.

Erica grew up in Syracuse, New York, where the agriculture-focused New York State Fair was held every year. Her father worked for his family's German meat-packing company. By default, her family ate tons of meat. She was an unlikely candidate to become a hero for farmed animals.

Compared to Erica's connection with animals, her family was pretty much indifferent to them. At a very young age, Erica grew up with a beagle, but at around eight years old, she bonded with Molly, the neighbor's black lab. There was a wooden fence between the yards, but part of the bottom of the fence was broken. "She would stick her head underneath it," Erica remembers. "I would lay there for hours just petting her, playing with her. She was my first memory of falling in love with an animal."

Erica remembers having a revelation when she was eight or nine years old. She was staring at the steak on her plate, and it occurred to her that this was an animal—and that Molly was an animal. She didn't want to eat Molly, so why would she want to eat this cow? She wasn't sure what to do with that thought, but it seemed strange to her. Erica's family brushed it off and life carried on as usual. But the question stuck with her.

It wasn't until she became an environmental activist in high school, cofounding an eco-group, that she was introduced to the word "vegetarian." She converted overnight. "That night," Erica says, "my mom made me chicken and tried to convince me that chicken wasn't meat, and that only applied to pigs and cows." She told her mom that she didn't eat anything with eyes. Her dad would jokingly say that potatoes were the exception.

Erica grew up to study environmental policy, hoping to enact ideas to protect the planet. While she was in college, however, she discovered a whole new world—the world of animal activism. "I had no idea that world existed," she says. "And when I found out, it was all over for me. This was my calling. This was where all my driving motivation was going."

After college, Erica worked for People for the Ethical Treatment of Animals (PETA) for several years. After that, she worked as an animal control officer in Washington, DC. The job had a law-enforcement component and a rescue component. It was a direct way of helping animals. As an animal control officer, Erica felt like the heroine of her youth—enforcing justice and fighting for animals.

In 2004, her government contract was unexpectedly delayed, and in early 2005 Erica took a job at Compassion Over Killing, a small nonprofit dedicated to exposing factory farming and promoting plant-based eating. She quickly rose through the ranks to become executive director. Now she found herself focusing on another type of justice—truth in labelling.

Polls show that people care how animals are treated, Erica explains, but they simply do not know much about where their meat comes from. "They don't know for a good reason: the industry is purposely shielding that information from them," she says. "There's a knowledge gap."

Polls from the industry trade group Food Marketing Institute, for example, have shown that animal welfare is critical to today's consumers. They rank it above other concerns, such as environmental impact. In their 2015 TRENDS report, FMI reported that "Shoppers want food retailers to prioritize animal welfare over environmentally sustainable practices." They report that "shoppers prioritize animal welfare second only to employment practices."

Companies have responded, not by changing the way they treat the animals they raise and kill, but instead simply by marketing products to people who care about these issues. Erica's organization has focused on how products are marketed to consumers, particularly consumers who care about animal welfare, in order to uncover the gap between what people want and what companies are really selling them.

In the early 2000s, the United Egg Producers (UEP) started a program called Animal Care Certified. The UEP is a voluntary industry group representing a large portion of egg producers. Through membership in UEP, farmers opted into the Animal Care Certified program. Any farm that opted into the program had to meet certain standards. Sounds good, right?

Not really, Erica explains. "Those standards pretty much codified the norm of what was happening on factory farms," she says. Farmers were required to give hens 67 square inches (420 cm^2) of living space. For comparison, that's substantially smaller than even a regular 8.5 by 11 inch (21 × 28 cm) piece of typing paper (which is 93.5 square inches/604 cm^2). That's not even enough space for a hen to stand comfortably, let alone stretch her wings.

The "standard" was essentially codifying the inhumane treatment of animals, but if producers adhered to these standards, they got to put a Care Certified "checkmark" on their egg cartons. To the average consumer, it looked like these animals were treated better than birds who didn't have that checkmark. In reality, it meant very little to the hens. Compassion Over Killing investigated non-Animal Care Certified farms and compared them to certified farms. The footage showed no meaningful difference in the birds' conditions.

"Our goal is to give consumers the information they need to make an informed choice," Erica says. "We aren't telling people what to do, we are just saying, at least give people the truth. By challenging these claims, we are saying that consumers deserve to know the truth about how these animals are treated."

Erica and Compassion Over Killing fought that meaningless checkmark for years. Eventually, in 2006, the Federal Trade Commission (FTC) ruled in their favor and required companies to remove the checkmark. So by the time Erica got to Kroger's Simple Truth brand, she was well-practiced in challenging misleading labels. Simultaneously, in a very similar case, the Humane Society of the United States was suing Perdue and the Harvestland chicken brand sold at Walmart.

I wanted to talk to Erica about how the case had gone. But when I asked her about the Simple Truth brand, she shifted in her chair. "I can only read you the statement we agreed to," she said. She pulled the statement up on her computer. Until five years after the settlement, she could not speak freely to anyone about the case. All she could do was read this legalese:

October 13, 2014:

The Kroger Co. (NYSE:KR) and Compassion Over Killing today announced the settlement of a federal case in California concerning Kroger's Simple Truth "raised in a humane environment" claim on chicken labels. The settlement requires plaintiff to dismiss her claims with prejudice, in exchange for Kroger agreeing to remove the "raised in a humane environment" label claim from its Simple Truth chicken packaging.

The proposed class action case was filed in 2014 by an individual consumer who contended that the "raised in a humane environment" claim on the packaging of Kroger's Simple Truth brand chicken was misleading. Kroger and its supplier, Perdue, vigorously opposed plaintiff's claims.

"We are pleased to see the claim removed from Simple Truth packaging, which we view to be inaccurate," said Cheryl Leahy, General Counsel for Compassion Over Killing. "We will continue to work to protect both animals and consumers."

"We stand by our assertion that the "raised in a humane environment" claim on our Simple Truth chicken label is accurate," said Gil Phipps, Kroger's vice president of corporate brands. "We are pleased to put this lawsuit behind us and will continue to work with our suppliers to ensure the humane treatment and welfare of animals. Customers should know that all of our Simple Truth chicken products have always been and will remain free from antibiotics and added hormones."

All parties have agreed that the conversion will be completed within the next 12 months.

The Humane Society of the United States's case against Perdue was settled around the same time, with an almost identical statement. Perdue and Kroger refused to admit any wrongdoing, but they agreed to remove the "humane" labels from their meat—the same labels I had questioned when I saw them in my local Kroger.

When I talked to Erica, I felt like Perdue, Kroger, and Walmart had gotten away with it. While the misleading labels were removed, the public remained none-the-wiser about the effort to greenwash ordinary (apart from being antibiotic free) factory-farmed products. And the companies didn't make any changes in the way they treated animals.

Hidden in Plain Sight

"It's unfortunate that we have to be the truthtellers," Erica says. "It's unfortunate that we have to work to expose information that should already be available to consumers." Consumers care about how animals are treated. They don't want to support the horrific suffering that factory farms inflict on animals—and yet they know so little about how meat production works that they can be easily fooled by a friendly-looking green checkmark or few buzzwords on a label.

Most people do not realize how few protections farmed animals actually have. If you see your neighbor treating a dog cruelly, you can file a complaint. Not so for farmed animals. Chickens have no federal protections at all. On a state level, they have very few. State animal cruelty codes often explicitly exempt farmed animals and what are considered "common agricultural practices."

Imagine a puppy and piglet. Both are adorable; both are sentient beings capable of joy, fear, pleasure, and pain. If you were to take a puppy and cut his tail off, you could be prosecuted for animal cruelty. You could go to jail or be fined, depending on what state you live in. But if you do the same thing to a piglet, in most states it is considered "common agricultural practice," simply because factory farms habitually do it. It's not that anyone has said that it is OK to cut pigs' tails off. No one has determined that cutting a pig's tail off is not painful or cruel. In fact, like dogs, pigs use their tails to communicate their emotions. But because enough farms do it, it is considered common—and therefore acceptable.

Most people buying ham, pork, or bacon have no idea how the pig has been treated. They don't know that it's common practice on factory farms to cut pigs' tails off because pigs kept in crowded, stressful conditions often bite each other's' tails. Animal activists have worked hard over the years to try to expose the rampant cruelty occurring every day inside factory farms and slaughterhouses, but this work has been difficult in the United States. By the time I spoke to Erica about her lawsuit in 2014, it had been more than 10 years since consumers had seen inside an industrial broiler farm.

In 2003, Compassion Over Killing produced a video exposé entitled *45 Days*. The video laid out the short, brutal life of a broiler chicken: panting, overcrowded, lame, limping, and even dead birds. The film showed a bird trapped in a feeder unable to reach water; birds in filthy, dusty conditions; and birds with chests so heavy that they were unable to move around with ease.

Separately, also in 2003, *New Yorker* writer Michael Specter wrote about his first visit to a broiler factory farm: "I was almost knocked to the ground by the overpowering smell of feces and ammonia. My eyes burned and so did my lungs, and I could neither see nor breathe... There must have been thirty thousand chickens sitting silently on the floor in front of me. They didn't move, didn't cluck. They were almost like statues of chickens, living in nearly total darkness, and they would spend every minute of their six-week lives that way."

Chickens raised for meat are 90 per cent of the animals we raise for food in the United States. They are the overwhelming majority of the animals on factory farms, and yet almost no investigations have been able to show consumers what goes on inside an industrial chicken house. It is trying and difficult to enter and expose these farms. In addition, there are no federal laws protecting these birds, which are denied basic legal rights and basic transparency. Thanks to a powerful agribusiness lobby, the federal government chooses to look away rather than confronting our mistreatment of chickens and other farmed animals. Consumers are kept from seeing the truth. Nobody sees inside those dark, crowded chicken houses. In the summer of 2014, when I first stepped onto Craig Watts's farm, the public had not seen the inside of a chicken factory farm in a decade.

CHAPTER FOUR

The Unlikely Alliance

M y collaboration with Craig Watts, a Perdue chicken factory farmer, was startling and unnatural. The animal activist and chicken factory farmer were worlds apart. We should not have met under any circumstances other than as adversaries. But somehow we broke free from our bubbles, and the result would turn the poultry industry's world upside down. Wyatt Williams of *Vice Magazine* later wrote:

> *Garcés filmed at Watts's farm over a period of months and helped put him in touch with media heavyweights like Kristof at the Times, Maryn McKenna at Wired, and producers at Fusion TV... The unlikely alliance between Watts and Garcés is, one might imagine, Perdue's worst nightmare. Without Garcés, Watts is a just a funny farmer out in the country, listing his complaints without anyone to listen to him. Without Watts, Garcés is just another activist leveling claims at a secretive industry.*

Prior to Craig and I meeting in 2014, there was little dialogue between the animal-protection movement and animal-agriculture industry. Unsurprisingly, relations were often hostile. Farmers wouldn't let activists—or the public—peek inside their facilities, so activists took jobs undercover. Wired with hidden cameras, these undercover investigators have documented the routine cruelties inflicted on farmed animals in the meat, egg, and dairy industries. Nearly 100 investigations have been released, each time exposing horrific yet often standard practices, such as locking hens in tiny cages and mutilating baby piglets. Rather than try to ban the cruelty, industry instead lobbied for laws across the country to ban taking photographs or videos inside factory farms.

Starting in 2011, a handful of states passed what *New York Times* food writer Mark Bittman dubbed "ag-gag" laws, as they gagged efforts to tell the public what was happening inside agricultural facilities. This was the industry's last desperate gasp to try to keep the public from seeing the inside of factory farms. Such laws—they are now in effect in Montana, Utah, North Dakota, Missouri, Kansas, Iowa, and North Carolina— made it difficult if not impossible for whistleblowing employees or animal activists to report animal cruelty or food-safety issues.[1] The intention is clear: to keep the public in the dark.

Despite this, farmers and workers were repeatedly being exposed for abusing animals. The usual response by the company that contracted the farmer or work was to fire, suspend, or end a contract with the farmer or worker for the misdemeanor. The farmer or worker temporarily lost all income, and the company simply carried on.

While the intention of ag-gag laws was to keep footage out of the hands of media outlets, they had the opposite effect. The media were not too happy at laws that criminalized journalists for distributing investigative video footage and photos. Media outlets chomped at the bit to combat what they saw as clear attempts to restrict the freedom of the press. In February 2014, NBC News showed an undercover investigation of an Oklahoma farm produced by Mercy for Animals. The video showed workers on the farm kicking, hitting, and throwing pigs, and slamming piglets into the ground[2]. The nation's largest meat producer, Tyson, terminated its contract with the offending farm. In July 2014, a second video emerged. CNN aired undercover video footage from Compassion Over Killing showing a North Carolina farmer throwing sick and injured birds, and dumping live birds into an outdoor pit where they were left to die from starvation, dehydration, or even suffocation[3]. JBS, the world's largest meat company, suspended its contract with the poultry farmer. JBS issued a predictable statement of apology and shock: "[T]he undercover video shows startling images of birds being mistreated. The actions in the video are unacceptable. Pilgrim's has initiated an investigation, led by our Animal Welfare Steering

Committee, and suspended our relationship with the grower."[4]

The pattern was clear. An accused company generally tried to put as much space between itself and the tainted contract farm in a highly calculated public-relations strategy. While groups like Compassion Over Killing and Mercy For Animals worked hard to hold the parent companies responsible, the companies always found a way out of the situation by breaking ties with the farm. More often than not, however, the contracting company was arguably equally responsible for the crime. The deviations from approved treatment happened under their watch, and they had no systems in place to ensure the abuses did not take place. In addition, the companies' demands for high output created pressures that all too often left poor farmers in desperate situations where they had to choose between a paycheck and pushing animals to—or beyond—their limits.

Companies turned a blind eye to such practices until the undercover cameras came in and made it impossible to do so. While abusive contract farms are certainly guilty, however, that does not mean that the companies are guiltless.

Most photos and video from factory farms come from undercover investigators who get themselves hired as workers and then secretly gather images for an external organization. This can be next to impossible in a broiler factory farm for the simple reason that there is hardly a "job" involved in raising broilers anymore. Often just one or two people—usually the farm owners—oversee multiple chicken houses, each of which is filled with tens of thousands of birds.

Chickens are put into long windowless "barns"—essentially warehouses—soon after hatching, and grow there. The main job of the farm owner is to remove, record, and dispose of dead birds on a daily basis. Typically, there are 30,000 chickens crowded inside each warehouse. The mortality rates have been rising in recent years, and are now at 4.8 per cent according to the National Chicken Council[5]. On average, that means that, over the six-week growth period, 1,440 birds die in each house—in other words, 34 birds die every day in each warehouse. That is the workers' main job: recognizing dead or dying birds, killing sick birds, and picking up and disposing of dead birds. The feed, water, and temperature are automated, and the litter is never changed during those birds' short life. The job is easily done by one or two people, so hired workers (including covert activists) are hardly required. Getting footage inside the barns had become near impossible, even without the ag-gag barrier.

The surge of proposed ag–gag bills was a sign of the industry's concern of what might be revealed behind the walls of factory farms and what impact these revelations might have on consumers. It was a desperate reaction by an industry whose worst enemy is itself.

In 2014, it had been nearly 11 years since the public had seen unedited images or videos of the short life of a factory-farmed broiler chicken in any detail. But the broiler industry could not hide forever.

It was uncomfortable, even risky, for me to befriend a factory farmer. I wasn't making any friends in doing so. I'd be accused time and time again—by both animal activists and the companies that contracted these farmers—of being too sympathetic toward factory farmers, of having the wool pulled over my eyes, of individual farmers being just "bad apples" and "squeaky wheels." But on this journey, I came to know just how desperate these farmers were, particularly through getting to know Craig Watts.

In the summer of 2014, the filmmaker Raegan Hodge and I were heading east from Atlanta, Georgia, to Fairmont, North Carolina, right on the border of South Carolina. No one but Raegan would be willing to join me on this sort of trip, and frankly I wouldn't have wanted anyone but her with me. We had hit on a seemingly impossible mission—trying to convince a chicken factory farmer to trust us enough to risk everything and bring truth and change to the industry. He risked his income, his community relationships, his property, and his safety to show us something very simple—the inside of his own farms. We had the car packed with batteries and cameras, snacks, flashlights, and protective biosecurity coveralls.

Raegan was more than the right person for the job. Her grandparents—Thomas Westin Hodge II and Frances Powell Hodge—hailed from Gainesville, Georgia, surrounded by one of the highest concentrations of chicken factory farming in the world. Raegan's grandfather went to seminary but ended up making more money farming chicken. "There was a dirty underbelly of what was really going on that I never saw as a kid, but it was going on all around me," she later told me.

Raegan's grandfather was very successful, like many at the time, and ended up selling his whole operation to Campbell Soup. The chicken business was treated with certain respect in her family. But somewhere in between Regan's grandfather and now, chicken farming went from something that delivered a family out of poverty to one that brought a family to the edge of bankruptcy. When Raegan asked her aunt about it, she said she dismissed it as something that was beneath them, something that the upper crust of Gainesville no longer did. Chicken farming was now only for poor Georgians, she asserted.

Despite her upbringing, the inside of chicken factory farms remained for the most part a mystery to Raegan. As she grew older and starting reading books about the food industry, however, it began to bother her. *Animal Liberation* by Peter Singer opened her eyes. In the years since I've known her, Raegan has more than once referred to a powerful Albert Schweitzer quote as a guiding force in her life: "Beware of the suffering of which you spare yourself the sight."

"I remember in Gainesville, there was a beautiful valley and it had these two long houses in it. As a kid, in my ignorance, I remember how the sun would reflect off of the metal and it being so beautiful down there. The metal was iridescent." Looking back, she says that same memory feels grotesque: "It is so strange how your whole idea can flip." She had all along been looking at what are referred to as longhouses, stuffed full of chickens. It did not even occur to her there might be live animals, suffering miserably, inside those warehouses.

Raegan recalls getting older and noticing transport trucks packed with chickens on their way to slaughter. Raegan's family had long stopped raising chickens, but their loyalty to the industry remained. When she commented to her aunt about how awful the trucks were and how bad they smelled, questioning whether the chickens were even alive, her aunt quickly shut her down. She looked Raegan squarely in the eyes and told her to not say a single bad thing about the chickens because they were why she had a roof over her head and would eventually be able to go to college.

"I was asked to stay silent," she told me as she took a deep breath. "It became this very dark looming element in the town. This town built on suffering. It gave me a suspicion of my grandparents. It was because it wasn't talked about."

Raegan and I first met in fall 2011 when she approached me after I spoke at a Georgia Organics event. I had been talking about all the detrimental impacts of chicken factory farming on the state. Raegan noted that hearing me talk about this—from the environment, to the workers, to our health, to the animals—was a lightbulb moment for her.

"I was struck by what a clear argument it seemed to be and how widespread it was. The wool was pulled out from over my eyes. I thought because I had family involved in the industry I could somehow get into these chicken houses. I could infiltrate, I could get someone on camera who had experienced the same kind of outrage that I had and have a change of heart."

She tried to talk to her cousins and aunt, but was told again, as she had when she was young, "don't even go there." But Raegan wasn't one to give up. She asked to meet me for lunch. As a documentarian, she had a strong drive to show people the truth, even when it was uncomfortable. This was something so close to home for her, yet so covered up, that she felt compelled and obligated to dig deeper. I explained that I had little money to pay her, but she didn't care. She just wanted to know how we could bring the truth to Americans. It was a truth she was determined to tell.

In spring 2014, when the opportunity presented itself, I knew no one more motivated than Raegan to do just that. When I called her, I barely had a chance to finish my sentence before she was on her way over to map out a plan.

Months earlier, I had received a call out of the blue. A Reuters journalist, Brian Grow, asked if I would mind meeting him to review some documents regarding antibiotic additives in chicken feed. I was curious, and never turned down a chance to work with a good journalist. I walked through the doors of a coffee shop in Oakhurst, near my home, and spotted Brian immediately. He sat with a furrowed brow, poring over the documents he had mentioned over the phone. This was good, old-fashioned journalism—something that was increasingly rare and which I very much admired.

What Brian presented me with was very unusual. He had got his hands on the list of chicken-feed ingredients that had been given to a specific farm, flock after flock. Details of what is actually fed to chickens are very hard to come by. They shouldn't be. This is something every American should be able to know—but it's not. It's guarded by companies as "commercially sensitive," part of their secret formulas for growing their birds as competitively as possible. For each flock, farmers are given a paper telling them the details of what their birds must be fed, usually in three phases: starter, intermediate, and finishing feed. The feed formula includes antibiotics, which help to keep the bird from getting sick in such dire filthy circumstances, but which also have an added bonus. Somewhere along the way, the industry realized that giving antibiotics to chickens helped them put on weight.

It looked as if Brian had a decade's worth of documents. Someone had given him their carefully filed records, sheets covering years of flocks and the exact ingredients, including antibiotics and amounts, these chickens were fed. Someone had handed him gold. I was stunned—this was deep-dive journalism at its best. He had got his hands on a great depth of information about a single farm, and a window into the whole secretive world of the poultry industry. Whoever had given this to him was either crazy or so fed up that he was ready to risk everything, or both.

I asked Brian who was his source. I figured someone had snuck these documents out, like an undercover investigator. I couldn't believe his answer. What he told me next would be the first step toward many changes in my perception of the issue to which I had dedicated my life.

Brian's source was a Perdue contract farmer named Craig Watts. Perdue is the fourth largest chicken company in the country, raising some 680 million birds a year on 2,200 farms. Not only was the source an actual farmer; he was still raising chickens for one of the biggest chicken companies in the world.

Within a few minutes, Craig Watts and I were connected. Our paths collided that day and our futures became irreversibly intertwined, for better or for worse.

The first time we spoke, Craig's birds were at the end of the line and about to be picked up for slaughter. I knew this was where the welfare issues were worse, and asked if I could come out to the farm right away. Craig refused. It was the end of the flock, when the work is hardest, with sometimes multiple all-nighters required to get the birds out to slaughter. He had blinders on and just wanted to get the job done. He didn't want an urban nuisance like me buzzing around asking questions. He meant no offense; he just couldn't spare the energy.

Looking back, the flock I didn't see was Craig's last ever non-antibiotic flock and, from the photos he shared with me, one of the worst. The flock clearly had health issues but, despite Craig raising the issue with his flock advisor, no antibiotics were supplied and no veterinary intervention was offered.

This was not the first time Craig had raised concerns with Perdue that his birds were getting sick. He had sent them DVDs and pictures three or four years prior to even meeting me. He said none of what we would later film should have been a surprise to Perdue. He also said it should not have been a surprise to the company that he had invited me down there, since he had become increasingly vocal with his complaints. The difference was that our film later went viral. Perhaps it's a lesson in not ignoring a squeaky wheel.

My contacts with Craig with as a series of conversations. We would text, speak on the phone, and email over the weekend as we felt each other out. These were not normal circumstances. I was someone who campaigned against factory farming my whole career. He was a chicken factory farmer. We were not meant to be on the same side. The only thing we had in common was our kids. His twins were the same age as my oldest. It was enough for us to build some trust.

In the media, we were pitted against each other. Investigations into the industry usually went one way. An animal-advocacy group sends an undercover investigator onto a farm, who documents the farmer or workers mistreating animals; the company is exposed and a few individuals are singled out for blame and fired. That was the atmosphere in which we were trying to establish trust. Since the poultry companies were not being transparent, even when I relentlessly called customer service or asked the meat manager at my local supermarket, I was going to bring transparency to them. The trust could not come right away on either side. I feared Craig would shut down and stop answering my calls.

Finally, one Sunday, I stood in the corner of my bedroom as my family ate lunch in the next room, took a deep breath, and asked: "Craig, do you think I could come visit with a camera and film your next flock?" "Sure, come on over," he responded without a pause. It was as if he had been waiting for me to ask.

After a month of planning, Raegan and I hit the road into unknown territory—invited by a chicken factory farmer to film inside his farm. Not undercover or with a button-hole hidden camera. We were bringing proper cameras operated by an experienced filmmaker. We were invited. No one had ever done anything like this before. I had no idea what Craig's motivation was, but I do know that Raegan and I had no idea what we were doing.

As we approached Craig Watts's county, we turned off the highway and passed by a few fields of tobacco. Broad leafed and swaying in the breeze, bathed in golden light, the fields seemed idyllic.

North Carolina and tobacco have a long relationship that dates back to when settlers in 1663 brought the first crop from Virginia, having struggled to grow anything else in the dry, sandy soil. Tobacco at the time was a luxury, and the markets in Europe provided huge opportunities for new colonists. Over the centuries that followed, tobacco became more and more ingrained in North Carolina's culture and identity.

For much of the 20th century, the tobacco industry operated within a system of government quotas. But in 2004, mainly due to health concerns around smoking, Congress legislated the end of tobacco quotas in exchange for a one-time buyout. Tobacco growing ended up concentrated in a few hands, and many small farmers fell through the cracks. This made for a big shift in rural North Carolina, where the economy had already begun to change.

North Carolina farmers had seen the writing on the wall and begun shifting away from tobacco. As early as 1997, 95 per cent of farmers there reported that they had grown or raised a commodity other than tobacco within the past year.[6] Contract chicken farming began to fill the hole that tobacco had left behind in rural areas where people had few other options for income.

It was around this time that a young man named Craig Watts from Fairmont, North Carolina, in one of the poorest counties in the state, signed a contract with Perdue Farms to raise their chickens on his land. It seemed like a good deal. Craig would have to borrow money to build the houses and equipment to raise the chickens, like any independent businessman, but the income was guaranteed. The loan was easy to get from the bank, thanks to the guaranteed contract from Perdue. As long as he kept raising chickens for Perdue, Craig would have enough cash flow to pay off his loan. Once the loan was paid off, the income looked tremendous and infallible. It seemed like a win–win. Craig's schoolteacher wife, Amelia, agreed and they began their life together with a lot of optimism for the future.

Nearly three decades and three kids later, still in debt, Craig asserted that, if he could go back in time and change one decision in his life, it would be the day he took out that loan and signed the contract. That decision determined the next 20-plus years of his path more than any other.

Despite a huge effort over many years to make the contract poultry system fairer for farmers, little change had come. Craig brought Raegan and me to his farm because he just couldn't take it anymore. He had seen a promotional video by Perdue earlier that year, which showed brightly lit barns and clean birds, and which referred to "doing the right thing like treating the chickens humanely". Craig says the video was a turning point for him. It simply didn't reflect the farming he was being asked to do. He could not be clearer about his motivation. He'd later tell me: "There's a lot of flaws in the system. The consumers are being hoodwinked. The farmers being jerked around."

But as we drove toward Fairmont, Raegan and I did not know any of this. We were not sure why a farmer would be willing to talk to us. But considering that we had failed to secure any other invitations to see inside a chicken farm— from a producer company, a farmer, even from Raegan's Gainesville family—we weren't going to ask too many questions. I had given my coworker and my husband the address we were going to. If I don't come back, I said, look for me rotting away in the chicken litter.

★ ★ ★

On the long drive to North Carolina, Craig was constantly sending us quirky text messages. We'd find out later that he kept sane and alleviated the tension by constantly joking. But at the time his texts only made us nervous. Raegan and I became convinced we were heading into an ambush where farmers would be waiting for us with pitchforks. Was this a trap?

When we reached the farm, there was an idyllic red barn at the top of the dirt driveway. A huge oak tree shaded the entirety of the house. There was a kids' treehouse, a basketball hoop, and a zipline—signs of normal family life. Back from the house was a field of wheat swishing in the warm summer breeze, and what appeared to be a small family cemetery (I'd later walk through there with Craig to see where his ancestors were buried). A small vegetable patch with tomatoes, peppers, and squash sat next to a modest house built during a period I couldn't place my finger on—perhaps many periods of additions upon additions and repairs upon repairs.

Craig was waiting to greet us when we opened the car doors, holding onto the rail on his back steps, wearing overalls stained with paint. Our visit was not an occasion to spruce up. He had a young face but peppered grey hair that suggested he had not had the easiest life. He also had warm brown eyes with crow's feet around them that suggested he laughed a lot. My mom always told me that was a sign of a good character.

Craig did not hesitate to invite us into his home. Shoes off at the door, in we went—there was no turning back.

CHAPTER FIVE

Crossing Enemy Lines

Craig Watts had never met an animal activist before, let alone invited one into his home. But that day in early summer 2014, it felt like the time was right. He was out of options.

Without realizing it at the time, 22 years earlier Craig had signed his life away. He was just 26 years old and had been traveling around working for a company called the Environmental Technologies Institute, which did research with agricultural chemicals, but he was ready to settle down. He had married his high-school sweetheart Amelia and they planned to have kids and be a family. Like generations before them, they wanted to do so on the land that Craig's forebears had been granted from the King of England in the 1700s. It was his heritage, and the land was his inheritance.

So when Perdue came around to the rural pocket near the North Carolina–South Carolina border with a contract that allowed Craig to stay on his land and run his own business, it sounded too good to be true. All he had to do was borrow $200,000 to build two chicken houses, which the bank was ready and willing to lend him, given the Perdue contract. Perdue would provide the chicks; Craig had to provide the feed, the houses, the land, the gas, and the electricity. As long as he could raise the birds, Perdue would pay him the money he needed to chip away at the loan.

Craig had a college degree. He'd gotten good grades and graduated from business school. While he didn't think that automatically made him smart, it did give him confidence that he could understand a contract and figure out a business. "I'm not stupid. I'm good at numbers. Raising chickens isn't rocket science," he thought.

The hard part would be managing the money and making it last. But he wanted to stay on the land, and this seemed to

him like a one-of-a-kind opportunity to run his own business
and hold on to the land of his ancestors. So he took the plunge
and signed on the dotted line. In December 1992, he started
his chicken farm.

At first, the business went exactly to plan. Perdue would
bring the chickens in then pick them up six weeks later for
slaughter. A couple weeks after that, Craig would get a check.
The money covered the bills and he had a small amount left
over. It wasn't a lot, but it was enough to keep his family
afloat. Business was so good that he expanded from two
chicken houses to four. He borrowed $200,000 more in 1994.
But it wasn't long before things started to go wrong.

Craig's first flock payment with four houses was an "uh-
oh" moment. His expenses had more than doubled—but the
money didn't double. He could not figure out exactly why.
Being an eternal optimist, though, he thought: tomorrow is
always going to be better.

It wasn't. At some point, Craig got so frustrated that the
money wasn't adding up that for one year he broke ties with
Perdue and took up a contract with Mountaire, another
large chicken company. Mountaire wasn't any better. The
contract system was the same, but Mountaire asked him to
grow the birds for more time to reach a larger size. The
birds were huge—up to 9–10lb (4–4.5kg)—and were
grotesquely overburdened by the size of their own bodies.
Craig started to lose sleep at night worrying about them. If
one ventilating fan went out in the warehouse, he thought,
the birds would quickly overheat and die of heat stress.
He'd get up to check the fans several times at night. It
would not be the last time he'd have insomnia worrying
about his birds.

Crig couldn't bear raising the chickens to a larger weight,
so he went back to Perdue. There were still plenty of problems,
but at least Perdue grew birds to a smaller size. They didn't
make him so nervous. Mountaire had been taking a lot of
farmers from Perdue in the area, and Craig knew that Perdue
would be happy to have him back. So he settled in again,
hoping to get ahead or at least to break even.

Craig kept a close eye on his debt. If his calculations were right, and nothing went too wrong with the chickens, then he'd be able to pay off all he owed by the end of 2004. And he did. After that, whatever money he earned went straight into his pocket instead of to the bank. He was excited and proud that he had stayed the course.

Then, in 2006, Perdue threw him a curveball. They said that if Craig wanted to keep growing chickens for them, he'd have to upgrade his warehouses. He'd have to invest a further $100,000. He was stuck between a rock and a hard place. He had just paid off his debt and finally was getting a return on his investment, but the only way to keep earning was to keep raising chickens—and the only way he could raise chickens was to borrow another $100,000, which would take him another 10 to 15 years to pay off.

With few good options, in 2006 he once again signed on the dotted line. He became depressed, realizing what he'd got himself and his family into. He saw no end in sight. What would stop Perdue from asking him to upgrade again in another few years? He was trapped. In over 23 years raising birds, he had only had a year and a half when he wasn't sending a check to the bank every month to pay off his debt.

To make matters worse, the chickens were incredibly susceptible to disease. They were overcrowded with poor immune systems, pushed to the limit of their metabolic capacities. In 2010 Craig's farm was hit by Laryngotracheitis (LT), a highly contagious viral herpes infection that makes birds have trouble breathing, and can even suffocate them. The virus is so contagious it can be spread on clothing, shoes, or tires.[1] Craig did some research and found out the farm was rarely the cause. The disease could have been prevented by a vaccine, but he wasn't allowed to administer any antibiotics or vaccines to his birds. Only the company could do that. Still, he knew he'd be blamed for poor management. Even worse, he'd take the hit financially when the birds died. Every time he got LT, more birds died. It started to feel as if he was spiraling down, out of control.

In 2014, Craig Watts was another three years away from paying off his second loan. That's when he invited me into his house, referring to me, half-jokingly, as an eco-terrorist. He told me he knew what he was getting into. He had done his research on my organization. He said we seemed fair, and concerned not just for the animals but the bigger picture. But he also knew that he could lose everything if we went out public together, so we'd only do this if we did it right.

For the first few hours of our visit, we were just sizing each other up. I was anxious to get inside Craig's chicken houses and get away with footage in case he changed his mind, but I knew I needed to take the time to ensure he trusted me. We sat on the floor of his living room and pored over his farm records. Minutes turned into hours. I got lost in the records of his decades in the poultry business. Janie and Dalton, his twin seven-year-olds, peeked into the room a few times to get a good look at me. I had so many questions. I took photos of the contract, the payment settlements, the antibiotics the birds had been given over the years, the letters he had been sent. Craig was a perfect record keeper—a journalist's dream.

As Craig told me the story of his life as a chicken contract farmer, I felt ashamed. I had until that moment been solely concerned with the birds. I hadn't had much empathy to spare for the farmers—until I actually met one. Until I heard Craig's story, until I really understood how he had got to this point, it was so easy for me to dismiss and demonize him.

I stared out the window at the hundred-year-old oak tree and thought about Craig's roots, and what it would be like to be from Fairmont, North Carolina; to burn inside with the desire to raise your kids on the land your ancestors had earned; and to have one of the only choices that made that possible be chicken farming. Would I have done it, had I been born here instead? I lingered on that question for a long time.

An idiom came to mind: "Before you judge a man, walk a mile in his shoes." It asks us to understand a person's

challenges, experiences, and perspectives. In essence, it is
asking us to practice empathy.

This was the beginning of my transformation; or, rather, it
was the beginning of the transformation of the so-called
enemy in my mind. This was the beginning of un-separating
myself from the likes of Craig Watts. I had always thought there
was us—the animal activists—and them—the meat industry
and its farmers. But this interaction with Craig would leave me
thinking that maybe there was no "them." And it that was true,
who, or what, was I fighting against?

I told my friend and coworker, Dave Soleil, a scholar and
activist who specializes in nonviolent movements, about the
curious new friend I had made—a factory farmer. When I
started to tell him, his face transformed and he hardly could
get his words out fast enough. I had fallen into the path of
"nonviolence." He urged me to read more on the teachings of
Ghandi and Martin Luther King, Jr. He referred to an
empirical study on nonviolent movements by Erica
Chenoweth and Maria Stephan that showed that nonviolent
approaches were more than twice as effective as movements
with violent elements, and are increasing in their effectiveness.
What's more, they accomplished their aims in a third of
the time.

When we employ violence, we only strengthen and unify
the "other." Dave explained that nonviolence was the
opposite, "a conversation while regarding the inherent
dignity and worth of all people, including your opponent."
He told me that in building a relationship with Craig, I was
creating a path toward building a more fair society. In
meeting and talking with Craig, I was erasing "the other."
If there is no "other," the enemy becomes something
different, as does the solution. The enemy becomes the
system, a system hurting us all. It means we can be not only
obstructive but also constructive in approaching the
problem.

Sitting in Craig Watts's house that day would be my first
introduction to seeing things through the so-called opponent's
eyes, but it would hardly be the last. It would open up an

entire new pathway for working to resolve the injustices in our food system—the same pathway of many nonviolence movements that have come before this one.

Organizations and individuals make decisions based on perceived benefits and costs, and changing those perceptions is at the root of fixing an unjust system. As my relationship with Craig grew, I would come to understand that perceptions and loyalties can change, and that happens through building relationships with the perceived enemy.

★ ★ ★

Eventually, I told Craig I was curious to see the birds he had now, which he had told me were a few days old, and then come back and see them at the end of their lives. From the science I'd read, they have real problems toward the end because of their genetics. We've selectively bred them over time to grow so big so fast that they have difficulty walking, breathing, and even moving. They sit still nearly all the time.

I was beginning to put it together in my head. No matter what Craig did to try to take care of the animals, there was little he could do to make life any better for those birds, because he was stuck in the contract factory farming system and the chickens were stuck with the genetics that made them miserable in the first place. Craig agreed: "You know that the genetic potential of each individual is done when he's in the egg. His blueprint for what he's going to do is done."

I paused and stared at Craig. This is when I first realized Craig was different. He didn't refer to the chickens as "it" but rather as "she" or "he." I still had coworkers who referred to animals as "it," as if they were a chair or some other inanimate object. But Craig had said "he." I started to feel optimistic about us working together.

"Remember that commercial, 'It's not nice to mess with Mother Nature?'" he asked me. I nodded. "That's what's happening here. That's why you are seeing all these problems.

They are grown for their breast meat only. What you have is two toothpicks sticking out of a grape."

We'd been sitting and talking for hours now. Without much warning, he asked if I was ready to see the birds. He had wanted to wait until later in the day, when there was less likelihood that his service tech might come by. He'd rather not raise suspicions with neighbors either. Now that dusk was upon us, he felt more comfortable bringing us down the dirt road between the houses. And so off we went, Raegan with her camera over her shoulder. Together, we got into Craig's truck and drove a mile down the road to where his four houses stood against the backdrop of a setting sun.

The houses were impossibly long, the length of a football field, and from the outside looked ominous. We walked toward one and he opened the wooden door. We stepped into a chemical foot wash, and through the first door into what reminded me of a decompression chamber. There were electronics on the wall, a clipboard with records of the number of birds that had died (the "cull sheet"), a few handwritten notes, and various quotes Craig had taped on the wall for inspiration. In a moment I would see Craig's chickens for the first time.

Entering the Nightmare

The first thing I noticed as the door swung open was an overpowering smell. Every muscle in my body tensed up. My eyes began to sting and tear. It literally took my breath away. I was too immersed in my own physical discomfort initially to even look around. I was truly shocked.

After the initial impact of the overpowering smell of ammonia wore off a little, two small yellow chicks caught my eye. One was a runt and was snuggling up under the other for comfort and warmth. As a mother, I was distraught to think they would never knew their mother. The runt followed the larger friend everywhere she went, perhaps looking for that motherly connection. I could immediately see the bond between them, and it broke my heart thinking of what the next few weeks would be like for them.

That runt would never find out. He didn't even make it to the end of the day. I know Craig spared me the sight, but he killed that little chick. He'd fallen behind too far and wouldn't be able to reach the water and feed without human assistance. It was part of the business, Craig said.

Next day, I witnessed it for myself as I followed Craig through his daily routine: finding sickly chicks, or runts like that little peep, and killing them by cervical dislocation—popping their necks outward with a swift firm action. The deformities were the stuff of nightmares: crossed beaks, splayed legs. One was even missing an eye. Par for the course, I am told. When you are churning out so many chickens, a few will inevitably have genetic defects. Craig moved through the barn like a machine, dislocating the necks of each deformed and sickly baby. It was baffling to see how this was Craig's basic job—to pick up dead and dying birds and put them out of their misery. What does that do to a person's soul?

As we walked through the barn, Craig explained all the problems he saw. Some problems stemmed from the time between hatching and arrival being too long. Chicks that hatched even a day earlier than the others would be more likely to have problems.

"This is just Wednesday," Craig said. "The first three, four days you'll see inflated mortality. It's just how bad is it going to get—that's the question. How bad is it going to get?"

Raegan asked Craig if he thought the chickens were suffering. His answer was simple. "What do you think? They are not loving life, that is for sure. They're not active and they are not happy. I can't speak for a chicken. All I can say is what I observe. And no, they are not happy. And they are definitely not healthy. Connecting the dots, that would be not feeling good. When you get to that point right there…" He pointed to a little chick, droopy-eyed, not moving. "Yeah you're suffering. It's just the acceptable losses with this kind of set-up." He leaned over and with a quick pop pulled the neck of the chick. She was instantly dead.

"They are really good at the bottom line, cost wise," Craig went on. "But at the end of the day this is a people business. People like me, people like the consumers. And they let that quest for the bottom line kind of blur that. Whereas if they would turn it into a people business, I think it would improve the bottom line, if you had a farmer who couldn't wait to be down here in the morning rather than one just grinding the day out to just pay off debt." By "people business," he meant taking better care of the farmers.

Then he turned and looked me squarely in the eye. "And what's going to happen when the public finds out that they've been fed a bunch of bull? There's going to be some major backlash. That's what it's going to take."

At that exact moment, I knew I was hooked. This was now my unlikely partner in crime, and I was ready to do everything I could to get his story out.

Craig had spoken up before, but he told me he had never attacked Perdue specifically—he had always talked generally about the industry: "I never singled Perdue out. So that's something we are going to have to think about." I knew he was right to be worried. I knew the risks. We would have to be completely certain of our facts and our plan before we went public.

During that first visit, I wandered around the expanse of the barn, contemplating the lives of those baby birds. Every 10 steps or so I found a chick that was deformed, mangled, unable to move, struggling to breathe. It wasn't all of them, but the number I saw was deeply disturbing.

Craig and I had both seen the same promotional video—one where Jim Perdue says that raising the birds humanely is important. Craig couldn't believe the disconnect between that commercial and the reality inside his barns. He knew the reason I was there was because I was curious—and suspicious—about the label on Perdue's packages that read "humanely raised." Now I was getting a front row seat to what "humane" really meant to Perdue.

"How is this humanely raised? This baby chick is two days old and she can't hold her own weight." I turned to Craig. I tried to gently rock the bird onto her feet and she just laid there, her breath labored. "She's waiting to die," I said.

"That's exactly right," Craig said.

"She can't walk, she can't move. If I try to get her to walk, she can't walk. She's collapsed. There's another one there and she's the same way." I pointed just a few feet away.

"That one is worse," said Craig

I leaned down and picked her up. She was hot and small and she felt slightly ... mushy.

"This is normal?" I waved around the chicken house.

"This is outstanding. This is a good flock," Craig said. He waited until I turned away, but then he killed the two sickly chicks.

There were thousands of birds in the barn, but it didn't feel as crowded as I expected. Craig turned to me and said: "When you return, with any luck, no disease that is, this house will be wall to wall a sea of white."

And sure enough, we returned just 37 days later and that is exactly what it looked like through the dust. The noise was frightening, squawking and flapping. My eyes and nose burned from the ammonia. I tasted it in my mouth, chalky and bitter. I was embarrassed that I couldn't stop coughing. I already had a slight chest infection on that visit, and the ammonia and the dust set me off on a violent coughing fit. In fact, the ammonia would affect me so badly that I'd have to go on steroids due to pulmonary inflammation after the hours spent in the chicken house. We had to keep stopping the camera so I could cough. I was embarrassed that I couldn't control it. Craig handled it, why couldn't I? My body did not want to be in that barn.

These chickens live their whole lives in this long windowless warehouse. What starts off as a seemingly spacious, albeit barren and dimly lit, environment soon changes. Thirty thousand animals defecate in the same enclosed space for 42 to 48 days. In that period, they rapidly grow from the size of a fist to the size of a soccer ball. This produces serious problems, including leg disorders, skeletal, developmental, and degenerative diseases, heart and lung problems, breathing difficulties, and premature death. If you grew as fast as a chicken, you'd weigh 600 pounds (275kg) by age two. The chickens are forced to breathe ammonia and dust-filled air. They never see the sun. As they grow, the space becomes more crowded, until they're eventually packed wing-to-wing. It is a sea of chickens from wall to wall, all of them sitting in their own feces, struggling to move.

My eyes search through the crowd of birds. I can easily spot a bird about 10 feet (3m) in front of me—what Craig calls a "hopper." Her legs are splayed out to the side, and she's using her wings to scoot and hop away from us. Craig picks her up and breaks her neck. Then I see another and another, all struggling to walk. They pick up their oversized bodies for a moment, only to plop down a few feet away. As I wade through the house, I find bird after bird with one leg that looks like it has been stuck on backward. Craig methodically moves through the house, picking up those birds, killing them, and plopping them in a bucket. It's easy to see how he might miss a suffering bird. There are just so many.

I look back and Raegan is on her belly in the litter and the feces, eye level with the birds, filming them. I see what she's doing—she's getting the literal bird's-eye view, seeing what they see. I squat down myself, and look them in the eye.

I have never noticed how a chicken's eyes are so intricate. They remind me of the glassy marbles of my childhood, with swirls of color, each so unique: gold, green, grey, blue. The bird closest to me, her eyes are complex—a golden yellow, with specks of brown. She's looking right at me.

Chickens don't blink like humans. They do the opposite. This one raises her lower lids to close her eyes—so quickly, in fact, I can't really see it. It is unnerving because she just seems to stare and stare right at me. Some of the more oversized birds are panting, heads turned up a little, presumably trying to gasp for cooler air—but still staring at me. At one point I become dizzy and lose my balance. I place my hand on the litter to catch myself.

It's then I notice that the floor, covered in litter, is hot. It is hot not by design, but by biology. The heat is caused by the build-up of composting feces. I ask Craig if he has a thermometer. He does. I place it on the litter, just on top. Out it comes: 87 degrees Fahrenheit (30.5°C). I was shocked. Those birds were sitting on a compost heap of feces day in day out. Their feet, their rears, their bare chests. This gives me the urge to pick one up and see her underneath. I lunge for one close by, causing a wave of bird movement throughout the chicken house, and I swoop her up.

My stomach turns at the sight.

Her chest is red, sore, bare, featherless. It is hot to the touch. She's been sitting and shifting on this hot litter. Her bare chest looks infected and sore. She's too heavy on her legs to stand up, so she's just been sitting on the litter, composting away along with the feces. Sitting on that hot litter, the pain in her red, sore chest must be a very close second to the pain in her legs.

It is that photo—me holding the bird with a red, bare, sore chest—that will end up in the New York Times six months later. It is that footage that New York Times journalist Nicholas Kristof will say gets to him: "Most shocking is that the bellies of nearly all the chickens have lost their feathers and are raw, angry, red flesh. The entire underside of almost every chicken is a huge, continuous bedsore. As a farm boy who raised small flocks of chickens and geese, I never saw anything like that."

In the midst of all this suffering, Craig had one main job: to dispose of and record the dead birds. The chickens that came out of this environment would be labeled "humanely raised" and "all natural." But, as Craig said, "Plutonium is all natural, so it doesn't mean anything."

Before we left on that second visit, Craig remarked how his chicken is marketed as "all natural." He turned to me and said: "I don't see how they get away with it. This isn't natural. Mass producing off of one breed is not natural."

By that night, after hours of filming, squatting in the houses, eye to eye with thousands of birds, I was more exhausted than I had ever felt in my working life. I was wiped out. I went back to my motel and got in the shower. I couldn't get the smell out of my nose. I couldn't stop tasting it. I felt like I had a fever—I very likely did, that simple cough exacerbated by the experience in the chicken house. I was sick and nauseous, coughing violently.

I didn't understand how Craig did that every day. What was it doing to his body, his mind? And I didn't understand how that could be all those birds ever knew. They hardly ever saw anything else. As the water ran over my body, washing away the filth and fumes, my mind wandered to the ducks of my childhood. I thought of how they left at the mere appearance of an algal bloom in a canal. These chickens had no way to escape. I couldn't imagine how much they must be suffering.

I collapsed in bed that night at my motel. Behind my lids I saw seas of white bodies shifting. I saw the earnest eyes of birds staring back at me, and Craig's furrowed brow and paint-spotted overalls.

Getting into that barn and filming those birds was an enormous opportunity. But it was also a burden. I had seen and filmed the true essence of America's favorite meat. I had the responsibility to tell people what I had seen. And it wasn't something they were going to want to hear. Perdue was not unique. Craig's farm was, in fact, probably much better than most. And it was awful. It was not what the public expected.

These were not my images to keep. I was just a vehicle for them to be put out in the world. I now had the heavy responsibility to bring this truth to the American people, come what may. I just hoped I could do justice to the story.

CHAPTER SIX

The Story Breaks

"If you're not living on the edge, you're taking up too much space."

—Stephen Hunt

Between May 2014, when I visited with Craig for the second time, and December 3, when we finally released our footage, we worried a lot about what might happen. We had a lot to do before we could go public with our story. Between May and December, I returned to Craig's farm a half-dozen more times—sometimes with Raegan to get more footage, and sometimes with others—almost every month. Craig, Raegan, and I tried to think of every angle where we might be wrong, where we might get sued or ignored, every piece of information we might not have understood, and every place where we might have assumed something incorrectly. We prepared in such depth, gathered so much documentation on contracts and communications and letters from the company, it became an obsession.

I became an insomniac, waking up in the middle of the night and working for hours before falling to sleep again, only to have to wake up early with my kids. There was so much checking and cross-checking that needed to be done to ensure the story was solid. I'd never done anything of this magnitude before—directly challenging a major poultry company. At the time, the entire staff of Compassion in World Farming (CIWF) USA was just me and my coworker Rachel Dreskin, who was on maternity leave. I felt the whole of the responsibility rested on my shoulders. I was scared to death. Craig could lose his livelihood or get sued. I could get my organization sued. Did I break any laws? I consulted lawyers again and again. I got Craig hooked up with lawyers

at the Government Accountability Project (GAP), who
provided pro bono legal advice.

I would drink pots of coffee daily to maintain my focus. I
forgot clothing in hotels, booked an airplane ticket going in
the wrong direction, and got two moving violations in a
48-hour period. My son was struggling at school, and I
couldn't keep up with everything the school thought I should
do for him. I felt judged as a mother. I battled daily with the
guilt of pursuing what I felt was a once-in-a-lifetime
opportunity to expose the truth—at the expense of my kids. I
felt pressured to deliver the biggest impact in media attention
I could for Craig, considering all that he was risking. And I felt
the weight of the chickens' suffering—their pain was always
on my mind. I felt like someone driving in a high-speed car
chase: just on the edge of losing control, I could not stop.

Craig felt it too. He thought about losing everything: his
home, his land, his friends. It kept him up at night. But he
also knew he couldn't stay silent anymore.

While we waited, I got to know Craig and his family
better and better. His children— Harrison, Dalton, and
Janie—are bright, respectful, and friendly. I found myself
going across their zipline, playing basketball with them, and
shucking corn with Craig's wife, Amelia. Unexpectedly, I
developed an attachment to the Watts family. I got involved
in their rituals. I came to understand just what Craig was
risking by speaking out.

Summertime is the time for husking corn at the Watt's
home. Harrison, their eldest son, Janie, their grandma, called
"Mema," and Amelia got up early one morning to harvest
corn from the field. They got about 100 ears of corn that day,
not as much as they had hoped. The weather had been weird
that season, and they had planted a bit late. But corn was still
a sought-after item in their household. Nothing tasted richer
or sweeter than fresh corn.

They had been growing corn for a long time in their
family. This season, Amelia had helped Craig's dad, known as
Papa (pronounced "pawpaw") plant it. "He's the planter,
Craig's daddy," Amelia told me as we sat down to shuck corn.

"Craig's mama and sister-in-law and before that, her mother, were the ones that would harvest. They've all got their duties. And they'd shuck together." She skillfully removed the kernels into a big metal pot. Some of it she'd freeze, some of it she'd make into creamed corn. I made a lame attempt to copy her shucking, but quickly gave up.

Amelia is careful with her words, even more so than her husband. While her hands were busy, I tried to get her to open up about how she felt about Craig working with me, and the risk to her family.

Amelia and Craig met in school. She was in sixth grade and he was in ninth, at a private school just 2 miles (3.2km) down the road from where they now live. "He saw me and thought I was cute. I saw him and thought he was cute," she laughs.

They got married young. She worked as school teacher. When the chicken business came to town, Amelia was not excited about the idea. "I thought, no way, that's crazy, that's too much debt. I never heard of that much money in my life." She laughs. "I couldn't imagine being that much in debt." But the idea of working for himself appealed to Craig. "I knew he wanted to be his own boss and have his own business."

Ten years went by before they had kids. In the meantime, the business kept them plenty busy. But now Craig was putting that business, their livelihood, on the line. I tried to ask Amelia what she hoped to gain out of us releasing the video. She just gave a big sigh and said she didn't know.

"It is hard. I think he thinks that as successful as he is—he undershot his potential. He's very smart and he works very hard. He's not treated with respect by the person he's in business with. I think he feels insulted and belittled. He thinks about it all the time. He spends a lot of time: when he's not working on it, he's thinking about it."

I'd spent enough time with Craig to know she was right. He had tried to get Perdue to listen to his concerns, and they had brushed him off. He wanted to make his voice heard as much as I wanted to get his story out there. But I wasn't sure if Amelia felt the same way. I asked her what she thought the best outcome might be for them, after all this was over.

"I lay awake thinking about that last night," she said. "I don't know what I think is going to happen. He needs a job and we need income—I know that." She considered for a second, and said, "I think I'd like him to move on from this. We've talked about it. People's natures are different. I am nonconfrontational. I'd prefer he move on."

I asked her what she'd do if her kids ever wanted to get into contract farming. For the first time, she responded immediately—she didn't have to think over her answer for a second. "Do not do it," she said. "Learn a trade. But not this." I could see her love for her kids in her face as she spoke. "I hope they do something that makes them happy and feel fulfilled, and makes a living. A doctor or a barber or a professor or a plumber. Whatever fulfills you," she said. "But not this."

I was getting to know her kids myself—they were bright, funny, and curious. I certainly wouldn't want them to spend their lives in debt, surrounded by suffering birds. These are the same things I hope for my kids, for them to feel happy and fulfilled and to make a living. And yes, definitely nothing like this. The longer we spent together, the more they were curious about why I was vegan and what it was like. In particular, they couldn't understand how I didn't eat bacon. When he first learned of my baconless existence, Dalton looked at me, wide-eyed. "You don't eat bacon?!"

I shrugged. I've been a vegan for many years and I'm used to questions like these. "Next time I'll bring you some veggie bacon," I offered. "It's pretty good."

They all burst out laughing, incredulous.

One time, Craig and I went to pick up the kids when we hadn't had a chance to have any lunch yet. There was nothing to eat for miles, so we went with the kids through the Burger King drive-thru. I challenged Dalton to try a veggie burger. At first, the kids didn't even believe Burger King had such a thing on the menu. Dalton was skeptical, but he agreed to try it. "Dalton tried a veggie burger and it was actually good!"

Janie burst out to Amelia when we got home. Amelia just smiled kindly.

Selling Dalton on one burger alternative was easy. Finding alternatives for the whole family if things went south would be a bit harder. As I sat in their kitchen, trying to help Amelia shuck the corn, I asked her what she thought Craig might do if speaking out cost him his business.

"What would he be good at?" I asked.

"Anything!" Amelia exclaimed. She has a kind, warm, infectious smile.

"He seems like a good dad," I offer. Every day, at around 2:00pm, Craig would start looking at the clock. He didn't want to be late picking the twins up from school. Sometimes he'd pick Harrison up, too, if he didn't have football practice.

"I think Craig would be a good teacher," Amelia offered. "He can fix things. Everybody has things that need fixing."

Bred to Suffer

I didn't know what impact Craig's story was going to have on the poultry industry. The problem was huge—the birds that were suffering on Craig's farm were suffering not just because of how he was forced to treat them, but because of how they were made. They were built wrong. The problem was in their genes.

Many people know the story of how the agrochemical giant Monsanto sued hundreds of farmers to keep them from saving seeds from one crop to replant for the next crop.[1] The company contends that this amounts to patent infringement—that the genetically engineered seeds are their intellectual property. They have won a number of court cases affirming their position, including in the US Supreme Court.[2]

Like genetically modified corn or soy, our table chickens today have been redesigned through selective breeding to serve the purposes of industrial agriculture. In the same way that dogs are bred for specific traits, chickens were bred to grow enormous breasts, very quickly. As with genetically modified crops, chicken genes are controlled by a few companies. Significantly, the farmers who raise these chickens do not keep a few of the best for breeding the next flock, as farmers have traditionally done for centuries. They can't, because today's chickens are "dead-end" birds who do not produce commercially viable offspring. Instead, farmers return, flock after flock, to the same few companies that provide the day-old chicks.

Farmers don't have much choice about where to get their birds. Some 80 per cent of all chicken produced globally—about 44 billion birds—come from one of three companies: Cobb-Vantress, Hubbard, and Ross. While these companies are fiercely competitive, the birds they market are almost identical and all of them can suffer from profound welfare problems, most of them caused by fast growth.

Compared with the more traditional breeds that were common in the 1950s, which took around 120 days to reach market weight, table birds today eat less but reach the same weight in around 42 days. The industrial breeds of chicken have been selectively bred to grow so large so quickly that they can collapse under their own weight, have difficulty walking in the final stages of their life, and suffer musculoskeletal, heart, and lung problems. When they're slaughtered, they're essentially obese infants.Even worse, the special "broiler breeders" who produce the billions of birds destined for supermarket shelves are so distorted that the birds only feel full if allowed to get severely overweight. As a result, these birds must be put on restricted feeding regimes. This violates a basic tenet of good animal welfare: giving an animal sufficient food. It not only produces great suffering—a state of chronic hunger—but its legality is questionable, because the law requires that animals be provided with adequate food.

It became clearer to me than ever: the distorted chickens raised for meat today are essentially living in a something worse than a physical cage: a biological cage. Their cage is their own body.

Putting a Team Together

In September 2014, Raegan assembled our raw footage into a media package, and we began the process of trying to court media partners to help us break the story. We needed the story to be big enough that, if it came to it, it was worth Craig losing everything. We knew that Perdue could break their contract with him for any number of reasons that they would claim had nothing to do with us. We knew that this can and does happen throughout the industry when farmers speak out.

With the help of contacts from Mercy for Animals, I was introduced to Mariana Van Zellar from Fusion TV. She and producer Alice Brennan poured months into what would become an award-winning documentary called *Cockfight* about Craig, the contract system, the "humane" label claim, and Compassion in World Farming's work with him. Alice was a charismatic, loud, blonde Australian. Craig refused to call her by her name, instead referring to her only as "Croc." We'd just roll our eyes, which I think he enjoyed. Mariana was a Brazilian journalist who had just broken a story on the opioid epidemic through a documentary called *Oxytrain*. She was ahead of her time, as a couple of years later opioids would dominate national conversation. The two of them were relentless. They labored and dug and asked Perdue questions without revealing Craig's identity.

Each time we thought we were ready to release, Fusion TV's lawyers put the brakes on it. They kept asking questions, asking for more evidence, more i's to be dotted and t's to be crossed. We couldn't get the film out the door. Alice and Mariana worked around the clock to answer the questions, to cover every angle, but to no avail. No one was willing to come out first with the story. We started to worry that, if we wanted to get the story out, we would just have to go it alone. Nothing like this had been done before, and no one wanted to risk being first. Everyone who saw the footage worried that it was too explosive to touch.

At the same time, Craig, Raegan, and I were worried that it wasn't explosive enough. What if, after all this risk and work, we finally released our story, and Perdue and the public just ignored us?

Eventually, in October, we got our lucky break. With an introduction by Bruce Friedrich, a long-time leader and advocate for farmed animals, I wrote to Nicholas Kristof, the most widely-read *New York Times* columnist. I've long admired Kristof's ability to tell an important, complicated story in a simple and direct way. I couldn't believe it when he wrote back to say he was interested in writing about our work with Craig. He'd only written one other story about factory farming at the time, as he usually wrote about politics and human-rights issues. But he had grown up on a farm, and Craig's story spoke to him.

Kristof agreed to cover the story and the release of our film. Around the same time, I also got the opportunity to bring the award-winning journalist Maryn McKenna to the farm. She'd been working on a book called *Big Chicken,* and had written insightfully and beautifully in *Wired* and *National Geographic* about food, antibiotics, and, well, chicken. I showed her our film, and with her feedback I completely rearranged it. Her insights may have made all the difference between a mediocre short film and one that would be viewed by millions. She also agreed to cover the release.

Even with coverage secured, Fusion's lawyers wanted more time to ensure everything was correct. It was making me nervous: what risk did they see that we didn't? Finally, Craig and I couldn't wait any longer. We were too worried that Perdue would find out and fire him before we came out with the story, which would take the wind out of our sails. Being an ex-farmer with an ax to grind would be a far less potent story than a current farmer risking it all to tell the truth.

We told our partners that it was now or never.

Live from Georgia

We took the plunge. On December 3, 2014, the video went live on YouTube, and Nicholas Kristof's piece appeared on the *New York Times* site. I was on the phone with Craig and several coworkers the moment the piece and the video went online.

The story, called *Abusing the Chickens We Eat,* described how Craig had a crisis of conscience when he saw Jim Perdue's promotional video, and what he did after:

> So Watts opened his four chicken barns to show how a Perdue chicken lives. It's a hellish sight. Watts invited an animal welfare group, Compassion in World Farming, to document conditions, and it has spent months doing so. The organization has just released the resulting video on its website.

But it's the ending that I read over and over and over again:

> Torture a single chicken and you risk arrest. Abuse hundreds of thousands of chickens for their entire lives? That's agribusiness.
> I don't know where to draw the lines. But when chickens have huge open bedsores on their undersides, I wonder if that isn't less animal husbandry than animal abuse.

"Are you reading this?" I asked Craig. I couldn't believe how strongly Kristof had stated our case. We couldn't have hoped for a better story. "Yeah, but are you seeing the video numbers shooting up?" he responded.

I kept refreshing the page. Each time I refreshed the video, the numbers went up a few thousand. I collapsed in my chair with the sheer relief. "It's done. It's over," I thought. By the end of the evening, before I went to sleep, half a million people had seen the video. After 24 hours, 1 million people had seen it. It was the definition of viral.

I slept well that night. Craig said he hadn't slept that well in years. Our relief lasted a little more than 24 hours.

Paying the Price

Hours after we released the video, Perdue turned up at Craig's farm to conduct a surprise animal-welfare audit, the first Craig had ever received in 22 years of raising chickens.

Perdue handed CIWF's video over to the Center for Food Integrity (CIF) for review. They issued Craig with a "performance improvement plan" and said he wouldn't be getting any more chickens until he retrained. No more chickens meant no more money to pay the bills. Perdue Farms maintained that it was Watts, not the company, that was negligent.

"It is clear from the video that he is not following our guidelines and has been negligent in the care of his flock," the company said in a statement.[3] "We sent a team of poultry welfare experts to visit his farm and assess the condition of his current flock, and will take whatever steps are needed to assure their well-being."

The game was on.

On that same day, the National Chicken Council, which represents the majority of the chicken industry, issued its own statement.[4] As soon as the video had been released, it called upon its Center for Food Integrity's (CFI) Animal Care Review Panel to review our video and give a so-called "expert opinion." The panel had been formed in 2013 by the chicken industry to "review undercover investigations." CFI claims to have created the Animal Care Review Panel program to engage recognized animal-care specialists to examine video and provide expert perspectives for food retailers, the poultry industry, and the media. However, CFI's CEO, Charlie Arnot, has made clear the true purpose of the "review panel": "This program creates an opportunity for animal agriculture to re-frame the public conversation related to undercover-video investigations."

Predictably, CFI's "re-framing" was to blame Watts for poor management. The industry press regurgitated the panel's review. Most of the criticism revolved around the claim that Craig should have euthanized sick and dying birds. One scientist on the panel wrote in the review, "Many animal welfare programs require farmers to inspect their birds twice daily. If you walk into a chicken house and see birds that are sick, immobilized, with gait problems, etc., they should be humanely euthanized immediately, at any age. So, if what is shown in the video is correct, the farmer was negligent in his husbandry obligations."[5]

This struck me as the strangest of responses, and as an indication that the industry was massively out of kilter with the public. In the industry's eyes, a farmer's job is to walk the barn, look for sick and dying birds, and kill them. That's what modern chicken farming has come to. Did they not see that the public would question why the birds were sick, deformed, lame, and suffering in the first place?

The industry was closing ranks against us. *Feedstuffs*, a farming newspaper, wrote that the "video misrepresents the broiler industry" and tried to blame both poor management and selective editing of the film. But they failed to check Craig's history and records. Not only were the conditions of Craig's farm within industry norms, but Craig had actually been recognized by Perdue as a top producer.

Now that the story was out, however, Perdue seemed to have changed their opinion of Craig overnight. Perdue representatives continued to drop in and review Craig's farm—more than 17 times after the release of the video. As part of his performance improvement plan (PIP), the company made Craig take a biosecurity and animal-welfare course.

The truth fights back

On December 5, GAP announced that it would represent Craig. It was a warning shot to Perdue—and all chicken companies—that whistleblowers would be protected. Amanda Hitt, the director of GAP's Food Integrity Campaign, said: "This is about the public's right to know and whistleblowers' right to tell. The reality is that consumers simply could not stand the sight of what happens on industrial farms. It takes brave truth-tellers like Craig Watts to let the public know what's really going on behind the closed barn doors. He's risked a lot coming forward, and GAP's Food Integrity Campaign is committed to standing by him if Perdue retaliates."

The public wasn't going to be fooled by Perdue's stonewalling, either. Perdue would post recipes on their

Facebook page, and a barrage of posts would question them on their treatment of both farmers and chickens. One Facebook user, Rickie Colonna, wrote: "Nice retaliation against a farmer who wants his unhealthy chickens to see the light of day. I will never buy Perdue again."

From Japan to the United Kingdom, Brazil, and all over the United States, people heard Craig's story. Press attention went worldwide. People were inspired by the risk he had taken, and they started to take action. More than 22,000 consumers sent emails to supermarkets across the country asking for better treatment of chickens. Heartfelt letters of encouragement poured into our office, thanking Craig for his efforts and hoping other farmers might do the same.

Our story wasn't the only one catching the public's attention at the time. While Craig and I were working with our partners and lawyers to get our story ready for prime time, a Compassion Over Killing investigator got herself hired by a North Carolina contract farm for Pilgrims' Pride, to work inside the shed where the birds were. The shocker was that the footage she collected in fall 2014, just like that from Craig's farm, looked remarkably similar to what Compassion Over Killing had documented a decade earlier. Nothing seemed to have changed. There were tens of thousands of birds packed into the chicken house, with very few people tending to them.

For six to eight weeks, the chickens occupied barren warehouses, which become overcrowded as the birds' bodies filled in the space around them. One or two people worked in the chicken house, but their main job was just to pick up the dead birds. The investigator wore a hidden camera, and the images she captured were shocking. The footage was grainy and dark, but any more clarity would have made it unwatchable. If anything, it was worse than the footage from Craig's farm.

The video documented the usual stuff: the misery these birds endure. As they get larger, they suffer from living, eating, and sleeping in their own waste. The flat floor of the chicken house collected the waste from flock after flock after flock, and was never truly cleaned out. There were birds having a hard time walking and birds who were completely unable to move. There were birds who had recently died and birds who had died a long time ago and were trampled on.

The birds appeared terrified of people, scattering at the slightest human movement. The investigator documented the farmers throwing birds across the room to move them around. The dead birds were picked up and put in buckets. Sometimes the birds weren't dead yet—although they were going to die, because they couldn't walk to get food or water. The workers would put them, still alive, in buckets full of dead birds, or throw them across the room into a pile to collect later.

The footage also showed the investigator moving outside. It was sunny and bright and you could see birds still moving in the buckets. They were peeping. They were talking. They were blinking their eyes. The farmer loaded up the buckets of peeping birds onto a truck and drove them out back behind the sheds, where he dumped the birds into an open pit. The footage showed live birds hobbling around inside these pits. On the tape, you can just hear the farmer say to the undercover investigator: "We're gonna drop them in the pit just as they are. Mother nature will take care of the rest." Then the farmer slams the door shut.

"We turned all the evidence over to the authorities," said Erica Meier, the executive director of Compassion Over Killing. "We were certain that, if this was not a cruelty code violation, that it must be an environmental regulation violation." They thought they had a smoking gun. But they were wrong. "North Carolina specifically exempts poultry operations from these codes," Erica told me.

At the same time, a so-called "ag-gag law" was moving through the legislature in North Carolina. Such laws make it illegal to do undercover investigations and expose animal abuse on farms. That law successfully passed shortly after the investigation, making it virtually impossible to do another similar investigation. Farms like the one Compassion Over Killing had filmed would never be held accountable.

No one was ever held accountable for what their investigation had uncovered, either. The farmer was fired, but Pilgrims' Pride carried on and never issued a public policy to stop future farmers from burying chickens alive. The investigation and the company's reaction—or lack of a reaction—made it crystal clear to me that, bad as Craig's farm was, it was, in fact, better than most.

What We Won

Craig risked everything to tell this story. He risked his friendships with his neighbors, his livelihood, and his family's future. He had nothing to gain, and everything to lose. Luckily, he didn't have to do it alone. In February 2015, the Food Integrity Campaign (FIC) filed a whistleblower retaliation complaint on his behalf. The complaint alleged that Perdue had initiated intimidation tactics against Craig after he published animal-welfare concerns.

This was an historic event, the first case and filing of its kind in the United States. A contract farmer and whistleblower had filed a lawsuit against one of the largest poultry producers in the nation. FIC said, "This landmark filing marks a first step in an effort for contract farmers to have the right to speak out against unfair and inhumane conditions on large-scale farms."

FIC director Amanda Hitt said in a statement: "Craig Watts spoke out against misleading labels and food-safety concerns and paid the price. His truth-telling is legally protected under a federal law that is meant to protect whistleblowers from the type of retaliation that Mr Watts is now facing. Instead of retaliating against Craig Watts, Perdue should be listening to him and start implementing practices that are better for animals, farmers, and consumers."

With the eyes of the media on Perdue, and Craig receiving *pro bono* legal counsel from the Government Accountability Project, the company did eventually honor his contract, despite making him jump through a few hoops. Thanks to his courage, the treatment of chicken in our food system was now in the public eye again. The gates were open, and a flood of public outrage was descending upon the industry. Light had been brought into the darkness of all those chicken houses.

Craig Watts's story not only woke up the public; it also energized animal protection groups across the country. A lot of animal-welfare groups had been focusing on securing corporate policy that would phase out cages for hens, but that campaign was wrapping up by mid-2016. Thanks to concerted efforts by Compassion in World Farming (CIWF), the Humane Society of the United States (HSUS), The Humane League, and others, the last of the major retailers, Publix, had agreed to go cage free. It was time for a new focus. Now, thanks in large part to Craig, this army of advocates had a new issue to organize around.

The American Society for the Prevention of Cruelty to Animals (ASPCA) and Farm Forward developed a platform around the need for higher welfare standards in the chicken industry. Meanwhile, Mercy For Animals conducted six undercover investigations into broiler farmers in an 18-month period, recording video after video of chickens suffering immensely on farms supplying some of the largest companies in the poultry business. HSUS turned its attention to this growing issue, too. CIWF, with broiler welfare now squarely in the public eye, strengthened its commitment to drive corporate policy change.

The chicken industry was now presented with two options. One was to continue to blame "farm management" as the culprit every time a new video revealed the cruel realities of factory farming. This approach had clearly backfired in Craig's situation. Trying to silence farmers who question the status quo was not an effective way to win Americans' trust.

The other option was to listen to what consumers—and farmers—were saying. To go beyond the National Chicken Council's anemic guidelines. It was clear that if the industry didn't take its head out of the sand soon, the chasm between it and its customers would only continue to grow.

To everyone's surprise, Perdue would start looking at the latter option. By 2015, they were working quietly from within to reorganize their own company.

CHAPTER SEVEN

Farmers Coming Out of the Woodwork

Late on a January afternoon in 2015, I arrived at Teresa Herman's farm for the first time. The winter sun was already starting to sink lower in a pink sky. Wet brown fields stretched out for miles in most directions. Leafless trees were silhouetted on the hills. Teresa's house was modest. She lived in the foothills of North Carolina, hours north of Craig's farm. This region was dominated by growers for Tyson Foods, rather than Perdue.

I pulled into the gravel driveway and before I was out of the car a large dog named Gator was at my door to greet me, tail wagging, shaking his long-haired body. I stepped out and Teresa came out from behind the house with her eight-year-old son Eli. Not far behind them was a lamb, Daisy. Daisy had been bottle weaned by Eli and followed him wherever he went, just like Gator. Eli, Daisy, and Teresa had been checking out the cows in the field. They had recently decided to stop growing chickens for Tyson and start raising cows in pasture.

Teresa had long blonde hair, a strong-looking body, and a confident stance. I'd call her a firecracker. She greeted me, wiping her hands on her jeans before stretching out her hand. "Come on in," she said, "They are waiting for you."

"They?"

"Yeah," Teresa said. "The farmers."

I hadn't been expecting to meet anyone else, so I was a little nervous as I followed her into the house, wondering what she had gotten me into. This definitely wasn't my world. There were coyote pelts on the wall and animal skulls on the coffee table. There was a photo of Teresa receiving a prize for a rodeo contest. I couldn't help but think of everything I knew about animal cruelty in rodeos—the electric prods that make animals act aggressive, the broken backs and necks. But I wasn't here to talk about rodeos. I followed Teresa into her kitchen, where four men and women were leaning and standing around her wooden kitchen table. Their faces were weathered and worried. When they saw me, they got up. They eased toward me, introducing themselves.

They asked me not to use their names, or even to describe their appearance. This conversation would be off the record. They wanted to talk and to be heard—but not to be exposed. Most would not even tell me their names. In the few hours I sat around hearing their stories, they kept looking over their shoulders at the driveway. Some of them would not even sit down. They were too nervous someone might come up the road and see them talking to me. It soon became clear to me that they were trapped by the factory-farming system, just like their chickens were.

A Tournament with No Winners

In the film *Under Contract*, Christopher Leonard, author of *The Meat Racket,* describes the typical poultry farmer as "someone who owes $500,000 to $2 million on their farm, and lives flock to flock or paycheck to paycheck. The people who rely entirely on this business for their income are living, if not on the poverty line, certainly on the edge of bankruptcy."[1]

In total, contract chicken farmers across America owe $5.2 billion dollars.[2] Saddled with this debt, they have few options for improving their own lives, let alone the lives of the chickens they raise. One of the biggest problems is something called the tournament system. Fusion's investigative team described the tournament system as follows:

> It works like this: Farmers are divided into groups called complexes, kind of like sports leagues, and they compete against each other. The goal is to raise chickens to the right weight at the lowest cost. The company sets an average price per pound of chicken and according to their formula they rank the farmers

from best to worst each flock. But here's the catch, it doesn't really matter if all of them do reasonably well, they're still ranked. So theoretically the top farmer can get 70 per cent more pay than the guy on the bottom of the ranking sheet. What's more, it's not easy to predict where you're going to fall on the ladder and so farmers find it difficult to do any financial planning.[3]

One farmer I met described the system this way: "If I do really well in a tournament system, that means my pound of feed per pound of gain is less than everybody else's. Then I move up on the sheet. They take money away from the people at the bottom of the sheet to compensate me for doing well. But at the same time, those growers are being punished, not necessarily because they did anything wrong, just because the birds that I had are better than their birds."

When a farmer "wins" this rigged tournament, he is literally taking money away from his neighbors. When he loses, he's paying his neighbors out of his own paycheck. And it gets worse—farmers can't even determine their own strategy for playing this rigged game. They don't choose the type of chickens they raise, or the conditions they keep them in, or the number of chickens in each house. They don't choose how much they feed the birds, or what they eat, or what kinds of medicines they get. The company determines all those factors. The company determines every single input, but the farmer takes financial responsibility for the results.

One farmer showed me his actual paycheck. The numbers were confounding. The flow of cash meant tens of thousands of dollars moving around for the chickens bought, the feed, the propane, the electricity, the spraying of the houses, the insurance. After all of those expenses, there wasn't much left to feed a family. According to the Poultry Site, depending on the size of bird produced, gross income per house will generally range from $28,000 to $35,000 annually. Most farmers have to borrow money to set up their houses, so net returns per house are generally minimal—$3,000 to $10,000—during the 10- to 15-year payback period.

In fact, pay for most farmers is actually going down even as their costs continue to rise. In 2018, a typical farmer might be paid 5.55 cents per pound of chicken he raised. For a 4-pound (1.8kg) chicken, he'd make 22 cents. Poultry companies can and do adjust the end weight for the chickens, and this impacts the final paycheck for the farmer. They're still paid by the pound, but if the chicken weighs less, the farmer makes less. But their bills keep going up. I've spoken to farmers who have invested more than $2 million in their farms and are still struggling to pay for groceries and canning vegetables "just in case."

These are the farmers producing America's favorite protein. The chicken industry is worth $90 billion annually[4], but the farmers who raise the birds all too often live on the edge of poverty. Chicken sells on the commodity market for a dollar a pound.[5] Farmers make five cents a pound. They take home only 5 per cent of the total amount consumers pay for chicken. A 2001 study by the US Department of Agriculture (USDA) and the National Contract Poultry Growers Association found that 71 per cent of those who made their living solely from chicken farming lived below the poverty line[6].

These were the people I met at Teresa's house. Two of those farmers together owed more than a million dollars in loans for the construction and upgrades of their chicken houses. They were both over 60 years old, so they wouldn't live to repay that debt. They were barely keeping their heads above the water financially. They talked about how their children would inherit their debt or, if they didn't take over the debt, they'd lose the land. They talked about the tournament system, the diminishing returns of chicken farming, how there seemed to be no way out for them. They talked about getting unhealthy birds, asking for help in getting them better, and just getting more sick birds. They were not experts. They didn't know how to deal with the constant health issues their birds suffered from. They only knew how much those sick and dying birds were costing them.

The farmers felt as if the companies they worked for had forgotten them. They felt as if America had forgotten them.

Yet the birds they raised still made their way onto the plates of Americans. They were still a part of the food system. They were just lost in the shadows.

One farmer I met at Teresa's house was open to me visiting his chicken house. With dusk upon us, I followed him a few miles to his property. He didn't want me to give his name, but he did want me to see, smell, and feel how things were not going well.

As he cracked open the door to his chicken house, one word came to mind: dungeon. This place was medieval: dank, damp, dark. It felt like a cave where dark deeds might happen. The floor squished beneath my feet. The area had flooded recently, and water had seeped in through the sides of the house. It was winter, but the air was warm—and thick with dust and the scent of ammonia. I coughed, my eyes streamed with tears. The smell was familiar from my time at Craig's farm, but this was so much worse.

The farmer hardly spoke to me. He didn't even watch for my reaction. He seemed to have given up.

It was barely light enough to read a newspaper. I couldn't see the end of the house. I shuffled around, wading through despondent birds. Most scattered as I moved toward them. Some couldn't scatter: they were too lame, sickly, or weak to move.

I got out of there as fast as I could, but that damp and dark dungeon would remain imprinted in my mind. I'd thought the conditions on Craig's farm were bad, but now I had walked into the forgotten shadows of the food system. Now I knew things could get much, much worse.

Get Out

When I later told Craig I had been accused of just going out of looking for an "angry farmer" when I visited his farm, he said, "You're damn right you did."

Why was Craig so angry? When farmers have sick birds, that doesn't just hurt the birds. Every bird that dies means less money in the farmer's pocket, and therefore less money for all their expenses, including that mortgage-like loan they took out to be in business in the first place. That loan is their whole life: their home, their land, the future for their kids.

After Craig Watts went public with his story, other farmers began contacting Compassion in World Farming. From all of the major companies, from multiple states, I heard the same thing over and over again. The system was rigged; the birds were sick; the farmers were trapped. But most farmers were not willing to go on the record. They just wanted to talk.

Teresa and her husband Rich were some of the few farmers who would actually let me use their names—possibly because they had recently quit raising birds for Tyson. On that first visit, Teresa was sizing me up. Afterward, we started emailing and talking. She invited me back, and this time I came with Raegan and her camera. I wanted to tell Teresa's story, and she was willing to tell it to me.

In 1996, the Herman family borrowed $350,000 to build three industrial chicken houses. They hoped to pay that debt off before their son hit college age . But all along the way, they were asked to make upgrades, which meant they had to keep borrowing more money just to meet the new requirements set by the chicken companies. By 2014, they owed $400,000 on the houses. What's worse, they were losing $30,000 each year in sick and dying chickens. They realized they would never get ahead, so they made a decision that would change their lives forever. They quit Tyson. They quit chicken factory farming.

The math just didn't add up. In 2013, Teresa realized that it was costing them more than they were making to grow their chickens, if she took into account the electricity, the propane, and the upgrades the company demanded. In 2014, the Hermans' expenses were $33,000 more than what they made growing chickens for Tyson.

"At some point," Teresa says, "you have to step back and say this is not sustainable. When we built the houses, it cost somewhere in the region of $350,000. Today we owe close to $600,000 on those same houses. It's not sustainable. There is absolutely no way to get ahead."

Teresa and Rich knew they had to do something to get their family out from under this crushing debt. "We made the decision that we are not going to be able to please these people, it doesn't matter what we do," Teresa says. "We bent over backward to meet their demands. It was never good enough." They did the math and realized that if they took the $30,000 they were losing every year on chicken farming and put it toward their debt, they'd be able to pay it off in 15 years. "It will be a difficult 15 years, but at least at the end of the 15 years we'll have the farm paid off." If they didn't quit, they realized, their son Eli would inherit their debt. "It's not fair to leave him with a $600,000 debt that he'll never be able to pay off," Teresa says.

Sick Birds, Sick System

It wasn't just the debt. Teresa and Rich had also started to notice that there wasn't something quite right with the birds they were being given.

"They have designed the chickens so they just sit and eat," Rich explains. "And it's so dark in there they won't move around." The darkness is part of the design. "They don't want them wasting any energy. The chickens can't deal with any bright light. They are real fragile."

The fragility of the birds became a concern for Teresa and Rich. During her last year or so of growing chickens, Teresa, who has a background in animal science, started noticing some troubling things about the health of their birds. "You see these birds and they have crooked necks, and they have weird deformed legs, and I started asking questions. 'Why are we having these diseased birds?'"

Teresa wanted to know more about the way antibiotics were administered. She couldn't figure out why she and her husband were being asked to run low levels of these drugs in the birds' water. "It's not something farmers do as normal practice," Teresa explains. "It's not economically feasible." But Tyson advice was to run low levels of a drug called Tylan—just 20 per cent of the recommended dose. But the birds were sick. Why were they being given only a partial dose of antibiotics?

Teresa began to dig around, and soon learned enough to know that running very low doses wasn't just about fighting disease. It was about stimulating growth. Somewhere along the way, the industry discovered that giving antibiotics to chickens in low dosages was a great way to make chickens get bigger faster. Teresa knew enough about antibiotics to know that overuse on farms was a key factor in creating antibiotic resistance. It concerned her. When she starting asking questions, she was told not to worry about it. But she knew enough that it was starting to keep her up at night. "If you listen to any of the news stories," she says, "we have overused and misused antibiotics for so long that we've developed superbugs."

Bad Bugs

The problem of the misuse of antibiotics in our food system is one very close to my heart: my grandmother and then my father suffered from antibiotic-resistant infections. In her 80s, my grandmother was in and out of the hospital for six months because of an infection to a cut on her toe. The cut just kept getting worse, and an infection set in and began to spread. The doctors were worried it would move up her leg. If it infected her blood, there was no telling what would happen. At her age, they could not take the risk of not taking action. They tried various interventions, cocktails of drugs, but eventually there was only one solution left: amputation. Her toe had to be removed to stop the infection from spreading and potentially killing her.

A year later, my father acquired a multidrug-resistant infection. Again, he had a simple cut from working on his sailboat. Usually this sort of thing couldn't rattle my dad. He treated it in the usual way, but like my grandmother, the cut took a menacing path. Over months, the infectious-disease doctor tried different mixes of drugs of increasing strength. The antibiotics were destroying my father's gut health and energy, but not having an impact on his infection. The doctors started to worry that the infection would spread and move up his arm. Surgery became the only option—to physically go in and try to remove the infection. This resulted in a jagged opening on his finger, held together by stitches, that took many more weeks to heal. It looked gruesome, but the worse was now over.

Sitting with my dad in February 2016, he was in the middle of his antibiotic cocktail course. At the time, I had just completed an investigation into Pilgrims Farms, and it was just a month before we would release the video. My father was visibly drained. This is a man who swims a mile a day, sails every weekend, and builds handmade cribs for his granddaughters. This man now couldn't cut his own dinner because of an out-of-control infection on his finger. My mom was leaning over him, cutting his meal. I couldn't watch. The drugs he was on were destroying his energy and appetite.

I had a passionate rant at the table that day about wasting our antibiotics on farmed animals who have to be kept alive through drugs because that is how bad their conditions are. At one point, my family demanded evidence that antibiotic resistance really comes from using drugs on farms. Isn't it caused by overuse in hospitals or doctors' offices?

The Center for Disease Control (CDC) has a handy diagram[7] that describes how exactly resistance can emerge. There are only two ways. One is through farmed animals and the other is through humans using antibiotics. For farmed animals, the CDC describes the following path:

1. Animals get antibiotics and develop resistant bacteria in their guts.
2. Drug-resistant bacteria can remain on meat from animals. When not handled or cooked properly, the bacteria can spread to humans.
3. Fertilizer or water containing animal feces and drug-resistant bacteria is used on food crops.

4. Drug-resistant bacteria in the animal feces can remain on crops and be eaten. These bacteria can remain in the human gut.

The CDC states that, according to data published by the Food and Drug Administration (FDA), more antibiotics are sold by weight in the United States for farmed animals than for people. This use contributes to the emergence of antibiotic-resistant bacteria, of which animals serve as the carrier. [8] The CDC reminds us that, no matter what, we should only use antibiotics when there is defined illness. Despite these warnings, 80 per cent of antibiotics distributed are for farmed animals.[9]

While it is hard to know if my grandmother's or father's problems are directly due to farmed-animal uses of antibiotics, it is certain that overuse of antibiotics on farmed animals is contributing to the overall problem of resistance. With more than 2 million people getting sick[10] every year with antibiotic-resistant infections, and at least 23,000 dying as a result, this could not be more serious[11].

Years earlier, I spoke on a panel at the CDC with Robert Lawrence, founding director of Johns Hopkins Center for a Liveable Future, to talk about antibiotic use in the food system. I remember him saying that, if your child had to receive antibiotics every day of their life just to survive in their environment, you would definitely think there is something wrong with that environment. That is factory farming for chickens. In 2013, the industry begun to take antibiotics out of the chickens' feed without improving their environment—leaving them in the worst possible situation. They had removed the birds' only protection but kept them trapped with disease and death on the rise in our food system.

This would prove a critical pressure point for getting the chicken industry to wake up and change its ways.

Maryn McKenna, expert science writer, goes into great detail in her book *Big Chicken* about the connection between antibiotic use and the chicken industry. While my experience was personal, her book lays out the wider impact antibiotic resistance is having on our world. She writes that: "Resistant bacteria are a grave threat and getting worse. They are responsible for at least 700,000 deaths around the world each year: 23,000 in the United States, 25,000 in Europe, more than 63,000 babies in India. Beyond those deaths, bacteria that are resistant to antibiotics cause millions of illnesses—two million annually just in the United States—and cost billions in health-care spending, lost wages, and lost national productivity. It is predicted that by 2050, antibiotic resistance will cost the world $100 trillion and will cause a staggering 10 million deaths per year." [12]

It also cost my grandmother her toe and my dad some bits of his finger. They were lucky it was brought under control, but it was horrifying to me that we as a society could be so short sighted, so casual about something so critical. It was horrifying to me to imagine a post-antibiotic era when so much as a cut could kill you.

Dr Kellog Schwab, a Johns Hopkins researcher, stated the problem elegantly: "It's not appreciated until it's your mother, or your son, or you are trying to fight off an infection that will not go away because the last mechanism to fight it has been usurped by someone putting it into a pig or chicken.[13]"

Teresa's sense that antibiotic overuse was a problem was just an instinct. For some of the farmers I met later, it was a crisis. But Teresa and Rich were already asking themselves whether they might be a part of this growing problem. That, combined with the fact that they kept losing money on these diseased flocks, made them wonder if chicken farming was worth it.

"We did a lot of praying," Rich says. He told me that he offered to grow chickens for Tyson if they would just pay the power and gas bill and pay him $75 a day to look after the chickens, which is actually less than minimum wage. If they were guaranteed minimum wage, he thought they could make it work. They had already invested so much. "But they wouldn't do that, because that would cost them more," he says.

Teresa knows the issue is not just at the integrator level. She is clear that customers are at the end of the string, constantly demanding more cheap chicken. "I know a lot of

moms that buy chicken from Wal Mart," she says. "They pay
five bucks for a pack of chicken, and it's a cheap way to feed
their family, but in reality, is it a cheap meal? I mean, what's
the final cost of that five-pound pack of chicken to their
family? The cost to us is about $600,000. That's not cheap.
That's not cheap at all."

Teresa and Rich spent many long, late nights crunching
the numbers. In the end they came up with their own plan to
pay off their enormous loans by diversifying their farm. They
broke ties with Tyson and ventured out on their own.

CHAPTER EIGHT

How Healthy Is Chicken, Really?

In August 2015, I attended a meeting of farmers and ranchers in Kansas City, Missouri, arranged by the Organization for Competitive Markets (OCM), a nonprofit that represents family farms and advocates against the corporate takeover of the food system. I was definitely not their usual attendee. When the man sitting next to me crossed his legs, I saw a pistol strapped to his ankle. These were not people who felt at ease in the world. In one way or another, these farmers and ranchers had been let down by the food and farming system. I was there to learn more about their lives. After hearing from so many contract growers, I was hungry for more stories, more people willing to speak out. When one of the speakers mentioned my work with Craig Watts, I stood up and said I'd be happy to speak to anyone else wanting to tell their story. I said we needed more people to speak up and be truth-tellers.

Mike Weaver made his way to me without much hesitation and introduced himself as a grower for Pilgrim's Pride, the second-largest poultry producer in the United States. He said he'd be happy to have me come to West Virginia to see his farm and to meet with another grower, Eric Hedrick. Eric was the largest grower for Pilgrim's in the state, with 12 chicken houses on his property. I did the math quickly in my head: Eric was overseeing close to 300,000 birds at a time. Staggering. Mike said Eric was on the verge of bankruptcy because his birds kept getting sick. Everyone's in the valley did, and they didn't know why and they didn't know what to do about it.

Three months later, Raegan and I flew to Baltimore and then drove three hours straight west into the Shenandoah Valley. Mike had given me directions that involved things like, "When you see the pond on the left, go three miles and take a right." I didn't write them down the first time, thinking I'd just use my phone. But when I told him I had Google Maps, he laughed, "That's no good out here." I dutifully scribbled down his directions in a notebook.

About two hours into our drive, the highway seemed suddenly to empty of cars as we entered a valley of bright red, orange, and yellow fall color. Raegan and I pulled over just to take it in. It was already very cold, and our breath hung in the air and floated off in little clouds. There was a fog rolling slowly through. It was such a peaceful and beautiful place—a stark contrast to the darkness we were about to uncover.

Deeper and deeper into the valley we drove. We didn't talk much. The few houses we passed were run down and seemed abandoned. True to Mike's warning, cell phone service cut out, and I had to refer to my notebook for directions for the rest of the way. We were just a couple of hours from the nation's capital, but it felt we were no longer in the same country. We were somewhere foreign— somewhere forgotten.

Our goal for this trip was to learn more about a disease that was decimating flocks in the region. Mike had told us about an horrific bacterial disease called gangrenous dermatitis that was not only causing immense suffering for the birds, but also bringing financial ruin for farmers. It seemed no one knew how to control it. Birds would be seemingly normal one day and then, within 24 hours, they'd essentially be eaten from the inside out. The disease always seemed to strike toward the end of the last week of growth, by which stage the farmer had paid for all of the feed. Not only were the animals suffering and dying; the farmers also did not get paid for the birds that don't make it to market.

I wanted to bring the truth about this disease to light, but Mike was taking a big risk in even allowing me to visit his farm. Months earlier, an anonymous source had sent me a copy of a letter that Pilgrim's had sent to all of their farmers, threatening that if they let activists like me or media into their chicken houses, it was considered a terminable offense.

The stakes were high, and I wasn't sure how we've ever get images out of these chicken houses.

We arrived at Mike's place as the sun was setting and the temperature dropping. In the distance we could see two silver chicken houses with the sun reflecting off their roofs. With not much time to look around, Mike had us jump on his RTV to tour the property, passing the chicken shed without much comment. We weaved up a dirt path, up hills and down through woods, as Mike pointed out where bears, turkeys, and deer could be found, including places where he'd set up feeding stations so that he'd be able to hunt the animals more easily. Once again, I was in a world I didn't know and wasn't comfortable with. But I'm sure Mike wasn't that comfortable hosting us, either. We were both pushing our boundaries.

Raegan and I stayed that night at a motel that doubled as a liquor store and pizza place. The walls were thin and the rooms came equipped with fly swatters and TVs that didn't work. The continued lack of cell phone reception made for a feeling of unease and disconnect from anything familiar.

The next morning, we met Mike at a local diner for breakfast. We continued to feel each other out, looking for common ground. We narrowly avoided an argument about hunting. I felt as if, up until the very last moment of that meal, he was trying to decide whether or not to deliver me to Eric Hedrick, the largest Pilgrim's Pride farmer in the state. In the end, for better or for worse, he decided that he would.

Driving up to Eric and Rachel Hedrick's house, I tried to prepare myself. I could not look too eager. I would need to be patient, hear their story, and assess the risk for them and for us. We drove up on the crest of the road and I could not believe what I was seeing. Twelve silver houses were tucked in the valley below. And inside those houses were hundreds of sick and dying birds.[SM1]

Through a half-day conversation over the kitchen table, Raegan and I sat with Mike, Rachel, and Eric, immersed in their world and their story. It wasn't until many hours into the conversation that they agreed to let me turn on a camera to document their words.

Eric told me he had 12 houses, each 42 by 400 feet (12.8 x 120m), where he raised broilers for the Moorefield complex of Pilgrim's. He had one goal: to get each bird to 3.75lb (1.7kg) in 35 days. He oversaw 315,000 birds at any one time, with about 26,000 birds in each house. That's about 0.75 of a square foot (70cm²) per bird.

I told him I'd seen the letter Pilgrim's Pride sent to their contract growers, saying they should not let anyone like me into their chicken houses. I told him I was there to find out what the company didn't want me to see, and to learn more about what was behind those closed doors. I told him I wanted to hear what he thought the public needed to know about the system. I wanted to understand not only what was happening to his chickens, but also what he was going through as a farmer.

Eric and Mike looked at each other. After a moment, Eric told me that what the company was trying to hide was, basically, everything—the overcrowded conditions inside the houses, and the diseases and physical deformities affecting the birds. The disease was worse than I had ever imagined. Eric told me that, just a couple of weeks earlier, he'd picked up 400 dead birds in one house one morning—and when he went back in the evening he found 900 more dead birds. Every single dollar he'd spent raising every single one of those dead birds was a loss he had to bear.

With mounting deaths, Eric asked the company for help. Their answer? Hire more people to pick up the dead birds faster. Not a drug, not a procedure—just pick up the corpses up faster. At this point, Eric threw up his hands. He felt helpless. He had 12 chicken houses, and he told me it took an hour and a half to walk through each house to pick up 100 dead birds. At the rate his birds were dying, he had to do that three or four times a day. That's 54 to 72 hours of work to get through every single day. That's not a small job. Between Eric and his wife and whatever help they could hire with the cash they had, that was a lot of bending over and collecting dead chickens. Eric wanted to hire more people, but he couldn't afford it. When disease hit, the number of dead birds jumped up and his income plummeted. Because of the losses, he had even less cash to hire more people. If that was the only solution, it was no solution at all. It was a vicious cycle: "They say to hire more people, but it's hard to spend money you don't have."

Rotting Alive

Gangrenous dermatitis (GD), the disease Eric and Mike and their neighbors were experiencing on their farms, has been called the number-one health problem facing US chicken companies. The bacteria infects soft tissue and causes loss of feathers, lesions that are dark red to blue green, and macerated skin areas. It typically begins from the wings and adjacent areas and, once infected, birds can die as soon as within 24 hours.[1]

Mike had taken photos of his last flock, which had been infected. They were nauseating. The birds looked like pulped purple and green flesh, loosely resembling a chicken shape, disintegrating on the inside. I thought I had been desensitized to chicken-house conditions over the years, but even I grimaced at the times. Mike just shrugged and told me the disease was common. I could not believe I had never heard of it.

We would come to learn that the disease was not limited to these Pilgrim's Pride farms. As many as 25 per cent of flocks at some companies have been affected by gangrenous dermatitis, with 4 per cent or more of the birds dying from the disease. The disease is now the considered a leading health problem amongst chicken integrators. In one industry survey, 12 out of 17 broiler company veterinarians listed GD as their biggest disease concern.[2]

Losing thousands of birds from each flock to disease was bad enough, but Eric and MIke were worried about something else. They were concerned that birds with undetected disease might actually go to slaughter. If the disease is detected at a slaughterhouse, the carcass may be condemned—but it may also simply have visibly infected areas trimmed off.[3] The carcasses of infected birds could end up on Americans' plates.

Of course, the way modern chickens are raised does not help. The majority of chickens raised on conventional farms today live in dirty, warm environments, which are perfect conditions for bacteria to thrive. The birds have also been selectively bred to grow very big, very fast. One unintended consequence of this fast growth is poor immune function. So, we have taken a bird that has a weakened immune system and put her in an environment perfect for growing bacteria. On top of all this, we are now starting to remove antibiotics from the system.

As Teresa Herman had discovered, daily inputs of antibiotics and other antibacterial drugs in chicken feed have been a crucial prop for the factory-farming system for decades. Removing this crutch without improving living conditions or chickens' immune systems is a recipe for disaster. Too often, antibiotics are simply removed from birds' feed. Antibiotic-free chicken typically commands a premium price, but welfare standards for these chickens are not necessarily improved; nor are the farmers raising them getting higher wages.

In 2014, according to the National Chicken Council, mortality rates rose[4] in the US chicken industry for the first time after a long period of decreasing mortality. This trend continued in 2015. It's no coincidence that mortality started rising around the time several big chicken companies began to remove antibiotics from feed.[5]

Who pays the price for the higher mortality levels? It's not the big companies like Pilgrim's, Tyson, or Sanderson. The chickens are paying through increased disease and suffering, but the farmers are literally paying the price. The farmers only get paid for the live weight of birds they can sell, so, even though they have little to no control over the health and genetics of their birds, they take the hit when diseased birds die.

Thanks to public pressure, chicken companies have also recently begun removing arsenic—yes, arsenic—from daily feed. Arsenic was used to control coccidia, a parasite that causes diarrhea, but it also promoted faster growth. In 2013, the FDA withdrew approval for three arsenic-based animal drugs because of reports of unacceptable levels of arsenic showing up in food.[6] But solving the arsenic problem would end up creating another problem. According to Dr David Chapman, who specializes in coccidial research, as long as chickens continue to have constant contact with their own feces, the disease will continue to be a problem. In other words, as long as factory farming remains the norm, so will the disease.[7]

Gangrenous-dermatitis infection is thought to follow coccidiosis infection. As arsenic is removed from feed but conditions for chickens are not improved, it is not surprising that diseases like gangrenous dermatitis are becoming a problem.

As Teresa had guessed, antibiotic overuse had become a real threat to sick humans—yet reducing antibiotic use in chickens without improving their living conditions created perfect conditions for disease. Most major producers were starting to remove antibiotics from chicken feed. In April 2015, about 5 per ent of Pilgrim's chickens were antibiotic free, but Pilgrim's planned to be 25 per cent antibiotic-free by 2019.[8] Perdue and Tyson have also made public commitments to reduce their human-relevant antibiotic use. As of 2017, Sanderson was the only major integrator without an antibiotic-free policy, and its CEO had said he does not plan to budge on the issue[9,10].

Eric and Mike were aware of all these problems. They weren't sure exactly what the solutions were, but they knew things weren't right. When I asked what they hoped for, their answer was simple: fair treatment.

"Fair treatment is the main thing," Mike said, "for us and for the birds. Basically, that's all it boils down to. None of us have asked to become millionaires. But we expect to be treated fairly, and make enough money to pay our bills and feed our families and do some things that we enjoy."

When a Plan Comes Together

Eric and Mike no longer believed they could get that fair treatment from Pilgrim's without applying some pressure. So we set a plan in motion. They agreed to work with us, but given the letter that said Raegan and I could not step foot in their chicken houses, we had to find another way to get images out of their farms without getting them cut off by the company. Eric and Rachel were already on the verge of bankruptcy. They have three daughters. They had to find a way to limit their risk.

We brainstormed and tossed different ideas around until one stuck: we'd leave a camera with Eric and Mike. They would film inside their own houses—that way Reagan and I wouldn't have to set foot inside. The farmers would show the reality of the conditions inside their own houses, through their own eyes. At the end of the flock, Reagan and I would pick up the cameras, review the footage, and find a way to get the images out to the public. Together—animal activists and chicken farmers—we set out to reveal the truth.

Weeks later, when Raegan and I returned to collect the footage, we were welcomed warmly, with no more hesitation or doubt. We were all in this together now. Mike kindly let us stay at a trailer on his property. The motel was too far away, and we wanted to stay close by so we could get to work. The "trailer" turns out to be a place Mike and his buddies use during hunting season. It's full of hunting paraphernalia: target instructions, rifles lying around, photos of animals they've shot, and even Frantic Fawn, a fake baby deer that makes a panicked bleating noise to attract animals to shoot. I didn't sleep very well that night, and I'm not entirely sure Mike wasn't having a little chuckle to himself about having us stay there.

The next morning, Raegan and I found our rental car had about a thousand house flies in it. When we arrived, it had been raining. We left the windows and trunk open and soon learned that flies go where it's dry. Rookie mistake, Mike told us (Raegan later had to pull over while driving a mountain road through thick fog when a fly committed suicide in her eye and she was unable to see). While we managed to get the flies out of the main car, we eventually returned the vehicle to the rental company with a surprise army of farm flies still living in the trunk.

Despite the comic relief, the situation on the farm was as bad as we had been told it would be. GD had struck both Mike's and Eric's farms, and both gave us grotesque footage of infected birds. And it wasn't just GD. Another disease, called enteritis, had also come to light. This one caused the birds to have bloody poop.

Rachel, who ended up doing some filming, told me about what she had seen: "There were dead birds laying on top of a bird that was already dead, and there's bloody poop all over it. That's what people are eating. Consumers do not know anything about how their food is being grown, or they would be disgusted, they wouldn't eat chicken at all." She looked at me and added, "I'm not sure I'm going to eat it anymore."

"Do you think there is a better way to do this?" I asked. "Not having so many birds in the houses would help a lot," she said immediately. She put herself in the chickens' place for a moment: "I would feel I was smothered, just because there is no room to move, at all. You're fighting for food, you're fighting for a drink of water. That shouldn't be." She was clearly upset, for the birds' sake as well as her own. If she knew in the beginning what she knows now about how chickens are raised, she says, she would never have gotten into the business: "The further you go along, the more they see you are bound to them because they own you as well the bank owns you. You have to do what they tell you."

Without people like Rachel speaking up, I don't know where we'd be. "You are being very brave, you and your husband," I tell her. We both know what she and her husband are risking to speak out. "Are you afraid?"

We're standing outside the crowded, disease-ridden chicken houses. It's raining, and Rachel is wearing a gray sweatshirt with the hood pulled up, nearly covering her eyes. She's looking out toward the hills, and I can tell by the turn of her mouth that she's holding back tears. "We are to the point where something has to give," she says. "If we close down, we close down." She's crying now, no longer able to hold back. "I'm sorry," she says, wiping her eyes. "Nobody wants to lose everything they have, your home, nobody wants that, but that is what we are facing."

Rachel is a mother just like me. She's risking everything to get the truth out. Talking to her reminds me of the obligation I have to do right by her and make sure this risk she's taking makes a difference.

We spent months reviewing the footage, sending it to a veterinarian and legal experts to help us understand exactly what Eric, Rachel, and Mike have recorded. The disease, gangrenous dermatitis, is like nothing I've ever seen. Birds turn from one day to the next. One day they are walking around; the next they are a lump of flesh on the ground, covered in hideous dark red or blue-green lesions.

The video also showed some of the more familiar health problems related to these birds' genetics. Birds bred for unnaturally large breasts grow very big, very fast. The unintended consequence of this is that they can be "genetically lame," unable to walk because their bodies are out of balance, and also can have poor immune function. The birds' welfare is further compromised by being denied natural light and enrichment. They are housed in crowded, dirty, warm environments—perfect conditions for bacterial disease to thrive—without even antibiotics to keep them healthy.

Although broilers are not kept in a cage, they are trapped in a physiological "cage." They are bound by fast-growth genetics that result in inherent welfare problems such as lameness, heart attacks, footpad dermatitis, and hockburns, among other problems. Consumers have become more aware of the suffering caused by crates for pigs and battery cages for laying hens, but fast-growth genetics deserves just as much attention.

The Truth Comes Out

Before releasing the film, we made extensive efforts to reach out to Pilgrim's Pride to discuss our concerns. They stonewalled us. So, on April 16, 2016, we partnered again with *The New York Times'* Nicholas Kristof, who wrote a Sunday column[11] on our partnership with the two brave farmers, Mike Weaver and Eric Hedrick. Kristof called the video and the disease "stomach churning," saying that "to watch the video is to develop an appetite for soy." He called national attention to the problems affecting both chicken and farmer.

This time the reaction from the industry was not what we expected. The National Chicken Council for the first time remained silent about an undercover video investigation, although the Center for Food Integrity did their own review[12] of our video[SM5][13]. Despite their unbiased-sounding name, CFI are an industry group whose self-stated goal is to "create an opportunity for animal agriculture to re-frame the public conversation related to undercover video investigations." But their tune had changed since our the release of our Craig Watts video. For the first time, they actually agreed with some of our concerns.

CFI's Animal Care Review Panel three members agreed with the key points that fast-growth rate genetics are a problem, and that simply removing antibiotics without improving living conditions and chicken immune systems is only going to increase the spread of disease throughout the industry. Dr Bruce Webster specifically agreed that the chickens' leg problems and inability to move around were related to their rapid growth. Dr Patricia Hester also conceded, "Genetically selecting broilers for rapid growth and broad breast has led to more inactive chickens with leg problems ... Broilers spend about 76 per cent of their time sitting."

Commenting on the enteritis seen in the video, the third panel member, Dr Sacit Bilgili, said, "The current push to eliminate antibiotic use in poultry production will likely increase enteritis in commercial flocks." In response to a comment in the video by one farmer that there is "bloody poop laying all over the floor," Webster observed, "We could see more of this type of disease as we move away from using antibiotics in poultry production."

The experts pointed to consumer demand for large, white breast meat as the culprit behind today's fast-growth genetic lines. Bilgili said, "There are many genetic strains available to the broiler companies to choose from based on their target markets and business plans. This includes fast and slow growing strains, as well as those with low or high breast muscle yields. Given the expansion of foodservice and consumer appetite for 'white meat,' the 'economics' will continue the demand for more breast meat."

Some industry press did try to find parts of the panel review that defended the industry and blamed the farmers,[14] but for the most part this response was new. Had we turned a corner? Had the industry started to realize that somewhere along the way they had taken a wrong turn?

White Striping, Woody Breast, and Spaghetti Meat

It wasn't just the unexpected response from the industry panel regarding the video. It was becoming clear that the industry was concerned about the rapid and grotesque growth of the birds for a whole other reason.

In the United States, chicken has long been one of the most popular sources of animal protein, and its consumption has consistently grown since the 1950s, surpassing that of both pork and beef, according to the National Chicken Council. In 2015, almost 9 billion broiler chickens were produced, weighing a total of 53 billion pounds (24 billion kg), and more than 40 billion pounds (18 billion kg) of chicken meat were marketed in the United States.

One of the reasons for the popularity of chicken is that, like other "lean" meats, it has been reported to be healthier than other animal protein sources [SM6].[15] Major cancer-research organizations have declared that certain red meats are probable carcinogens, and poultry and fish are healthier alternatives.

What these cancer researchers don't say, however (or perhaps don't know), is that the chicken you're eating today is very different from the chicken our grandparents ate. In 1925, before fast-growing broiler strains became so popular, an average chicken raised for meat took 112 days to reach its market weight of 2.5 pounds (1.13kg); in 2016, broilers are ready for slaughter at 47 days, with an average weight of 6.18 pounds (2.8kg).[16] These birds don't just grow faster, they grow different. In 2001, an average Ross 308 broiler (a fast-growing strain) weighed 4.7lb (2.1kg) at 43 days of age, with the breast weighing about 0.8 lb (360g).[17] In 2012, this bird's total body weight at 35 days was very similar, but breast weight had increased to over 1 lb (450g).[18]

It turns out that changing these birds so dramatically has consequences for the quality of their meat. Genetic selection for fast growth of larger muscles is believed to play a central role in the recent increase in muscle disorders known as myopathies in fast-growing broilers. New types of breast-muscle myopathies have begun to emerge: deep pectoral myopathy (DPM), white striping (WS), wooden breast (WB), and an even stranger one called spaghetti meat.[19] The name tells you exactly what that one looks like.

DPM involves the death of muscle fiber, presumably due to poor blood circulation in disproportionately large muscles.[20] In both wooden breast and white striping, normal muscle tissue is replaced with fibrous connective tissue. You can actually see and feel the difference in the meat. In wooden breast, the tissue feels harder. With white striping, you can see thin white lines running across the breast muscle.

These problems are so obvious that consumers were actually starting to notice. The industry was projected to lose up to a billion dollars producing meat consumers would not want to buy. No wonder they were starting to talk about the problems with fast-growth chickens. In a *Wall Street Journal* interview, a chief executive from a major US broiler company admitted to receiving complaints from restaurant and retail customers, forcing the company to implement additional quality checks at their processing plants.[21]

The chickens were finally coming home to roost. The treatment of these creatures was now being directly reflected in the quality of the meat. It was becoming increasingly clear that the chickens had been pushed to their limit.

Unfortunately, Eric and Rachel had reached their limit as well. While Mike managed to stay afloat and keep advocating for farmers, the situation for Eric and Rachel got much worse. Pilgrim's Pride ignored the video and never engaged with either Compassion in World Farming or the farmers. The Hedrickses continued to suffer losses from diseased birds until, like the Hermans, they couldn't take it anymore. They had been the largest Pilgrim's Pride grower in West Virginia. They ended their contract with the company. I had deep anxiety about their financial situation. I worked to connect them to alternative options but, at the time of writing this line, Eric and Rachel still hadn't found a solution and were preparing to file for bankruptcy.

Eric and Rachel's situation is not unique. It's a story that is all too common, and deeply tragic. The system thrives on the back of farmers often living at any given time just one flock away from poverty. In order to end factory farming, we cannot ignore these farmers and their struggles. We must create a future with them in it.

CHAPTER NINE

The Radicals

As I became deeply immersed in understanding and undoing factory farming, I wasn't only getting to know the farmers. I was mixing with both the executives inside the companies purchasing the chicken and the activists outside campaigning for the birds' better treatment. I took a deep dive into these seemingly opposed forces and got to know some of them very well.

Picture an animal rights activist in your mind. What does someone look like who spends their working life making a difference for suffering animals? Chances are the person you're picturing looks something like David Coman-Hidy or Aaron Ross. David is covered in tattoos, including images of cats on the backs of his calves, while Aaron looks like a nightclub bouncer with his broad shoulders and shaved head. And then there's Cheryl Queen. She has silver hair cut stylishly short and chic black-framed glasses. She dresses practically but elegantly. She looks like what she is—a successful corporate executive.

Aaron and David have a punk-rock sensibility. Cheryl is all Southern charm. They couldn't be more different. And yet all three of them, in their own ways, have helped make huge strides for animals.

By the end of 2016, more than 200 food businesses in the United States, including the likes of Walmart, McDonald's, and Costco, had committed to switching from caged to cage-free eggs. The industry estimates it will cost $6 billion to build enough cage-free systems to satisfy current demand[1][1]. By the end of 2017, the same thing was starting to happen in the meat-chicken industry. More than 50 companies and rising had committed to giving chickens more space, slower growth, and better living environments. The cost would likely completely overshadow the cost of switching to cage-free eggs. There are 313 million egg-laying hens in production each year, but there are 9 billion—that's billion with a "b"—meat chickens that move through the system annually. Recognizing that they need better lives would have major cost implications, but that wasn't stopping companies.

Aaron and David represent one face of that sweeping change. Cheryl represents the other. They are two sides of the same coin: the woman who speaks for the system, and the guys who rail against it. They don't know they are working together. They'd never admit they need each other to cross the finish line. They may even hate each other. But together, they're making millions of animals' lives better.

War Is Hell

Aaron Ross and David Coman-Hidy are two of the people food companies hate the most. They've made more than one food-corporation employee leave the industry altogether. They've made people cry. In person, Aaron is soft-spoken and gentle, while David has a kind and empathetic heart. When it comes to confronting the companies that control the lives of farmed animals, however, they are ruthless.

Aaron and David's weapon of choice is shame. They make companies fear being publicly associated with farmed animal cruelty. They create websites with dripping red blood splashed on top of logos and videos of dead and dying birds, and systematically dangle this shame in front of anyone working with the target company: the donors, investors, franchisees, and clients. They are relentless, clever, well-resourced, and organized. They claim they have never lost a campaign. They always get what they want.

Hannah Thomson, the communications director at the Animal Agriculture Alliance, whose organization supports animal agriculture, paints a wicked picture of David. She reported about him in the industry publication *MeatingPlace* when he was addressing activists at a conference in Washington, DC. According to Thomson, he told activists: "When the competition is drowning, stick a hose in their mouth."

When I asked David if those really had been his words, he said the quote was taken out of context. He said he was actually quoting Ray Crock, the founder of McDonald's, and half-jokingly claimed that was where he got his inspiration: "That's his quote, not mine." He says another quote more accurately represents the Humane League's campaign philosophy, this one borrowed from General Sherman: "War is hell." He adds: "The crueler it is, the quicker it's over."

At a 2017 animal-rights conference in DC, the packed room is filled with young, eager activists. There are as many shaved heads and tattoos as there are suits and high heels. People are sitting on the floor, leaning up against the wall. They have their Macs out and are taking notes. David stands at the podium wearing a jacket, a thin black tie, and slacks. He's not overdressed, but he's dressed well enough to be taken seriously and to cover the many tattoos that line his limbs. But nothing can cover his mischievous, boyish grin. He's still not even 30, but he commands the room.

David tells the crowd that food companies "don't make policies due to altruism, they do it because of the pressure." He goes on to tell his audience to research deep into a company and find ways to make them look like hypocrites. He says the goal is to damage their reputation and brand. He emphasizes that activists are there to be a "pain in the neck," not to negotiate. He adds: "I recommend adding blood drips to their logos."

To the activists in the room, David is a superhero. To the companies he targets, he's more like a supervillain. Either way, he's super-effective.

Aaron Ross also has no remorse about the tactics animal-rights activists employ: "The way I look at it is that these few people are the ones standing in the way of improving the lives of billions of animals. I don't feel bad when they get upset with us for making an inconvenience for them because they're not willing to produce a policy that just improves the lives of animals." To Aaron and activists like him, the world is black and white. You are either helping to get animals out of their cages or helping to keep them there.

Aaron got his start in activism in hyper-aggressive campaigns to shut down the most abusive animal-testing laboratories in the early 2000s. By the mid-2000s, he was following campaigning tactics from Europe to end egg-laying hen battery cages in Austria and Australia. He was particularly inspired by the Australian activist Patty Mark, who started the open-rescue movement in the 1990s, which had spread to the United States by 2001. The concept of an open rescue is one of direct action. Animals that are in pain and suffering are illegally taken from a farm and given veterinary care and sanctuary. In the process, the conditions of the animals are documented so they can be brought into the public eye.

"The first major open-rescue and expose of a battery-cage farm happened to be in Maryland less than an hour from my house," Aaron tells me. "This rescue marked the beginning of the battle for egg-laying hens in the US and sparked a series of open-rescues and investigations of cage facilities across the country which would continue for the next decade."

One of those open rescues was conducted at a farm owned by a fairly small but rapidly growing retailer of the time called Wegmans. In 2004, a public campaign was launched against Wegmans for keeping hens in battery cages. This was the first ever major cage-free campaign in the United States. It was long and brutal, and lasted three years.

"We gave them all we had," Aaron recalls. "I had a little scrappy organization back then called the Baltimore Animal Rights Coalition and we spent literally every weekend protesting Wegmans up and down the East Coast. We did a lot of civil disobedience like banner-hanging, stickering egg cartons, locking ourselves in cages in front of stores, and regularly storming their supermarkets with bullhorns and getting tackled into the fruit stands and dragged out screaming by security. It was a dramatic and brutal campaign."

After three years, Wegmans sold their farm in order to distance themselves from the controversy. "Personally, I loved the idea of using these radical tactics for a pragmatic ask," says

Aaron. "No matter how radical our tactics were, the retailers were perceived by the public as the unreasonable ones for refusing to adopt even basic animal welfare standards."

David Coman-Hidy was 21 years old when he started working with Aaron, and the two of them started to test their joint strategies on a cage-free campaign in 2011. David had graduated a year early from Emerson University with highest honors. While at Emerson, he worked a bunch of jobs on campus, including at the Aramark dining hall, in a convenience store, and as a resident assistant. He was a memorable character on campus thanks to his big mohawk.

While David was in the sixth grade, Ralph Nader was running for US President and David's mom was a supporter. David was inspired by his mother's passion for justice and politics. By the next election he went with her, door to door canvassing. It was his gateway drug to activism. He began to push every issue he could get his hands on. He started the Gay Straight Alliance at his high school and ended up leaving after he was beat up in his sophomore year. He turned to community college and went on to study politics at Emerson, where David went vegan and settled on his true cause: farmed-animal rights.

David decided the best place to start was a place he knew. He worked at Emerson during the summers, helping run and manage the dorms, so one day he approached the university with a threat. If Emerson didn't go cage free, David's small grassroots group, the Humane League, would wage a "horrible campaign." It must have sounded childish at the time, but David and Aaron's horrible campaigns would become the signature approach of the now-global organization.

David had learned basic campaigning tactics from more experienced activists, including Aaron, and he was in a good position. He was connected to all the activist groups on campus and had worked at a radical bookstore, so he knew plenty of people born to challenge the status quo. "There's just this feeling in that punk community," he says. "There's the deep DIY attitude of, just, if there's a problem you just bash your head against it until it's solved, you know?"

David started his first cage-free campaign by gathering signatures from the students. And when that didn't work, he and Aaron began reaching out to donors and alumni of the school, asking them not to contribute more funds until Emerson went cage free on their egg supply. They wrote to hundreds of donors whose names they found published at the end of an alumni magazine. They then got 20 or so student groups to sign a letter asking donors to pledge to not donate again until Emerson committed. They got dozens of letters of support back. Then they walked into the school's development department and unveiled a list of donors who would not longer donate until Emerson went cage free.

The tactic worked. Emerson committed to going cage free for 100 per cent of their supply. "That was the killing blow that won the campaign," David says. "We'd done a bunch of other stuff, but that was by far the most impactful thing, so we started using that on every campus." With Aaron in Baltimore and David in Boston, they started using those same tactics in other schools. Soon, nearly every school in those cities had a cage-free policy.

Most of those schools' dining services were run by one food service company: Aramark. Aaron and David won campaigns against more than 50 Aramark schools. "This was a trench warfare campaign against Aramark staff members for years and years and years," Aaron says. It didn't take long for the activists to realize the company was using the same press releases again and again, every time they were attacked. "They had this playbook of, when you get this email from the Humane League, respond with this form email and then send this press release to the school newspaper," Aaron says.

"The year after my Emerson campaign," David says, "Aramark lost their contract, and they switched to Sodexo. I have that cage-free victory paper framed above my desk from Emerson from that first campaign."

That cheap red Ikea desk sits in front of the window in David's small Brooklyn apartment, where he lives with his girlfriend and two cats: the ones tattooed on his calves. Today, he is president of the the Humane League, which now has more than 70 staff around the world. Above that desk are the few things that keep him going by reminding him of the progress he's making: a team photo, a state-ballot-initiative victory, a few newspaper articles. On the filing cabinet next to David's desk are two stickers. One is for Dungeon and Dragons. I remember kids in my high-school student lounge playing the game, building a secret world in their heads that only they could see. David is those kids all grown up, envisioning a world free of animal suffering.

The other sticker reads "Soylent," which is the equivalent of adult vegan baby formula. It smells faintly like paint and looks like pancake batter. It's all the nutrients you need to survive in a drink, because who cares about wasting time eating when there are battles to fight?

David has always been quick to adapt his tactics when his targets start to catch on to his game. At Harvard University, when David tried to get into the development office to look for an alumni magazine to find a list of donors, the staff seemed to know who he was. They wouldn't give him the magazines. So he did some more research and learned that the most generous donors got their names inscribed on a marble wall in the development office. So David went back to the office, snuck in behind an employee, and filmed the wall. He researched the names and addresses and got a number of them to withhold donations until Harvard agreed to go cage free. David celebrated by sending the Harvard president flowers and by framing the article announcing the change: it's in one of those neat frames above his desk.

David and Aaron got more than 100 campuses to go cage free in just two years, but there were a few holdouts. They decided to set their sights higher, on the parent service company that provided the food to the dining halls. Instead of going campus by campus, what if they went right to the top?

They started off with a smaller food-service company, Delaware North, and launched their first national campaign. They contacted every single one of Delaware North's clients, and launched campaigns against them for contracting with the company. When I asked how the campaign was finally won, Aaron and David laughed. Aaron was at a punk show when his cell phone rang. He stepped outside to take the call and heard a woman crying. It was an executive from Delaware North begging him to stop the campaign.

In October 2014, Delaware North conceded. The Humane League put out a press release about the announcement, and David, who had by now become the organization's executive director, was quoted saying: "We appreciate Delaware North's announcement to improve animal welfare within its purchasing practices. This move is one that will impact the lives of tens of thousands of animals.[2]" It was a cordial comment to conclude a nasty, no-holds-barred campaign.

This was the first national campaign David and Aaron won, but it only whetted their appetite for more. At that point, they were still running campaigns more or less in their spare time, with few resources. Their tactics were minor in comparison to what they do now—but nothing feels as good as that first win.

The pair still had their sights set on Aramark, but they also targeted the massive company's competitors. Their progress wasn't all straightforward, and they did have to rely on some lucky breaks. They were sure they were about to lose their campaign against Centerplate, for example, when Centerplate's CEO was caught on film abusing a puppy in an elevator.[3] "It was honestly like the hand of God moving down and winning the campaign for us," says David. "Imagine campaigning against a company for months. We honestly felt like this was the first time we were going to face defeat. And then, you look up at the TV: 'Breaking news. Food CEO caught abusing puppy on camera.' And then the Centerplate logo."

Centerplate's CEO was forced to resign, and the company decided that a cage-free announcement would make a great distraction from the PR disaster. Although David was disturbed by the incident, he could not believe its silver lining. The CEO's abusive behavior toward a single puppy had resulted in the company creating a policy to reduce the suffering of tens of thousands of other animals.

Sodexo—another major food-service company that operates college and hospital cafeterias—folded soon after

Centerplate. Aramark, the campaigners' original nemesis, was still holding out. After Sodexo's announcement, Aramark said they needed six months to look at the issue. The Humane League impatiently launched a campaign with an online petition, a website, and a video detailing the incredibly sad lives of hens that laid eggs for Aramark. They reached out to all of the company's key clients, informing them of conditions for chickens in Aramark's supply chain and urging them to drop Aramark and switch to a company like Sodexo instead.

"We launched the campaign on a Saturday to ensure the maximum annoyance and disruption to the company," says David. "I remember getting a call from the Director of Sustainability within hours of the campaign launch. The first thing she said when I answered was 'Thanks for ruining my weekend.'" Within eight days, Aramark produced a cage free commitment.

Winning Without Fighting

The last major food-service company on David and Aaron's list was Compass. They'd already made a cage-free commitment on their shelled eggs, which are the kind sold in grocery stores— eggs still in the shell.* But many restaurants use liquid eggs, where they are precracked and come in tubs or frozen blocks. Within a month of Aramark's announcement, Compass announced they were going 100 per cent cage-free. Between Aramark, Compass, Delaware North, and Centerplate, this meant that more than 90 per cent of the entire food-service industry had committed to go cage free. From David and Aaron's perspective, Compass went down without a fight. "Centerplate took five months, Aramark eight days," David says, and Aaron adds: "Compass was won without even campaigning."

Animal activists aren't used to easy victories; they're used to fighting dirty. But they do know that once one company in a sector has made a commitment, competitors will follow

---

* As a note, I think the term shelled eggs is confusing! You'd think it would be the other way around! Eggs outside their shells!

quickly. No one wants to be left behind as consumers increasingly demand companies let every hen out of her cage. I once heard a food-company executive say, "The question is not what will it cost to make these changes, but will it cost to NOT make these changes." A whole industry could ignore the risk of cruelty being exposed. But once someone broke rank, the whole house of cards would come crashing down. For activists like David and Aaron, that means it's worth throwing everything they've got at that first target.

When they targeted Subway, for example, the Humane League systematically disrupted its business model. Subway is a franchise company. They license the ability to use Subway's name, and order the company's food. Typically, it's very easy to open a Subway. The company delivers everything. The owner pays a premium for the name and supplies, and makes money on the small margins for food sales.

Subway is only successful as long as people keep wanting to open Subways, so David decided to target potential franchisees. The Humane League specifically targeted the meetings where Subway was trying to recruit new franchisees. Volunteers attended the company's group phone calls and meetings. They repeatedly asked, "Is it true you are part of this horrific animal-abuse scandal?" They would actively try to convince potential franchisees to go to Quiznos instead, because Quiznos had already gone cage free. That strategy worked, and Subway followed Quiznos in adopting a cage-free policy.

Campaigning against investors is another effective avenue. The Humane League meet with investors and present a clear case: "Here's the company you're investing in. Here's how we will hurt your investment, and we will make clear that you are investing in cruelty." David and Aaron know that they're fighting for animals that are living miserable lives. They'll target anyone with any tactic they think will succeed, barring physical harm.*

---

* Compassion in World Farming does not believe in taking radical actions to achieve change. Regardless, these actions played a role in putting pressure on companies.

On the other side of the fence

Of course, all of David and Aaron's targets are people. Real people, with mortgages and children and dreams. People like Cheryl Queen. Cheryl has to navigate a very different world from Aaron and David in Compass Group's nondescript headquarters in Charlotte, North Carolina. It looks like any other offices in corporate America. Executives pore over spreadsheets, worry about shareholders and competitors, and oversee a quarter of a million employees.

Cheryl talks about having to "socialize" an idea, to present it carefully in order to make it stick. Like David and Aaron, she cares deeply about improving the lives of farmed animals. But her tactics are a little different from theirs.

From the outside, it looked as if Compass went cage-free without a campaign urging them to do so. But Cheryl Queen had launched her own kind of campaign from within—and her company would commit to going cage free by 2019, sooner than their competitors. Compass were also the first to commit to better standards for chickens raised for meat. The Humane League has waged and won hundreds of campaigns to improve the lives of chickens, but Cheryl Queen has won her own impressive victories.

I first met with Cheryl in 2013, along with the Compass procurement team directly responsible for the purchase of 60 million chickens every year in the United States alone. Cheryl's team were polite and engaged, but after the meeting Cheryl wrote me to say that broiler-chicken welfare was not a priority for them. It was nearly impossible for her to bring this sort of policy change to the boardroom when it was not of major public concern.

This would be the same message I'd hear again and again as I did the circuit, pitching to food companies that they needed to care more about chickens. They were 90 per cent of farmed animals in our food system, and their lives were miserable. But the answer was always the same: not a priority. Too expensive. No one cares. Of all the executives I met with, Cheryl gave the clearest advice: if you want me to move this issue, she said, go make a stink about it with the public.

She was right: after Craig Watts's story went viral in 2014, those same executives who had brushed me aside started returning my calls. Activists like David, Aaron, and me, we did our job. We made a stink in the media and put pressure on companies from the outside. But executives like Cheryl did their part, too.

The Insider

Cheryl Queen has a deep, hearty laugh. "When they see me coming, I'm sure they think, oh here comes Cheryl to talk about pigs or chickens or whatever cause, and they duck under their desk," she says. I remember going to her office once for a very serious meeting to negotiate a policy her company should be following. She wore her chicken clogs especially for me. They were shiny yellow gardening shoes with chickens patterned across the whole of the shoe. She took them off as soon as the meeting was over. I loved her for wearing them to a serious business meeting. I imagined it was a subversive coded message to me about whose side she was really on.

Cheryl had never particularly aspired to be in charge of public relations or corporate social responsibility at the largest food-service company in the world, serving more than 9 million meals per day in North America alone. It just sort of happened. These days, as she nears retirement, Cheryl is a force to be reckoned with. She commands attention. She's somehow able to navigate the most challenging of confrontations with a smile. It's hard to imagine her making any compromises for anyone, but earlier in her career she did, for her kids. Today she works long hours, seems to live on an airplane, regularly presents at global forums, and has received numerous awards for her work.

At the start, she was a young single mom. She would begin work at 5.00 a.m. and do a lot of catch up on weekends. She had to juggle her work schedule to meet her children's needs. She found she had a knack for PR, and in between ballet, carpool, and fixing dinner, her business thrived until one day it got the attention of one of her clients, Compass

Group. Her kids were nearly out of high school, so when they offered her the role of leading communication in 1998, she was all in.

Cheryl would end up being one of the most influential business executives in the United States with regard to farmed animals, but she didn't set out caring about the issue. Today most companies have Corporate Social Responsibility departments, but there was no such thing when Cheryl started at Compass. She was asked to create the company's social-responsibility initiative, and she approached the task with her typical focus and drive, reading every book she could get her hands on.

Her first project was with the Environmental Defense Fund. They approached her and explained that they were targeting Smithfield Foods, in North Carolina, to try to get them to use fewer antibiotics. They weren't really getting anywhere. They thought Compass, which was one of Smithfield's biggest clients, might be able to help. It was the first time anyone had asked Compass to do anything like that. "I didn't know what would happen if we said yes," Cheryl remembers, "and I didn't know what would happen if we said no."

She took the plunge and said yes. It took about 18 months to hammer out the agreement, but when Compass sent out the press release in 2005, it was groundbreaking for the industry. No one back then was talking about antibiotic use in the industry. The Environmental Defense Fund saw it as a simple, successful campaign. But for Cheryl and Compass, it was revolutionary. The company received 10,000 letters, emails, and phone calls from consumers—all from people thanking them for doing the right thing.

Cheryl says this experience taught Compass two things: "People really did care about this kind of stuff, to the point that they would take the time to write a letter or send an email or make a phone call to a company they'd never heard of. And second of all, that there was a real value in working with a non-governmental organization (NGO) who understood the issues, because we didn't"

That campaign was a big "aha" moment. So when the Humane Society of the United States (HSUS), one of the largest animal protection organizations in the country, called Compass Group to talk about going egg-laying hens going cage free, they were ready to listen.

"I will always appreciate how [HSUS] approached it," Cheryl says now, "because it wasn't hysterical. It wasn't demanding, 'You've got to do this.'" She remembers the meeting. "They treated everybody as if they were rational adults who, if they understood the problem, would want to engage and make a difference. And it wasn't like, 'Now I'm going to show you a twenty-minute video that's probably going to make all of you get sick over lunch.' They took a piece of paper and said, 'This is amount of space a chicken has in a battery cage. You all know what a chicken looks like, right?' They won more hearts and minds that day. And it changed everything."

Compass committed early to going cage-free for their shelled eggs, in 2006, but it wouldn't be until 2015 that they'd make the same commitment for all of their eggs. By that time, the THL campaigns and Mercy for Animal investigations were raging all around them.

By the time I met Cheryl in 2013, she had already made a personal commitment to work to reduce animal suffering. She had been instrumental in Compass's decision to go partially cage-free in 2006, and she knew exactly what she was up against because not everyone was happy with the leadership role Compass had taken in farm-animal welfare. "We had conventional ag clients as well as industry organizations who took exception to our work in this space. There were challenging meetings where we tried to explain the business decision that led to our policies and commitments. We believed consumers really cared about the issue and I think trends and history have proved we were correct. I will always be proud of the company for standing behind its commitments. And it challenged us to listen, try to understand and respect every view, and give thoughtful consideration to decisions we made."

At times, the process came with unexpected consequences, like the time Cheryl was invited to visit a poultry-raising operation. "I knew they were very proud of the work they were doing but in fact the conditions were heartbreaking, with dead broilers in a barn that was overcrowded with birds. It was my first look at the broiler industry. When I met you and you told me you wanted to change conditions for broilers, I immediately went back to that visit and I knew [you were] on more than I could imagine," she told me.

When I first came in 2013 to ask Cheryl to change Compass's policy on meat chickens, she says she thought, "I know what you're saying is right and true and real, but you're trying to boil the ocean. Chickens? Oh my God. Is there a more ubiquitous farm animal?"

How Change Happens

It's remarkable what can change in just a few years, how the impossible can become possible. Craig Watts's story broke, and the issue of chickens rose in public consciousness. Activists like David and Aaron kept the pressure on with their campaigns. And John Mackey, the founder of Whole Foods, created a new animal-welfare standard for his stores. He dreamed of a way of animal farming that both animal advocates and cattle ranchers could agree to support. That dream became the Global Animal Partnership (GAP), a certification for which meat producers could apply. GAP was a stepped approach, providing guidelines for how to have a better farm, complete with auditors, standards, and approval from the animal-protection community. When Compass started looking for a way to solve their broiler-welfare conundrum, GAP seemed like the perfect solution.

The program had picked up steam when Anne Malleau became its executive director. Within just a year or so of accepting the role, she recognized the need to "blow up" the current GAP broiler standards. She proposed no longer allowing the fastest-growing breeds of bird, and requiring that birds be given the environment they needed to express their natural behavior.

When Anne proposed that change in a GAP board meeting, I knew, in that moment, that change was coming. Whole

Foods Market announced in March 2016 that they would do away with fast-growth breeds and give birds more space and enrichments. The first domino had fallen.

In May 2016, Josh Balk from HSUS and I visited Compass to give them the heads up that broiler welfare was about to become a priority in the public eye. This was our signal that the Humane League was coming to town. We also wanted to let them know that this campaign would be different. For the first time, groups across the animal rights spectrum, from the more radical activists like the Humane League to very conservative household names like the ASPCA, were coming together. Eight groups in total were united behind a single set of demands.

Even after that meeting, Cheryl still wasn't sure how in the world Compass could change such a huge part of their supply chain. But she reasoned, "Leading in sustainability has been a great differentiator for us. Sometimes we're the only ones who will have done it for a while, or we were the first to do it. And our guests care about that." Knowing that being first appealed to Compass, in fall 2016, Josh Balk, Anne Malleau, and I flew up to present on broiler welfare to the entire executive team and propose they pilot with GAP to be the first company in the United States to step up to the plate for broiler chickens.

At the same time, the Humane League was waging its full-blown war against Aramark, and by the time we arrived, it was clear that Compass had decided to make the change. Cheryl had done the heavy lifting to "socialize" the idea internally. The Humane League had put the pressure on from the outside. GAP's new standards provided the path. By that point, the decision was easy to make. Shortly after our meeting, Compass announced they would adopt GAP's new standard for chickens by 2024. An hour later, Aramark made a similar announcement. The rest of the food service industry followed by the end of the year, impacting more than 100 million chickens annually.

Compass was never targeted by the Humane League. Maybe Cheryl saw the writing on the wall; maybe Josh and I helped her see it; maybe she saw her competitors being targeted by campaigns. She has told me more than once that she doesn't care for the kind of vicious campaign David and Aaron tend to pursue. But I believe the pressure they created helped make it an easy decision for Compass to change their standards. It took pressure from both inside and outside companies like Compass to make them change.

It's not just that the Humane League and groups like them are a bunch of relentless, fearless activists with no off-button. They also represent something. They shine a light on a possible opportunity for a company to do better. They shine a light on where we as a society have taken a wrong turn. They sift through the many choices a company has, and present one—just one—that a company can actually to do something about. They offer companies a chance to win in the public eye. Cheryl saw that. She saw the opportunity, and we provided the road-map out of the mess. Even if Cheryl did not think highly of activists like David and Aaron, in the end, change required both the carrot and the stick.

CHAPTER TEN

The Year the Impossible Happened

"Do I not destroy my enemies when I make them my friends?"

—*Abraham Lincoln*

"I feel like a lamb being led to slaughter," Jim Perdue told me, a boyish grin on his face, slightly nervous. I could understand the sentiment. We were on my home turf, at the Compassion in World Farming (CIWF) conference on Livestock and Extinction in London, UK. The previous panel had spent most of its time discussing the devastating impact of industrial-scale animal agriculture and explaining why eating a sustainable diet has to mean eating less meat. As the third-generation leader of a company responsible for thousands of large-scale broiler-chicken farms and billions of slaughtered chickens—and the target of the CIWF exposé video I'd produced with Craig Watts—I could see why Perdue was afraid this might be a tough crowd.

I was nervous too. Perdue and I were about to be interviewed by the esteemed journalist Maryn McKenna. It would be the very first time we would appear in public together to speak about the journey we had been on, a journey that had taken us from being adversaries on either side of a nasty media battle to something almost like colleagues. I was worried about a million things. What if I slipped up on the panel and said something offensive to him? What if I destroyed the delicate relationship that had taken more than a year to build? What if I betrayed my values or appeared too close to Perdue? What if someone in the audience decided to shout at him—or at me? I knew Craig Watts was planning to watch the panel on Facebook Live, as were many of my other contacts. What would these farmers who had risked their livelihoods to speak out think when they saw me sitting shoulder to shoulder with Jim Perdue?

I'm sure Perdue was worried about his peers too. He'd gone out on a limb to work with me. He had mentioned that he was not loved by his chicken-industry peers. Going to meetings had been difficult lately. This wasn't going to make his life any easier.

We were both making enemies in the process of becoming friends, but we'd come too far to turn back. The progress we were making was coming at a cost for both of us, but we kept going. What other choice did we have? Refusing to move forward was not an option. Working together was the right thing to do, maybe the only thing to do.

Backstage, waiting for an audience that had reason to distrust both of us, waiting to expose a relationship that involved so many risks, Jim Perdue paused and looked me right in the eyes. "I trust you," he said.

★ ★ ★

This was the year the impossible happened. It was also the year my husband and I adopted our daughter, Andrea. We had decided to adopt for many reasons, but one thing shone brightest from our hearts: we had a good family and we wanted to share that with someone who didn't have one. We wanted to expand the meaning of who we were as a family, expand what that meant to us, to our two boys. We wanted to connect to something greater than ourselves and expand our sense of who we were.

We had been trying to adopt for more than two years. I remember our lawyer telling us to be patient. He said our match had already been made in the universe and we just had to wait for it to reveal itself to us, but three times now we had been put before a panel for a potential child, and three times we hadn't been chosen. Each time was an emotional rollercoaster. Each time we had to pick ourselves up again and keep going, keep hoping.

I had been ready to give up, thinking that it wasn't meant to be. I was already trying to convince myself that I was too busy for a third child, anyhow, and that it was better this way. But as Nelson Mandela famously said, "It always seems impossible until it is done."

The day I got the call from the agency was like any other day. I was working from home, had a million things to get through. But that call would change my life forever. "Are you sitting down?" Denise, our case worker, said.

"Yes." I wasn't. I couldn't move. I was frozen. I knew this was it.

"We have a little girl for you."

The rest of what she said was a blur. When I got the email with Andrea's photo, I started shaking. I fell apart. That was our daughter, beyond a doubt. I knew she was ours and we had finally found each other. People tell us sometimes she is lucky to have us, but I feel the opposite. We are lucky to get to be her parents. She's expanded our hearts in ways I never thought possible.

Making change at Perdue Farms had seemed impossible for years. My colleagues and I were certain the company wasn't listening. Most chicken companies weren't. They just played a public relations game with us. Any time we made a dent in their image, they'd figure out the best way to regain public trust without actually changing the way they did business. The industry set up a scientific panel via the Center for Food Integrity, a big-ag spin group whose stated purpose[1] is to redirect public opinion whenever undercover investigations come out critiquing the industry's practices.

That's where things stood when, in February of 2016, two years after the release of the Craig Watts video, Perdue invited me to a meeting, along with Josh Balk from the Humane Society of the United States (HSUS) and Jaya Bhumitra from Mercy for Animals. We were invited to address a group of 40 or so people from the company's senior leadership teams in Ocean City, Maryland.

My expectations for that meeting were low. After all, we weren't on very friendly terms with Perdue at the time. But I knew that if change were going to happen, the people in that room in Maryland were going to have to be a part of it.

Of course, I am not the first to realize that the most lasting change comes from within institutions. Gandhi once famously met with a South African official, General Jan Smuts, the head of the Transvaal government. Gandhi explained that he planned to fight the government for the rights of South African Indians, opposing legislation that had been introduced to deprive them of civil rights. He told Smuts, "I am going to fight against your government." The official laughed and asked if there was anything else he'd like to say. Ghandi said, "I am going to win." Smuts was apparently shocked and asked how he planned to do that. Gandhi stared into his eyes and, in a kind voice, said, "With your help."

No change can be achieved without the opponent's engagement. Not if we aim for long-term, permanent, sustainable change. Dr Bernard Lafayette, a civil-rights leader in the inner circle of Dr Martin Luther King, Jr, once said: "We have to win people over. If they disagree with what we stand for, we don't alienate ourselves from them, we need to engage them.[2]" We must gain belief and trust. That is a very difficult process, and requires patience, perseverance, and far more failures than wins at the outset— more failures than most people can tolerate. It also means that inevitably your own path will adjust, shift, and adapt. You can't engage your enemy unless you're willing to listen and trust.

I did think of Gandhi in that moment, when I stood at the front of the conference room in Maryland and prepared to address the leaders of Perdue Farms. I didn't mention him—I figured they probably already thought I was a crazy lentil-weaving hippy—but I did say to them, clearly and slowly, that this change, improving the lives of farm animals, was in their hands. Without them, progress was impossible. They had a great responsibility, and a great opportunity to reduce suffering in the world.

I told them chickens needed more space. They needed to see sunlight through windows. They needed an enriched environment, and they needed to come from healthier, slower-growing strains. The folks from Perdue were surprisingly humble and attentive as I told them everything that was wrong with their business.

After the meeting, they took me and my fellow activists on a tour of one of their experimental farms. From the outside, the long chicken warehouse looked like all others I had seen … until we got closer, and I could see that this house had windows. This was a radical change, this invitation to look inside a chicken warehouse. It spelled transparency and confidence in a farming system that was so different from the usual closed doors and blank walls of chicken farms.

I followed the Perdue staff into the warehouse, and I had to take a moment to appreciate what I was seeing and hearing. With calm pride Bruce Stewart-Brown, Perdue's chief veterinarian and animal-welfare expert, pointed out to me the shafts of autumn light coming through the windows. He pointed out how the birds were dust bathing in those rays. Dust came up and floated in the air above birds engaged in that simple, pleasurable activity. Then he pointed to the shaded part of the house and explained that that was where the birds could rest. "We want birds to be doing four things," Bruce said, "Eat, rest, drink, play. And you should walk into a house and see all four of those happening at once within a flock."

Here was the fourth-largest poultry company in the country telling me how important it was for birds to play. Bruce said they were actually measuring play, and their new policy committed to doubling play activity levels in birds in just three years. These experimental farms were also using a slower-growing strain of bird—a mix between a fast-growth Aviagen bird and a slower-growth Hubbard bird. The result was what Bruce called the "party mix," an array of colored birds, speckled black and white, some brownish. Here we were, nearly two years after we had criticized Perdue with a damning video, looking at chicken houses that had made significant progress toward what we'd asked for: more sunlight, more space, enrichments, and slower-growing breeds of birds. I knew these warehouses were experimental and didn't reflect the typical Perdue farm, but I was still heartened by the visible signs of progress and the evidence that the company had heard us.

Our hosts took us to a set of houses they were comparing side by side, one with windows and one without. The difference in the activity level between the two houses was visible and audible. The house without windows looked very similar to Craig Watts's house. It was crowded wall to wall with birds, all of them motionless except for an occasional shifting individual, which would create a sea of shifting throughout the house. Some birds got up to eat or drink, but they were mostly doing nothing at all.

Birds do not squat or sit by nature. If you look outside, you'd be hard pressed to see many birds sitting plotted on the ground. They perch to rest, but they spend most of their time pecking, foraging, and dustbathing. But in that windowless chicken house, more than 20,000 birds were just sitting still, waiting. Waiting to have the light and activity the chickens had in the house next door, thanks to those windows.

The house with windows had visibly more activity and the birds were noisier. They still weren't as active as the "party mix" crew, but it was an improvement, and Bruce believed the windows were measurably having an impact on activity level—and that the increased activity was reducing leg problems later on. In adding windows, Perdue discovered something else unexpected. Farmers liked windows, too. And farmers were spending more time in the houses with windows, with the chickens, because it was more pleasant to be there. This meant the chickens were being looked after more often, assessed more frequently, and in better light. Bruce told me that, even if the windows had no benefits for the birds, they still might have invested in them, because of the effect it had on the farmers.

Seeing those farms made me much more optimistic about the prospects for change in the industry, but developing a relationship with Perdue still wasn't easy. We had plenty of conflicts. The on-farm changes CIWF were asking for were, admittedly, huge: more space, different breeds with better welfare outcomes and better environments. Each of these changes would impact the bottom line of one of the largest companies in the world. It wasn't easy to sit at a table with people who saw me as an enemy and ask them to make these changes. In order to build a relationship, we both had to get comfortable being uncomfortable.

There were many moments of grace along the way. I'll never forget the moment in the fall of 2016 when my coworker Rachel and I walked into a hotel lobby and were surprised to see Jim Perdue, chairman of Perdue Farms, sitting waiting for us. I would have recognized that face anywhere. Jim has crystal-blue eyes that remind me of my grandmother's. He is softly spoken and thoughtful in his words. He stood up and stretched out his hand: "I'm Jim Perdue. It's nice to finally meet you." I smiled and said: "I know who you are, and it's nice to meet you, too."

This would be the first of many meetings with Jim. I would come to respect this man whom I'd made the villain in the video with Craig Watts. In my eyes, Jim Perdue became a redemption story, a foe turned into an ally. While we didn't see eye to eye on everything, we both found common ground in getting out of our comfort zones and pushing the needle forward on animal welfare together.

That first meeting was awkward. I was there with a major national restaurant company touring Perdue's hatchery and farms. I'd been invited to the company's headquarters in Salisbury, Maryland. But it was still just two years after we had put out the whistleblower video, which arguably resulted in the most negative publicity the company had ever had.

No one had mentioned that Jim Perdue would be joining us. After we'd introduced ourselves, he returned to his conversation with someone else and I was saved by Bruce Stewart-Brown striking up a conversation. Eventually Jim returned to me in that hotel lobby. I had recently missed a speaking engagement with him at Niman Ranch because I had been in Colombia adopting my daughter. He remembered the story and asked how my daughter was adjusting.

That fall morning, November 9, 2016, was crisp and blindingly sunny. Many of us were still reeling from the previous night's presidential election results, trying to make sense of Donald Trump's surprise win over Hillary Clinton. As an urban liberal in rural Maryland, I was very aware of being different on that day more than most. I was aware of the need to understand the other perspective on that day more than most. And I was grateful that Jim Perdue, someone who had every reason to distrust and even dislike me, had remembered something about my personal story and taken the time to ask me about my daughter. That's how relationships get built: through moments of empathy.

★ ★ ★

After this visit, Jim Perdue and I exchanged a warm email. He wrote: "One of the issues around a company like ours and an organization like yours is how do you develop TRUST, which, at first, seems impossible."

Trust between apparent opponents is not easy to build. Where I started off with Perdue was very different from where I ended up: sitting next to Jim on a stage, ready to talk about what we'd accomplished together. And that has everything to do with the dialogue, transparency, and change the company committed to.

Jim Perdue would later tell me: "I think there's a stereotype out there that we were used to back in the 1980s and 1990s that was just, there was no way you could come to any agreement because there was no common ground whatsoever. The fact that there were groups out there that truly had an interest in animal care, and you could actually have some areas of agreement, I think that was the big 'aha' moment."

On the London stage, interviewer Maryn McKenna didn't let us off easily. Her first question out of the gate asked about our beginning, our investigation, and our oppositional relationship. Jim was measured and calm, but his leg was shaking under the table—as was mine. He talked about the investigations. He described how in the end the company called the groups involved and said they appreciated the information and thanked them for letting them know about the conditions on their farms. He talked about how it was hard to watch the videos, especially the second one produced by Mercy for Animals.

I talked about the *New York Times* article a year after the exposé, where I read a quote from Jim saying "We need happier birds," and how I knew it was time to try and sit down. I explained how I'd met with Bruce Stewart-Brown and found we had more in common than we expected. Jim agreed. "It turned out 90 per cent of what they were trying to do and what we were trying to do were in agreement," he said. He explained how they called on us to help develop their first "animal care policy" to carve out their ambitions to improve the lives of farmed animals.

I told the audience that we remain Perdue's critical friend. We are the ones who will say keep going, you aren't there yet. I said Perdue are the most transparent and accountable food business I know. I explained that they'd revealed that, the previous year, only 3 per cent of their houses had windows. Now they were saying that by July 2016 it would be 17 per cent, and by the end of 2017, 25 per cent. "They are tracking their progress," I said. "They are putting it out there. And I don't know another company that is being that clear in percentages."

When Maryn pressed me on what we could draw from this example when working with the larger industry, I said, "What this journey has taught me is that there is always common ground, and you need to find it, and build from there. It's from there genuine solutions are created." I looked at Jim and went on. "This journey has been the surprise of my life. If you had told me a few years ago I'd be doing this right now"—I gestured to Jim, sitting next to me on the stage—"I would have laughed. That shows those relationships are possible, and they are critical for a better food system."

The audience, as I looked out from the stage, was very still. They were captivated by this story I never expected to tell.

Jim looked at that audience of activists and said, "We are not a small company. The question in the US is, can a big company be trusted? That's a challenge I put to our people every day. I still don't know the answer. For Leah and others, if you can get a large company like us, then it gets the attention of our competitors for sure, and will help move the pendulum faster."

And that is exactly what happened.

In July 2016, Perdue announced that their first animal-care policy would work toward many of our goals: enrichment for birds, natural light, better slaughter, better breeds. In 2017, they reported they would meet their goal of 25 per cent of their houses having windows. They were experimenting with slower-growing birds, and they were applying enrichments throughout their houses. They were committed to completely converting their slaughter system away from electric, live-shackle stunning to the less cruel method of controlled atmosphere stunning, which at least renders the bird unconscious prior to being shackled or even being handled by a human at the slaughterhouse ...

From there, the dominoes started to fall. In November 2016, Compass Group, the largest food-service company in the world, committed to be fully certified by Global Animal Partners by 2024. Cheryl Queen, the company's VP of communications, had agreed to meet with me, Josh Balk from HSUS, and Anne Malleau from the Global Animal Partnership (GAP). We asked if Compass would be the first company to sign up to these improved standards for chickens. They asked direct questions about the cost, about the standard itself, and about the tools and resources needed. But ultimately it was clear about five minutes into the meeting that they were already 90 per cent of the way decided. It only took a week or so after the meeting for them to go public.

Within minutes, so did Aramark, one of the largest food-service companies in the country. Within months, the entire food-service sector followed along similar lines. Panera, after many months of negotiations and discussion and that first farm visit, announced in December that they too would commit by 2024 to giving chickens more space, better genetics, a better environment to live in, and a less painful death. By the spring of the following year, giants like Burger King and Subway had also committed. By mid-2018, nearly 100 companies had followed suit.

Now that the leaders had stepped into place and solutions had been identified, the market had a roadmap and there was no stopping it. There was only one direction to go. Perdue became more and more confident in leading in the way. They announced in July 2017 they would be able to provide chickens for any company that wanted to meet the higher welfare standards that groups like CIWF, HSUS, the Humane League, and Mercy for Animals were asking for.

The Power of Human Connection

That wasn't all. Other chicken companies started to wake up to the changes happening in the market. Wayne Farms was the sixth-largest chicken company in the market, with annual sales exceeding $2 billion[3]. In June 2017, they announced a new line called Naked Truth that would meet GAP standards for chickens. They had never offered such a product. They said they would be there to meet supply for the "Class of 2024,"[4] referring to the many companies that had already committed to meet the new standards for chickens by 2024.

Our connection with another major chicken company, which prefers not to be named, was entirely unexpected, but it would be one upon which I would reflect deeply. It would be one that would make me consider the vast opportunities the lie beyond the walls we erect between ourselves and our enemies.

The first time Rachel Dreskin, CIWF's head of Food Business, met with an executive from this company—he asked to remain anonymous, so let's call him Mike—she received a cold reception. They were at the Menus of Change conference when they were introduced by a mutual contact from Stanford University. Mike recalls saying to Rachel: "Honestly, I'm not sure what we have to talk about. I'm not sure where we would find common ground." Rachel brushed this off; she was used to being met with suspicion. She barreled ahead with her friendly tone, searching for some commonality. Before too long they were talking about his grandkids and her son and laughing warmly. From there, the relationship opened up.

Months later, Rachel and I were in the car, headed to Mike's company headquarters. It was the first time an animal-protection group had ever been invited to their premises. We did not know what to expect.

Like many places we had been, it was a nondescript corporate office with a vast parking lot along a nondescript road. We could have been anywhere. Mike greeted us warmly as we entered the building at reception. The receptionist seemed very eager, definitely expected us. We signed in and were given badges indicating we were clear for entry.

Mike led us down a corridor. Out of the corner of my eye, I felt someone watching me. I turned to get a glimpse of a woman quickly dropping back down inside her cubicle. As we moved through the building, it became clear that the staff wanted to have a look at us. What did an animal activist look like exactly? Rachel and I, in our suits and jackets, were probably a disappointment.

We finally reached the meeting room, where we met an executive in charge of poultry-meat quality (let's call him John). After short introductions and handshakes, John sat back down and crossed his arms. His body language made it clear he was not comfortable. I'm sure mine did too as I fumbled to open my laptop and pull up my presentation. As I did, my background photo popped up on my desktop. It was a photo of my three kids. Clearly, Andrea looked different with her beautiful ringlets and coffee colored skin, and John noticed. I saw his face tilt and his arms uncross. He leaned forward: "Are those your kids?"

I proceeded to tell him about my recent adoption of Andrea. This was the first month I was back at work and it wasn't easy, but things that are worth it rarely are. I was adjusting, and so was my daughter. My emotions were raw. I probably blabbed more than I usually would have. His face softened. He had two adopted kids himself. His wife and he ran a ministry that worked with foster care. We spent the next 20 minutes talking about the joys and difficulties of adoption. We compared adoption stories. In those moments, I forgot who we were supposed to be. I forgot why we had come to the table. In those moments, the walls came down and a bridge was built.

As Rachel and I drove back from the visit, a story came to mind from the civil rights movement. In February 1960, students marched from the First Baptist Church Capitol Hill to the downtown business district in Nashville, Tennessee. It was a peaceful march, headed toward Woolworths department store to protest segregated lunch counters, but Bernard Lafayette and Solomon Gort, prominent figures of the civil rights movement, walked cautiously. Their teacher, the Reverend James M. Lawson, Jr, had warned them that violence could erupt in these situations. They should remember their nonviolence teaching; they should not meet violence with violence.

The students were relentlessly insulted by a group of white young men. Soon one of the group started beating Gort up. Lafayette stepped into to protect his friend by trying to shield the blows with his own body, but it was Lawson that diffused the attack:

> Lawson approached the situation with utter calm and politely asked the men to stop beating his colleagues. Looking up only long enough to spit in Lawson's face, the assailant continued to beat Lafayette. So Lawson asked him for a handkerchief. Amazingly, the young white man obliged. Wiping the spit from his face, Lawson realized he now had control over the situation. Seeing the man's leather jacket and ducktail haircut, Lawson asked if he owned a motorcycle or a hot rod. A motorcycle. Was it modified? It was. As the young white man described his customized motorcycle to the black Methodist minister, the

two seminarians quickly scrambled to safety and rejoined the
students marching downtown.[5]

The incident depicts how tension and distrust can be diffused
with the simplest of tools: the power of human connection.
It's what Rachel did with Mike when she talked about his
grandkids and her son. It's what happened between John and
me when we found common ground over our adopted kids.

* * *

In the months that followed my visit with Perdue, national
animal protection organizations became aligned around
common goals to improve the lives of broilers. The Humane
League, the HSUS, Mercy For Animals, Animal Equality,
Compassion Over Killing, ASPCA, World Animal
Protection, and CIWF were all asking companies throughout
the United States to do the same thing: improve the lives of
chickens in their supply chain. Not all companies were easily
won over, and organizations such as the Humane League and
Animal Equality had to campaign vigorously to bring them
into the fold. But in the course of a year, more progress was
made for farmed animals than ever before. Nico Pitney at the
Huffington Post[6] referred to it as "the most sweeping set of
animal welfare measures ever announced." The pace of
progress was unbelievable and unexpected.

As a critical friend of the largest food companies in the
world, I know they know that CIWF could never and would
never betray the animals or the farmers that are working for
a better food and farming system. Craig Watts, the
whistleblower farmer with whom we worked, risked
everything to partner with us: his livelihood, his safety, and
his community relationships. We risked everything to partner
with him. And then Perdue risked everything in admitting
they weren't doing the best they could, and committing to do
better. And we risked our relationship with farmers by
working with Perdue. There was so much risk on all sides—
but that was the only way we could move forward.

Months after our London panel, Jim Perdue and I reflected on our journey. I asked him what advice he'd give to companies and advocates alike. He replied: "You have to know that going forward there's going to be issues. There's going to be things that happen that aren't going to be the greatest things, but the question is, what do you do about it or are they going to react to it, or are they going to try to fix it? And that's where trust is. We're going to have problems, I can guarantee it; it's natural. So it's just a matter of making sure it doesn't become long term and if we fix those things."

Only time will tell where companies like Perdue and others end up and if they live up to their promises. I am heartened by the pathway they have laid out, and I do trust that the people I've met want to create something better. Our conversations are challenging, but I actually find that reassuring. Tension is the sense of the specific gap between where we are where we'd like to be. That tension drives change.

The journey that led me to sit on a stage with Perdue or inside the farms with others is not one I ever expected to take. The unlikely partnership I formed with Perdue contract farmer Craig Watts changed the course of my work. Credit must go to him and his extraordinary courage as being the catalyst for change in the chicken industry. I still don't understand exactly how it is we came to trust each other, but such stories show the kind of powerful force that can be unleashed when two apparent opponents find a way to work together. It turned out we had far more in common than we thought. And ultimately, we wanted the same thing—a fairer and more humane food and farming system.

That year was one where the impossible became possible.

Seeing change happen also changed the way I thought about my work. I started to ask if we were setting our sights high enough. What else could we correct? I wasn't the only one asking these questions. Maybe questions like these were what kept Perdue going in the right direction. Maybe a similar mindset made those within Subway and Panera and Aramark and Boston Market—all whom had committed to these difficult, complex and expensive improvements for chickens—shrug and think, "That wasn't so bad. In fact, it was good. Where else can we go?"

Perdue developed its second animal-care policy in July 2017. Mark McKay, the bright and energetic president of Perdue Premium Poultry and Meats, interviewed us in front of journalist, farmers, and Perdue executives. He asked us what future trends should they be watching out for. Josh Balk laid out the future of plant-based proteins and "clean meat," which is where meat is produced by in-vitro cultivation of animal cells, instead of from slaughtered animals. Josh said that competitors were looking into this already, and called on Perdue to diversify their protein options. I agreed, adding that the trend will only grow.

Later, in line at the lunch buffet, Jim Perdue turned to me and said how interesting the idea of diversifying protein was. "We aim to be the number provider of premium protein," he reflected. "Nothing in that vision says it just has to be from animals." I'd later ask him what he meant by this. He was thoughtful and measured in his response: "If we've got millennial consumers and we're interested in them and they want something more than what we're providing right now, if we're interested in staying in business we need to listen to our consumers. So I don't have a problem, and in fact we are pursuing other protein options."

Perdue is clear they want to try to remain a leader. If exploring alternative protein options will help that ambition, they will not hesitate to go in that direction.

Just a month after my last conversation with Jim Perdue, he went public with their interest in exploring plant-based alternatives to meat. While they continued to keep their cards close to their chest, Perdue said they were exploring all the options from smaller start-up companies, including pure vegan options and those that combine meat, plant-based proteins, and vegetables.[7] It was an unbelievable arc for me. This was the company I had set out to expose for their misleading claims about their chicken rearing conditions. They had committed to improving the conditions in their farms. And now, one of largest chicken companies in the world was exploring plant-based alternatives.

A few companies had already begun to diversify their protein sources. By early 2017, Maple Leaf Foods, a large Canadian meat manufacturer, announced they would spend £140 million to acquire Lightlife Foods, Inc., a leading manufacturer and brand of refrigerated plant-based protein foods in the United States. When asked why they would make such a move, president and CEO Michael McCain said: "Expanding into the fast-growing plant-based proteins market is one of Maple Leaf's strategic growth platforms and supports our commitment to become a leader in sustainability. Consumers are increasingly looking to diversify their protein consumption, including plant-based options. The acquisition of Lightlife provides Maple Leaf with a leading market position and brand in the United States in a category that is outpacing growth in the broader packaged foods sector." In short, they were doing it because it would make them money and consumers were looking for it.

This concept of "diversifying protein" became a buzzword in the months ahead, and would create a new roadmap for the meat industry, leading to even more radical changes—changes even I had never seen coming.

CHAPTER ELEVEN

Business as Usual Is Not an Option

"I would feel more optimistic about a bright future for man if he spent less time proving that he can outwit nature and more time respecting her seniority."

—*E. B. White*

In 2017, my precocious, sensitive son made me a Mother's Day card. When I opened it, I wasn't sure what I was seeing. It was a drawing of me, standing atop a mass of floating, multicolored balloons that spelled out "Happy Mother's Day." Below the message was a confusing gray scribble.

I have a folder in my closet of cards that he's made me for various occasions: birthdays, Valentine's Days, and Mother's Day. As he's grown older, he's put more thought into them, so I knew he'd put thought into this. I just didn't know what he'd been thinking.

"This is wonderful," I told him. "But what is that gray stuff at the bottom?"

He looked at me with his sweet hazel eyes and said, simply: "The gray is the pollution and the balloons are for you to ride away to another planet and be saved."

Deep breath.

On one hand, the fact that he wanted to rescue me from such a horrible fate was undeniably sweet. But on the other hand, I couldn't help but feel overwhelmed by one alarming thought: "We have to do better, faster, right now."

The dead zone

In August 2017, the National Oceanic and Atmospheric Administration (NOAA) announced[1] the largest-ever recorded dead zone in the Gulf of Mexico—an expanse of water roughly the size of New Jersey. In this zone, the marine life has either fled or perished due to high levels of pollutants. Shrimp growth was reported to be stunted. Only the most primordial of creatures, such as jellyfish, were able to linger in this toxic, low-oxygen soup. The culprit? Meat production. Or more specifically, meat consumption.

The environmental organization Mighty Earth identified[2] Tyson Foods as the only meat company with major processing facilities in each of the states listed by the US Geological Survey as contributing the highest levels of pollution to the Gulf. Mighty Earth also reported that Tyson, along with Smithfield, have the heaviest concentration of meat facilities in those regions of the country with the highest levels of nitrate contamination.

I knew what a dead zone looked like. In summer 2015, I had joined Philip Lymbery, CEO of Compassion in World Farming (CIWF) , as he researched his book, *Dead Zone: Where the Wild Things Were*. It wasn't a typical day at the office: we were planning to jump into the sea 15 miles (24km) off the coast of Louisiana, where the water was so polluted that nothing could live in it. I admit that I was not looking forward to the trip. We had come to see, with our own eyes, the impact that factory farming was having on life beneath the water.

As we hopped on a small motorboat with Dr Nancy Rabalais, executive director and professor at Louisiana Universities Marine Consortium, I didn't know what to expect. As someone who grew up sailing, I had always felt such happiness and peace at sea. I remembered the islands I explored, the glass-eyed dolphins and the seagulls calling overhead. I was lost in thought as Philip interviewed Nancy when, on the horizon, a strange sight began to come into focus. As we approached, I could see the jumble of objects more clearly: cranes and barges and what looked to be a floating construction site. These were oil rigs. And we were about to land next to one of them and dive in.

I expected to see no life at all, but what I saw instead surprised me. There was plenty of life—but it was all in the wrong places. The fish were clearly visible, swimming too close to the surface. I even saw crabs swishing by. As someone who grew up in the waterways of Florida, I knew instinctively that this was all wrong. Why were the creatures all near the surface? That, of course, begged a question: what was wrong with the bottom?

What was wrong with the bottom was that it was so polluted that the oxygen had been choked out. It was a story I knew well. It was the story of my ducks. A chemical had seeped into this once-magical place, and driven out all the life. Now nothing but the hardiest species could inhabit the sea floor; nothing but species that didn't need much oxygen. Everything else had either moved out, moved up, or died.

The strangest part to me was that we were 15 miles (24km) out to sea. Where in the world could the chemicals be coming from?

Tyson is the largest producer of meat in the United States, supplying meat to major outlets like Walmart and McDonald's, places where Americans eat and shop every day. According to a report[3] by Mighty Earth, Tyson slaughter 35 million chickens and 125,000 head of cattle every week, and those animals require 5 million acres (2 million ha) of corn a year for feed. All that land requires a lot of chemical inputs, which end up running down the Mississippi River into the Gulf of Mexico, ultimately resulting in the deadzone in which I was now floating with a snorkel, mask, and flippers.

In April 2018, Tyson recognized the need for change. They agreed to set a 2-million-acre (800,000ha) land-stewardship target, making this one of the largest ever sustainable grain commitments for a US protein company. At the same time, they committed to the not-so-small target of a 30 per cent reduction in greenhouse gas emissions by 2030. Achieving those targets would most certainly have them looking at their animal proteins.[4]

It's not just the Gulf of Mexico. We have known for a long time that factory farming is having a catastrophic impact on the planet. As early as 2006, the United Nations Food and Agriculture Organization (FAO) warned[5] in a landmark report that livestock posed a major threat to the environment and urged the world to consider the impact of farm animals. Henning Steinfeld, chief of FAO's Livestock Information and Policy Branch and senior author of the report, said: "Livestock are one of the most significant contributors to today's most serious environmental problems. Urgent action is required to remedy the situation."

The report referred to livestock's "long shadow." It makes it clear that livestock production is no friend to the future of our planet. According to the report, the livestock sector:[6]

> "...Accounts for 9 per cent of CO2 deriving from human-related activities, but produces a much larger share of even more harmful greenhouse gases... Generates 65 percent of human-related nitrous oxide, which has 296 times the Global Warming Potential (GWP) of CO2. Most of this comes from manure... Accounts for respectively 37 per cent of all human-induced methane (23 times as warming as CO2), which is largely produced by the digestive system of ruminants, and 64 per cent of ammonia, which contributes significantly to acid rain... Contributes to biodiversity loss; 15 out of 24 important ecosystem services are assessed as in decline, with livestock identified as a culprit due to its presence in vast tracts of land and its demand for feed crops.

Research published in the prestigious scientific journal *Nature*[7] in 2014 showed that our diets alone—with their high levels of animal product consumption—will take the world over the Paris target of limiting temperature rises to "well below 2°C."

This catastrophic damage isn't just a problem that's coming in the future. The damage is already happening now.

For my son's 10th birthday, we went to visit America's greatest national park: Yellowstone. What a tremendous place it is. The prismatic lake, in particular, is the stuff of other worlds. When early pioneers told people back home about it, no one believed them. I can see why. The rainbow colors and steaming clouds made me think I'd somehow escaped to that other planet my son dreamed of.

My son, Ruben, spent the majority of our week there with binoculars glued to his face, looking at the wild magic within the park's boundaries. When we spotted a pack of wolves, it was because we spotted a pack, not of wolves, but of people. Scopes and binoculars and long-lens cameras lined the edge of a cliff, along with their associated owners. There was pure joy in this, and it encouraged me to see people of all ages, from many different countries, captivated and unified by this common passion for the natural world.

But my joy was spoiled. I looked down at my three children who were hopping around, excitedly talking to a park ranger and showing off the photos they'd taken of the pack of wolves. A feeling of sadness welled up inside me and choked my pleasure. As I was approaching my 40th birthday, I knew that half of Earth's wildlife had disappeared during my lifetime. What will be left when my children are 40?

As Philip Lymbery explains in *Dead Zone*, in precisely my lifetime, the total number of birds, amphibians, mammals, and reptiles that populate global ecosystems has *halved*. The primary culprit is the global demand for food, and specifically the factory farming of beef, dairy, eggs, pork, and chicken.

Much of our arable land is used to grow feed for factory-farmed animals, and this has devastated wildlife populations, from once-common birds to Sumatran elephants to jaguars. In getting our food from farm to plate, our practices are inconceivably shortsighted: we overfarm our dwindling arable land and spray it with inconceivable amounts of chemicals; we overuse our drinkable water; and we cut down ecologically important habitats, such as rainforests—all to feed animals on factory farms. We use thousands of miles of valuable land to grow soy, maize, and wheat that could be used to feed humans directly, and instead feed it to animals cruelly crammed into warehouses.

The average American's food choices produce the same amount of greenhouse gases as his or her energy use. Taken together, the numbers are even more staggering: according to a 2016 study, animal-based foods in the US diet accounted for about 85 per cent of food-related greenhouse-gas emissions in 2009, and about 90 per cent of all agricultural land use.[8] Yet the global livestock population is expected to double by 2050, solely due to the demand for cheap meat.[9]

The question is, can we undo it? Can we repopulate and regenerate what we have destroyed? If not, what will my children's children have to see on their 10th birthdays when they look out into the majestic valleys of Yellowstone, or even into their own backyards?

How far we've come, how far we have to go

It's not like we haven't made any progress. Animal-welfare improvements are now a basic requirement for any food business. Removing antibiotics from factory farms has resulted in pressure to give animals healthier living conditions. This pressure, combined with increasing consumer awareness, has resulted in many food businesses making new commitments to animal welfare.

Many businesses have now incorporated five principles developed by the Farm Animal Welfare Council (an independent body that advises the UK government) known as the Five Freedoms. The principles promote the idea that animals have:

1. Freedom from hunger and thirst
2. Freedom from discomfort
3. Freedom from pain, injury, and disease
4. Freedom to express normal behavior
5. Freedom from fear and distress

Sadly, the US government has made no such move to adopt these principles at the government level, but they are now a key part of many businesses' policies regarding how they treat the animals in their supply chain. The largest business entities in the world, from Tyson to Walmart, have adopted them. Companies' acceptance of these animal freedoms provides a foundation for wider discussions about how animals should be treated. We can already see the effect of these ideas on the lives of animals on factory farms. Cages for laying hens, for example, are widely considered unacceptable, and more 200 leading US businesses, representing 70 per cent of the market,[10] have committed to phasing them out by no later than 2025.

Some companies have also agreed to implementing higher welfare practices for broiler chickens by 2024, including Panera, Chipotle, Compass, Aramark, and others. The list is only set to grow, and the whole industry is expected to come on board, just as the whole market moved to adopt cage-free eggs. Broiler welfare improvements agreed to by major food companies include committing to using a higher welfare breed of bird (likely a slower-growth bird that will live longer, yet less painful, lives before being slaughtered) and providing more space for chickens. These are consumer-driven demands, so they are unlikely to be reversed.

In spring 2017, progress seemed certain and unstoppable, as company after company jumped on the bandwagon of change, adopting policies to change the way they raised their chickens. For example, my coworker Rachel Dreskin worked with Subway to get them to align themselves with the animal-welfare certification Global Animal Partnership. Subway was by far the largest fast-food chain in the country—and in the world. They had 8,000 more restaurant locations than McDonald's. Getting them on the right path to better welfare standards for chicken meant certain change throughout the industry. Already, large companies such as Compass and Boston Market and even Burger King were aligning with Global Animal Partnership.

During this time of rapid change, I decided to drive back to White Oak Pastures to visit my friend Will Harris and to spend a few days sitting in the tall grass reflecting on our direction of travel. Time and again, I've found the practice of pausing and reflecting to be essential for keeping on the right path.

So much headway had been made since I first met Will. We'd exposed the "humanely raised" label, and Perdue was seeing the value of adopting better welfare policies and standards. I thought maybe going to see Will would cheer me up, that he might congratulate us on our progress. Instead, however, he was upset. He said that every time a new company signs up to our criteria, it cheapens what he's doing. He's raising his animals in pasture—a much better environment than any of the companies are signing up to. In his eyes, celebrating their progress is just greenwashing.

Talking to Will was a crushing reminder that we have much, *much* farther to go. For all the progress we are making, the problems resulting from factory farming are far from solved. We calculated that, in a decade of work, we had improved the lives of 1 billion animals through the new corporate policies. That's something of which to be very proud. But during the same period, 10 billion new animals had come into factory farming. As population grew around the world, so did meat consumption and production. By all empirical measures, we were failing.

Shortly after my visit to Will, I received a news alert that made me sink deep into my chair, struggling not to give in to despair. Global consumption and production of chicken has increased exponentially in the last half century. Between 1961 and 2014, production has increased more than 12-fold.[11] In 2014, it was reported that consumption of chicken and other white meat overtook consumption of beef for the first time in Britain.[12] Similarly, Americans are eating more chicken today than ever before. In 2017, the USDA predicted[13] that consumers would eat a record amount of chicken—92lb (41kg)— over the year. In Australia the trend is no different: chicken is now firmly cemented as the national favorite, and has overtaken all other meats.[14]

At the same time, consumer concern for how chickens are being raised and treated is also rising. This didn't make sense to me. How could there be raised concern and increased consumption both at the same time? James McWilliams, a professor at the University of Austin, has come up with an answer to the question. McWilliams writes[15]: "Morality might get dragged in every now and then by professors and activists, generating some interesting discussions in university seminar rooms. But the average consumer is going to eat more meat and drink less soda for economic rather than moral reasons." Chicken is cheap—if you don't count the cost to the planet or the suffering of the birds—so the consumption of chicken keeps rising, even as public awareness of the injustices of their production rises.

At moments like this, it's hard to remain optimistic.

The chicken industry often argues that intensive animal agriculture is feeding the world. In reality, however, industrial animal agriculture is leading us to a place where we may not be able to feed the world in future.

The answer to our future food supply is not to do more of the same. We cannot endlessly build more chicken houses, feedlots, or pig farms, and crowd the animals into infinitely tighter spaces to feed the exponentially growing world population. Food companies must take those limits seriously. The food system we've chosen is inefficient, cruel, and literally unsustainable. With our arable land and usable water diminishing, and our population growing by the second, we need to take a cold hard look at the future of our food and farming system if we want to have any future at all.

Unlike in my son's Mother's Day card, there are no escape hatches, other planets, or balloon rides away from this place we call home (at least not yet). The metaphorical chickens have come home to roost. Faced with the consequences of our actions, it's now our job to undo what we've done and hand our kids a better planet.

We have to do better, faster, right now.

I have times when I believe I'll never be satisfied by the speed of change. I see the entirety of the problem in front of me: the number of wildlife species disappearing, the land degrading, the water disappearing. When activists like myself compile the data and look at the facts, the problems can seem overwhelming, even paralyzing.

It's not just animals who are suffering. I am often overwhelmed by the enormity of the social justice issues around us: the #MeToo campaign, school shootings, immigration reform, Black Lives Matter, and income inequality. There are so many problems to tackle, and they are all so big. Where do we start? I see many solutions and I don't know why we can't get to them faster. It infuriates me that governments, companies, and individuals don't act more urgently to fix these enormous problems. And the more I see people around me who don't or won't act, the more responsibility I feel to fix the problems myself, as fast as possible.

My son often becomes overwhelmed by school assignments. Like me, he sees the entirety of the job at hand, all the possible pitfalls, all the exciting side trips, and the questions that need to be answered before he can even start. If he has to write an essay, he sits there and tries to plan out every passage, every sentence, every word, to answer every question in his head before he puts pen to paper. He thinks and thinks but doesn't write a word. Starting the job is the hardest part.

I can relate. As an activist trying to end factory farming, I can spend hours and hours, or weeks and weeks, staring out of a window, lost in strategic thought, imagining scenarios and counter-scenarios. Focusing on the size of the problem can be paralyzing. If you let it, it can stop you from even starting.

One day my son was struggling to start an essay, so we tried a new approach. We decided to break the problem down into small steps. We took out Post-it notes and on each we wrote down a top-line idea that covered what each paragraph would be about, with bullet points under each top-line idea. He still felt overwhelmed by starting, so we put away all the Post-it notes except the first one. I said, "Today, you only need to write the ideas on this Post-it note into your essay. Don't think about anything else, just get through this first step."

When he finished that first batch of Post-it note work, we pulled out the second in the series. By the end of the week, the task was complete. The essay didn't go exactly accordingly to plan. There were unplanned additions, and unexpected and exciting ideas emerged along the way. But by breaking it down and focusing on the task step by step, and feeling a sense of accomplishment as each step was achieved, he built up some momentum. The whole task got easier.

I try to apply that same strategy to tackling the very big task of "ending factory farming." We are on a long road, and we need a plan and a path. We need to set up milestones, like the Post-it notes. But it's also good to put many of the Post-it notes away, and just do one at a time.

The First Post-it

My work has made it increasingly clear to me that there is one simple thing we can all do to turn this giant shipwreck around: eat a lot fewer animals. Some people believe it's even simpler than that. Many experts have pointed specifically to beef as a main contributor to our ever-growing greenhouse-gas emissions problem. "The single most important thing is to eat less beef," writes Timothy Searchinger, co-author of a World Resource Institute report. "That is the overwhelming factor."[16]

However, turning down beef only to take up chicken, pork, and fish is like robbing Peter to pay Paul. It's true that raising cattle and dairy cows is terrible for the environment, exacerbating climate change and habitat loss, but encouraging people to stop eating beef and switch to fish, chicken, and pork would be a mistake from both an environmental and an animal-welfare perspective. Chickens and pigs, especially in intensive industrial-farm settings, require feed inputs from monoculture-intensive production, which is destructive to the soil. Growing monoculture corn requires chemical inputs—fertilizer, pesticides, and herbicides—that jointly deplete nutrients and any positive life-forms in the soil. Raising more pigs and chickens means cutting down more rainforest, destroying more wildlife, and using more arable land and precious water to prop up an unsustainable food system that hurts animals, our health, and the health of the planet.

The situation for fish is even worse. About 20 to 25 per cent of fish caught never reach a human mouth, but instead are used as feed for farmed animals. And we have already reached a point at which we have completely depleted the oceans of some critical species that are the basis for whole ecologies. Anchovies, for example, which are primarily used for fish feed in aquaculture, have now joined cod on the list of threatened species.[17]

What we really need is a food system reboot. We need a food system that isn't sending us on a one-way trip to self-destruction.

What does that look like? Greenpeace CEO John Saven offered some helpful words[18] in an article in 2017: "The most sustainable option is much smaller quantities of higher-quality, mainly grass-fed meat, along with less dairy, more fruit and vegetables, and less processed food. How much less meat? A lot less. Unless, that is, you can persuade all of your friends to go vegan."

To some people raised on a meat-heavy Western diet, getting millions of people to make this kind of change may seem impossible, but interest in plant-based eating and meat alternatives is growing. A recent survey by the research firm Mintel showed that 54 per cent of consumers said they need more protein as part of a healthy diet. But according to the same survey, nearly half the respondents were trying to eat less meat.[19]

More protein, but less meat? That sounds like a business opportunity. According to Mintel, the growth rate in sales of poultry in the US stagnated at 1 per cent between 2016 and 2017.[20] With the global plant-based protein market set to grow at 8.29 per cent annually,[21] there's reason for hope.

Reducing the meat in our diet has immediate effects. The National Resource Defense Council released a report in 2017 entitled *Less Beef, Less Carbon*,[22] which tracked the per capita change in consumption of 197 major food items tracked by the USDA. They found that there was a 19 per-cent decrease in beef consumption from 2005 to 2014. They calculated that this was the biggest driver behind a 10 per-cent per capita decrease in diet-related climate pollution during the same period. The report found that a drop in consumption of beef, pork, chicken, and milk contributed the most to the reduction of greenhouse gases over the period.

An individual person or family eating less meat is great, but it's even more exciting when companies or countries make these kinds of changes. China, the most populated country on the planet, has committed to a 50 per cent reduction in meat consumption,[23] and the German Ministry of Environment has decided[24] to serve only plant-based options at official events due to environmental concern over meat's impact.

Some US companies have also already committed to using fewer animal products, less often. Compass Group, the largest food-service company in the world, has committed to purchasing fewer animal products and promoting a "plant forward" diet. In 2009, Compass launched the Be a Flexitarian campaign,[25] which promotes substituting plant-based protein for animal protein one day a week. Panera Bread and Noodles & Company have similarly committed to expanding plant-based options on their menus. National burger chains Burger King and White Castle have introduced vegetarian burgers. By all empirical measures, the market trend is toward increasing and expanding plant-based proteins.

Away From Business As Usual

Under these circumstances, selling solely animal protein is a pretty risky commercial policy. For companies engaged in selling protein, continuing to invest only in animal protein comes with inherent risks with regard to food safety, health, and negative public and investor relations.

For example, disease outbreaks such as avian flu can threaten to disrupt supply. During the avian flu epidemic in 2015, there was a major shortage of eggs[26] in the United States, which drove egg prices up. In 2015, Compass Group announced it would replace eggs with a plant-based protein, because of the need to alleviate the pressure on the market. Within six months, they worked to eliminate 1.2 million eggs. They proactively expanded their protein offerings through a plant-based egg and simultaneously reduced risks related to a volatile egg market.

Undercover investigations showing abusive farmers, poor management, or poor welfare can also result in major risks to meat producers, due to negative attention from media, consumers, and investors. Food-safety recalls,[27] such as the infamous 2015 *Salmonella* Heidelberg outbreak linked to Foster Farms chicken[28], which lasted over 17 months and made at least 634 people ill, can result in significant financial loss, distrust by consumers, and concern from investors. These are important considerations to weigh for any business's future in terms of managing risk. Incorporating more plant proteins would be a viable way to reduce the risks associated with animal proteins.

Given the recent much-needed animal-welfare improvements to current industrial farming, we have likely reached a maximum limit as to how productive a square foot of chicken, laying hen, or pig farm can be. Continually building more houses for more farm animals won't work. Business as usual would not be smart business.

Staying the Course

Working on social justice can be exhausting. Even when we are making progress, it never feels like we're moving fast enough. My friend Dan Werner, who is a tireless civil rights lawyer at the Southern Poverty Law Center, was given an honorary PhD in Law from Grinnell College in 2017 for his outstanding contributions in the field. Our kids went to preschool together, our families camp together every year, and I consider he and his wife, Nan, and their three-kid family close friends. I was so happy to see him honored in this way, after his relentless efforts. He spoke at the commencement to students about to take their first steps toward impacting the world through their labors.

As someone who has worked over two decades in the difficult field of advocacy, Dan's words came from a place of deep truth. The work we do in social justice is hard, he said. It requires perseverance and the ability to accept that change takes a long time. We need to appreciate each forward step. We have to find ways to stay optimistic.

He said we should view Dr King's faith in the moral universe bending toward justice "not as an excuse to stand by and assume the bend will happen without engaging in the difficult work, but as a call to action to force that bend. Because in justice work, real change makers are optimistic activists. People who look to their day-to-day, hard, uncomfortable, often mundane and usually chaotic work, as a means for progress and not a sign of defeat."

This path we are on is not unlike long-distance running. As I write this, I have run seven half marathons. You train, you are disciplined, you plan, you get injured, you recover, you rework your plan, and you get back out there, again and again. The race day comes, and what is it that pushes you forward despite the pain? It's imagining the other side of the race. It's the thought of crossing the finish line and celebrating the completion of the task, your final achievement, even surpassing your goal. Especially in the moments of pain, imagining the task complete gives you the energy you need to keep going.

The other strategy that makes marathon running possible is finding good partners. Running partners keep you on task. They help you up when you fall. They distract you when things become painful. They shrug off your failures. They cross the finish line with you, and the victory is sweeter because you've done it together.

As activists, we have to keep that finish line in mind and find those partners. And we have to remember it is a marathon, not a sprint. We need to make measured progress. We may have setbacks or we may need to recover, but we must keep going forward, one step at a time, celebrating those steps, Post-it note by Post-it note, while remembering that we have to keep going.

I think of the future, of ending this destructive, cruel system that weighs me down as I race through my life. I try to remember that this is a marathon, not a sprint. Steady, measured progress is what we seek, all the while not losing sight of the finish line. We must stay on the road and come back to it, again and again. I imagine the end of suffering for billions of farmed animals—the caged hens and pigs, the crippled, crowded chickens, the trapped and suffering sentient beings of our food system. I imagine feeling lighter and being free of the dark and heavy feeling I carry with me everywhere I go—to dinner parties and barbeques where I politely and awkwardly decline the offerings while grimacing internally. I imagine that future and believe in its certainty. I imagine my children as adults never having to carry that dark and heavy weight around—being free. Imagining a brighter future keeps me going even when I am most tired and defeated. It's what gets me back out on the course, despite the setbacks, again and again.

We had made some important, measurable progress, but we still had a lot farther to go to reach the ultimate finish line. It was time to start down the path, one step at a time, toward the solutions that would truly get us to the end of factory farming.

CHAPTER TWELVE

Regeneration

On March 13, 2018, the US Department of Agriculture (USDA) dealt what was effectively a death blow to the hope for a meaningful organic standard when they announced that they would be withdrawing the Organic Livestock and Poultry Practices (OLPP) ruling. The OLPP standards would have greatly improved animal welfare, giving organically raised chickens actual outdoor access, as opposed to the tiny concrete pens they were currently permitted. "Organic" would have actually meant something with regards to animal welfare. But now with the new Trump administration, those standards were dead.

The result was catastrophic. Years of work were thrown out. It was nothing short of heartbreaking.

Hundreds of advocates had spent years working to improve the standard. I knew many people who had spent the past five years working on nothing else. I myself had given expert testimony at the National Organic Standards Board, explaining why the animal-welfare standards were insufficient and needed to be strengthened. For a brief moment, it looked as if we had won, but the USDA announcement marked the failure of all our efforts.

The administration's announcement cited "significant policy and legal issues." It noted that "changes to the existing organic regulations could have a negative effect on voluntary participation in the National Organic Program, including real costs for producers and consumers." But the real reason to abandon the rule was that some of the largest farms currently benefiting from the organic label did not want to do the right thing for animals because it would cost more money. It would cost money to give animals a decent life. It always came down to that.

Since its origins, the organic movement has focused not only on soil management but also on social justice and animal welfare. These were the movement's core principles, but when they were codified into regulations, some of the principles were lost.[1] The organic standard was originally imagined as a farming practice that would safeguard our planet and improve the welfare of all the beings on it while still delivering our food. Over the years, however, it had been watered down to such a degree that even many within the animal agriculture industry could no longer support it, let alone environmentalists or animal activists. For me and many other activists, the failure to revise the standard meant that the government could not manage and deliver a meaningful standard that met consumer expectations.

We had our period of mourning for the standard. But then we dusted ourselves off and began looking for a new path.

A year earlier, when President Donald Trump was elected, we had seen the writing on the wall. In spring 2017, I joined a new alliance of brands, farmers, and activists all looking to collaborate to create a new standard that would not rely on federal enforcement by a friendly administration. *Fast Company* would later call it "the ethical standard to rule them all."[2] We called it the Regenerative Organic Certification, or ROC for short.

Led not by activists but by two corporate CEOs, we committed to carving out a new path for the future of food and farming. It was not unusual for companies to take up solutions-based approaches. Whole Foods' John Mackey, for example, had done the same when he found that no standard for animal welfare existed in the market that met his vision. So he created his own, the Global Animal Partnership (GAP). This would later become the standard that would guide some of the biggest food companies in the world. But the CEOs who joined me and my fellow activists in developing the Regenerative Organic Certification were not just looking for better-quality products. They were trying to transform agriculture.

It was David Bronner, CEO of Dr Bronner's Magic Soaps, who drew me into the ROC team. Like me, David had been a vegan for many years. I knew he suffered from the same ethical dilemmas I did. We could not personally condone the killing of animals for food, but every year more and more animals were entering factory farms. Only 1 per cent of the US population is vegan. Today, we slaughter 10 billion more animals each year than we did 10 years ago. We couldn't pretend that wasn't happening. It was our cross to bear. We could not abandon the farmed animals left in the system, but our standard could steer them toward a less cruel system. When it comes down to it, if animals are going to be raised for food, it's better for die-hard animal advocates like David and me to have a say in how they are treated than no say at all.

The standards the ROC came up with were designed to incorporate the Five Freedoms of animal welfare. From the animals' perspective, the standard prohibits the absolute worst-of-the-worst practices in conventional farming. This means all close confinement is prohibited, including any cages, crates, and crowding. The ROC also prohibits painful mutilations, such as branding and debeaking, which are common in conventional farming.

While the ROC sets a higher standard for animal welfare, it also sets a higher standard for the production of crops such as coconuts and cotton. The ROC builds upon the organic standard in terms of protecting our environment and strengthens it.

Farming to Heal

The goal of regenerative organic agriculture is to heal what we have destroyed through our suicidal behavior—our reckless treatment of the soil, animals, and the planet. Through our careful, capable minds and hands, we can rebuild what we have broken. Regenerative agriculture promises that it is not too late. That there is still time.

Sustainability is not enough. "Sustainability" is a word that has been hijacked, and is mostly a meaningless, environmental gesture. To sustain is to keep things as they are, and how they are is not okay. We need to heal the planet, rebuild the soil, and get this planet into better shape. We do not need to sustain; we need to regenerate.

The regenerative organic concept was first devised by Robert Rodale, who was the son of the pioneering organic farmer Jerome Irving (J. I.) Rodale. Jeff Moyer, who now heads up the Rodale Institute, told me about the history of the family. Back in the 1930s and 1940s, J. I. Rodale worked on a system of food production he called organic agriculture. He did a lot to popularize the concept of organic farming and promote the idea that there is a link between the health of the soil and the health of the humans whose food relies on it. The organic farming industry grew slowly through the 1950s and 1960s into the 1970s as progressive and innovative people caught on to Rodale's ideas and read his writings. When he died in 1971, his son, Robert, took on the cause.[3]

Moyer observes that, at that time, the United States was beginning to latch on to the word "sustainable" as it pertained to many different facets of business, including agriculture and food production. But as Robert Rodale toured the world, he would say, "Boy, I meet a lot of people that aren't really interested in sustaining what they've got, because they have a really poor system." He was looking for a concept that would embody what he thought farming should be. That concept would become regenerative organic. He described its aims as "closed nutrient loops, greater diversity in the biological community, fewer annuals and more perennials, and greater reliance on internal rather than external resources."[4] This meant no fertilizers, no monocultures, no factory farms. Regenerative organic aimed to recover what we had destroyed in the soil, biodiversity, landscapes, water, and air, while still feeding us and making money. This, in Rodale's mind, was farming that could not only feed us, but heal us.

Regenerative agriculture is about a corrective action. No chemical inputs are used, so soil management is integral to the concept. Farmers must think carefully about how their practices can help bring the landscape back to life.

The Rodale Institute argued that moving the world toward adopting these systems could help future generations: "Changing farming practices to organic, regenerative and agroecological systems can increase soil organic carbon stocks, decrease greenhouse gas emissions, maintain yields, improve water retention and plant uptake, improve farm profitability, and revitalize traditional farming communities while ensuring biodiversity and resilience of ecosystem services. Regenerative organic agriculture is also integral to the climate solution."[5]

The Dream Team

In the early hours one morning in May 2017, Will Harris and I headed up from Georgia to the Rodale Institute in rural Pennsylvania to attend a small meeting of a determined few. We were going to meet with a powerhouse of a CEO, Rose Marcario of Patagonia, and the inspirational Cosmic Engagement Officer David Bronner of Dr Bronner's, along with about a dozen other motivated experts in soil, animal welfare, and labor justice. We had come to carve out the first regenerative organic standard in the country.

I saw Rose at the head of the table as I walked into the meeting room. It was rainy and cold, but the room had windows on almost all sides, and the natural light and warm wood put me at ease. I didn't know who Rose was, but she oozed a magnetic energy. I had a sense from the beginning that she was a force of nature, and I wanted to go wherever she was leading.

We sat all day, debating and considering the details of what might go into a standard. We were meeting at Rodale Institute intentionally. This was a place that believed in a better future, where life was breathed back into the soil. During a break, we took a tour of the farm and knelt in the rows of soil. The staff explained how, through decades of research, they were proving that regenerative organic farming would bring landscapes back to life—that over time, and with patience, it would have higher yields than our chemical farming did now. And what's more, it would keep going; it would last. It wouldn't exhaust the soil and then stop and dry up once that last breath of life had been sucked from the earth.

That was the first time I considered soil as a living thing. I remember holding a handful of it as Jeff Moyer explained just how alive it was, filled with microbes that power our food system. I considered the universe of invisible entities that lay in my palm. I thought about what would happen if we, through chemically addicted farming, killed them all. Where would we be?

That day at the Rodale Institute we dreamed up a model that could encompass all aspects of farming: soil health, labor justice, and animal welfare at the highest level. It was an answer to our disappointment. It was making a way when we had been told there was no way. In the months that followed, we consulted with experts and drafted the new standard. We put it out for public comment, and received hundreds. The feedback helped us create an even sharper set of guidelines.

Finally, a year later, we were ready.

Standing Room Only

Rose stood on a stage giving the keynote address to a room of business leaders at Expo West, the largest natural product expo in the country. She looked confident, standing tall and surveying the audience with an eagle eye. "Right now," she said, "in the U.S. alone we spray 300 million pounds of Roundup a year. Three hundred million pounds. Soil is a living thing, and we are spraying 300 million pounds of toxic chemicals on a microbiome so teeming with life that there are more living organisms in one teaspoon of soil than there are people on the planet. We live in an interconnected world. This is reckless, suicidal behavior."

She continued to rattle off alarming statements: "US soil is being lost at a rate ten times faster than it is being replenished ... The rise of chemical agriculture has coincided with an alarming rise in cancer rates, allergens, and diseases like ADHD and autism." She took a long pause. She wanted to make sure we had taken that in. "Pollinators are declining at shocking rates," she went on, "and I don't mean to be overly dramatic, but when they are gone it is game over for us."

I felt sick listening to her. It was the same panic I felt when I saw my son's Mother's Day card, the one where he'd attached me to a bunch of balloons to take me away from our gray, dying planet. *We are in trouble. We have to move faster.* I anchored myself to the fact that we had a plan, we had an answer.

During Rose's speech, she paid homage to the organic pioneers. Her purpose was not to tear them down, but rather to recognize that she stood on the shoulders of the giants that came before her: "I have so much respect for the great pioneers in the organic agriculture movement," she said, "many of whom are here today." She looked out into the crowd with a look of earnest gratitude. "You blazed a trail— you created an incredible $47 billion industry I personally think would be three times that if we didn't have financial barriers to entry like conversion of farm lands & infrastructure. You built a movement where now 80 per cent of all US households across the country participate in the organic marketplace. You took the long view, and you drew a line in the soil."

Rose had spent years trying to build on the great work of early organic pioneers. Years earlier, the founder of Patagonia[6], Yvon Chouinard, had made the financially risky decision to go 100 per-cent organic with their cotton. It was not easy. They had to create NGOs. They had to finance farms. They had to build supply chains and certifications. They had to roll up their sleeves to take the company to where their ideals were leading them. But they knew it was right. And they proved it was possible.

Rose never backed down from an ethical challenge. In fact, she seemed to seek them out. For example, she was a strong proponent of on-site childcare. It is something few companies offer, but she believed it held value, not just for her employees but for the company. Under her leadership and support, 100 per cent of working mothers at Patagonia have returned to work, thanks to their onsite childcare.[7] Patagonia has led the way on a lot of tricky issues, in large part because of Rose's vision. They were the first apparel brand to go to factories and convert them to Fair Trade, and she believes their action inspired others to follow.

"We have been the source of transformational change," she says, "because we've taken the first step. The path is difficult, it's always a bit scary to do something no one else has done, but why not take risks that make the world better?"

Under Rose's leadership, the company's profits have also tripled.[8] When she took over, she dove deep into Patagonia's supply chains, streamlining them both financially and environmentally. An article in *Fortune* reported Chouinard as saying: "Rose understands business better than I ever did, and she understands the need for revolution. She's the one who's going to lead us there."[9]

When Rose took over Patagonia, she had one goal. She wanted to show it was possible to be a very successful business in traditional terms without compromising on value. "We live in an interconnected world," she says. "There is tremendous stress on resources and the web of life, and so I wanted the environmental mission and our business North Star to be about the urgency of the problem: we are ruining the one planet we have because of greed and lack of vision for a better world." Her mission was to prove you can have it all as a business—solve the biggest problems facing all life on this planet and make money doing it.

Growing up, Rose lived a typical middle-class life until her parents divorced. With that, she went from being comfortable to living on food stamps. So when she started her career, she wasn't thinking about how business could change the world; she just knew she had to get a job and make money to survive. She knew she needed economic power.

The more power she got, however, the more she started to wonder about its cost. "I started to have real success, the kind of success my immigrant grandparents would have been very proud of, but that also caused me to reflect on the whole system, which to me seemed very flawed—all about chasing earnings. It was creating more human and planetary suffering. Participating in it seemed like fanning a flame unconsciously."

When she finally joined Patagonia, Rose says she found "a tribe of people who wanted to make the world better, who were working to save the planet, to change things for the better." She wanted to be part of that. "I think that's the only way to live," she says, "whether it's replacing a toxic material in the supply chain, or inspiring people to protect wilderness." Now she believes that business might just be the only thing that can really change the course of life on this planet for the better.

For the next decade, Rose has her sights set on Patagonia being a vehicle for transforming our farming system, because she sees this as one of the most pressing—and the most solvable— problems out there. As she puts it, she's focused on "reversing the chemical-agriculture model for good, and making healthier, regenerative supply chains." But for her, it's not just about making a few better choices. It's also about businesses having a longer lens, looking into their impact—both good and bad—and judging success beyond the "crazy quarterly earnings model," which she refers to as "the road to hell."

How soon can we expect tangible improvements? Soon, she thinks. "I believe that we can make this shift in a decade," she says. "It's hurting people and the planet, and why continue to do something we can improve? I think the great brands of the next decade will be the ones that were brave enough to take actions to make the world a better place, to develop healthy and regenerative supply chains. We need a more enlightened economy."

That day at the Expo, just as the USDA announced the withdrawal of the Obama-administration rules, our

regenerative-agriculture   alliance   stood   united—animal
welfare, fair trade, soil health, and market interests—presenting
our standard to the largest gathering of natural producers in the
country. The room was so packed they had to turn people
away. People sat on the floor, stood, and held up the wall. The
time was right. People were ready for a solution. They were
ready to be inspired.

Inspired to Serve

Earlier that same day, after a long flight into Los Angeles, I
found David Bronner—who had drawn me into the ROC
team to begin with—standing at an Advantage car-rental
counter. David was hunched over and looked exhausted.
He's tall and lanky, with hair to his shoulders, and I have
never seen him without an ethically messaged T-shirt. He
and his friend smelled like a campfire and looked like they
had been out in the wind and sun. I thought it the strangest
thing to find him there. There are so many car-rental
counters to choose from at a big airport like LAX, and
Advantage isn't near any of the rest, but there he was. David
did not think it strange at all, as he was just thinking about
me and the mission we were on together at Expo. He and his
friend didn't have a car reserved, and all the cars were sold
out. I had a car booked. So it was meant to be, and off
we went.

On the way to the Expo, they told me they had just come
from an all-night Peyote ceremony in Mexico. David told me
about his experience. I was glued to every word. He'd retell
this story to the entire Expo audience. It had solidified his
thinking and his commitment to the regenerative organic
ideal.

"Before I came here," David said on the Expo stage, "I was
attending a Peyote ceremony with the Huichol Tribe in
Mexico. They have been holding Peyote ceremonies for 8,000
unbroken years. We were visiting as part of a delegation,
because they're facing pressure from agricultural interests and
mining interests. We're strategizing how to preserve long-term

access to sacred Peyote lands. We got to participate in an all-night Peyote ceremony, which was really beautiful, and it was a world unification prayer."

David's grandfather on his dad's side was the original Dr Bronner, a third-generation German-Jewish soapmaker. He came over to the United States in 1929, at the age of 21, not so much because of the rise of fascism but because of generational conflicts with his dad and uncles, who were running the business that produced the majority of liquid soap in Germany at the time. They had a big factory in Heilbronn. David's grandfather came over and began a career as a consultant to the soap industry.

David tells me that, with the rise of Adolf Hitler, his grandfather became increasingly desperate to get his family out of Germany. Dr Bronner's two sisters got out, one in 1936 and one in 1938. But his parents, like millions of other Jews, didn't make it out alive. They were deported to a concentration camp and killed in 1942.

David's grandfather married and had three kids, but in 1944 tragedy struck again with the death of his wife Paula. In the midst of dealing with immense tragedy in his life, he became obsessed with a new mission. He believed that "all the faith traditions at their core were saying the same thing," David says. "That we need to get over ourselves and get down with each other and realize our transcendent unity across religious and tribal divides or we're all going to die in the next Holocaust or nuclear war. All perish. So he felt urgently called on this mission and set out to unite 'Spaceship Earth.'"

Dr Bronner felt so attracted to this mission that he effectively abandoned his kids. David's father grew up in foster homes. His grandfather paid for the foster care and checked in on them once in a while, but other than that he had completely checked out for the sake of unifying Earth.

David says that his grandfather was "like a prophet in a biblical tradition, just intense, touched, borderline schizophrenic at the time." Dr Bronner threw himself into the business of soap. He created the labels that describe the planet

as "Spaceship Earth" and talking about our need to unite as
one. The label is more than 2,600 words long and reads like
something between biblical scripture and frenzied poetry:

> *God alone knows man's far distant future! Towards which love's*
> *unfailing light shows clear the upward path to brotherhood-peace!*
> *Great tasks to nurture, with strength and knowledge happiness*
> *can last! Love when conquered after years of toil-sweat-blood,*
> *love can strike like greased lightning sent by God to spark mere*
> *dust to intense blazing fire and create new Love, faith-hope-*
> *guts-strength as only God Inspire! Unite the Human race in*
> *our Eternal Father's great All-One-God-Faith, as all mankind*
> *desire!*

With the rise of the counterculture in the 1960s and 1970s,
the lengthy-labelled soaps really took off, but as David's dad
Jim grew up, he wanted nothing to do with the soap company.
"My dad was 100 per-cent focused on family and community,
really rebuilding," David says. After a stint in the Navy,
David's dad moved to Los Angeles and worked for a chemical
company that made his grandfather's soap in bulk and shipped
it down to San Diego for bottling and distribution. Jim
worked hard and rose up in the company to become head of
operations of the facility.

One of the things Jim developed was a firefighting foam
for structure and forest fires that is still used in most
everywhere today. He then founded his own business, which
developed different products, primarily a fake snow based on
foam for Hollywood called Snofoam. "So I grew up working
for my dad," David says, "making different personal care and
household products for different companies." But primarily,
he recalls just making foam snow and blasting it all over trees
with his dad to simulate snow for fun.

"My dad was awesome. Everything we do today is still
because of him. He did not have the example I had, and was
the most amazing father," David recalls.

After David's grandfather got sick in the early 1990s, Jim
took over the company. He had already begun to work in

the company when Dr Bronner's health began to fail, assuming the position of president, with his brother Ralph as vice-president and spokesperson, and his mother Trudy as CFO.[10]

Like his dad, David also had an initial aversion to the family business. In his early 20s, he traveled through Europe. "I had my life kind of blown apart by some powerful psychedelic experiences," David says now. "That really reoriented my view of things." One night when he was out dancing, he had a series of visions on the dance floor, not unlike his grandfather. He said that, in one vision, Jesus was standing right in front of him: "Not like trying to explain it or rationalize it or complain." He said the vision was telling him his life should be about "stepping up and helping out and being rad*. I realized that I want to be like him and that I'm here to get down and serve," he says.

So that's what David did. He joined the family business, committed to the purpose of serving and making the world a better place. But tragedy struck again for the Bronners. Shortly after David joined the business, his father was diagnosed with lung cancer and given six months to live. "It was really intense, being with my mom and my dad and being with him as he taught me the ropes," David says. "He had to go through chemo and radiation. He actually rallied hard. We thought he kicked it and went into remission, and then it was a fast decline at the end. But he lived to see my sister married to my brother-in-law, Michael, which was so beautiful and his big goal."

David's dad had implemented a lot of progressive employee policies, along with his mom and Uncle Ralph. David decided to further that. He saw the company had "an activist engine.

---

*An abbreviation of 'radical'—a term made popular by the Teenage Mutant Ninja Turtles. Still primarily used by people on the West Coast who find words like 'cool', 'awesome', and 'tight' to be tired and overused; 'rad' is generally considered to be a much higher praise than the aforementioned superlatives.

This is not about making money. This is about changing the world, and that was the commitment." In practice, this meant implementing a five-to-one salary cap, so that all profits over and beyond that would go to the cause David wanted to get behind. In 2017 alone, Dr Bronner's gave $600,000 to organizations fighting factory farming.

David sees regenerative organic as a critical solution to get behind. "The problem with traditional industrial agriculture," he says, "is that it's systematically destroying wild ecosystems and the soil. Soil is alive, it's a living ecosystem—and in the wild it would nurture rich flora and fauna in a self-regenerative way, without external input. But instead of nurturing and growing healthy, vibrant soil, we're taking our crops to harvest via more and more chemical inputs and the soil is being killed and destroyed."

Toward Regeneration

Together, the ethics and drive of Rose and the moral compass and creativity of David made for a formidable, well-resourced leadership. I was honored to be part of their team, just for the chance to observe these visionaries. The standard was up and running as a pilot just over a year after its inception, which is lightning speed for a project like this.

Regenerative farming practices represent a better path forward for our food system, and I was honored to play an active role in driving that change and bringing about a better future by supporting Rose and David. Regenerative organic farming asks something else of us, too. It relies on businesses and consumers being forces for positive change, rather than destruction. That means businesses can be inspirations, thought leaders, and problem solvers. It means they must do something else besides review quarterly earnings statements. For good or for ill, their actions transform the planet, and our future. Their path is our planet's path. They can destroy—or they can inspire, collaborate, and drive change.

Rose Marcario believes there may be no other way to solve our world's most pressing problems besides problem-solving and collaboration, and the inspiration that follows. "We have big problems to solve," she says, "and we have to collaborate more than ever if we want to thrive and survive. Transparency is key, we are all inspired by each other. Sometimes I think leaders underestimate what an inspired and values-driven group of people are capable of, and I am continually impressed with what our teams achieve every year in continuous improvements and big shifts. There is always resistance, but you have to break through it. And like with any big aspirational change, the universe conspires to help it come about, and it's really the dedication of people who want to find better ways of working who see it through."

CHAPTER THIRTEEN

Tempt, Don't Bully, Darlings

On April 26, 2018, I was on my way to Berlin when I received a text message from my mom that would change my life for ever. I was due to meet with advocates dedicated to introducing more plant-based options into the market and reducing the use of animals for food. I had a layover in Amsterdam. I turned on my phone and a text from my mom blinked up in front of my eyes:

Last night I had to take Dad to the emergency room. He was in pain, nausea, jaw and left arm. They did blood work and hooked him up to a blood pressure machine immediately. Lab results showed there was something going on with his heart. There was not enough oxygen.

I couldn't get through to my mom at first and left a choked-up message on her voicemail. I could not put words to the fear I felt. My dad is the picture of health. He swims a mile nearly every day at the gym. He skis like a champ every year on the slopes, to the extent that only my equally adventurous 10-year-old can keep up with him. He sails and works for hours maintaining his boat. He's active and sharp. He had just retired a year earlier, and at 67 seemed to have exploded in energy and activity. The idea that there was something wrong with his heart didn't make any sense to me.

He had been doing laps in the pool when the pain had become unbearable. He's lucky he didn't drown, the doctor would later say. My nearly 90-year-old grandmother would call it a miracle. He tried to wait out the pain, but by the middle of the night he knew something was very wrong. He had had a heart attack. Two of his arteries were 40 per-cent blocked and one was 100 per-cent blocked. They were clogged by cholesterol.

The next few days were difficult for my family, as we came to terms with the fact that he'd had a heart attack. But it was most difficult for my father. Everyone has an idea of who they are. Dad had imagined himself living until the last day of his life without taking a single pill. And now he'd be taking several every day for the rest of his life.

I had imagined my dad would always be there, but human beings are not meant to last forever. We all have our expiration dates. I was not prepared for this moment, but I was grateful for the second chance he got—the second chance we all got.

That week, I went with my parents to my dad's first cardiologist appointment since his release from the hospital. There's no way to know exactly why he had a heart attack. Genetics didn't help. My great-grandfather had died in his 40s of heart failure, my great uncle in his early 60s, my grandfather at 69. Maybe it was the heat and dehydration from working on his boat that escalated his heart blockage. Maybe it was stress and a meat-heavy diet throughout his life, or maybe it was the rheumatic fever he had when he was five. Through tests, we'd later find out his doctor attributed it to just a bad diet.

One thing was for sure. Going forward, his cardiologist recommended a plant-based diet. He said my dad should not eat more than 6 ounces (170g) of meat—the size of the palm of one's hand he said—per week. My dad laughed and told the doctor I'd been trying to get him to eat less meat for years. But there was no joy for me in hearing this.

That night, after the doctor's appointment, I told my dad about a recent meeting I'd had with John Mackey, cofounder of Whole Foods Market. I had tried to tempt Mackey into talking about what the future might look like, what might 2040 look like. But he had halted me in my tracks. He told me: "Twenty-two years ago, Google didn't exist. Facebook didn't exist. Amazon was kind of getting started. There was no Twitter. There was no Netflix. There were no smartphones. No iPods. No iPads. "

I tried to remember how I would have booked my flights, my hotel, or my taxi, or mapped my way to this meeting 22 years ago. It's mind-blowing to think of how quickly our world is changing. "Look at how different the world is today compared to 22 years ago," Mackey told me. "Then imagine for a second that change is accelerating. There will be bigger changes in the next 22 years than there were in the past 22 years."

Change is happening so fast that it's almost impossible to imagine what the world will be like in another 22 years. But I told my dad that there was one thing Mackey was willing to speculate about. John told me: "I absolutely, categorically will state that people will be eating fewer animal foods, whether it be the kind that people are growing today in factory farms, or whether it comes from vat-grown meats, or whether it comes from higher welfare sources. Because animal foods are not really good for our health."

I asked him why he was so certain. He pointed to his wrist, to a device counting his steps and measuring his sleep. While today we might count our steps, Mackey said, tomorrow we might see the instantaneous result of our meals on our cholesterol and blood pressure. Imagine how quickly that would re-route your eating habits.

"We'll probably be able to monitor the overall nutrient makeup of our bodies," Mackey said. "At every instance, we'll see our deficiencies. The science is overwhelming," he went on, "Animal foods promote cancer growth. They clog up your arteries and produce heart disease." He told me that, ultimately, animal agriculture companies will lose, just like the tobacco companies lost.

I asked my dad what he would have done if he had a watch that told him his lifestyle was increasing his cholesterol numbers and blood pressure. He didn't hesitate to tell me he would have changed if he'd had that information. I was taken aback by how quickly he answered, how sure he was.

Even without these futuristic health devices, I've noticed over the years my non-vegetarian extended family starting to eat more and more plant-based products. All my family cares about is food that's healthy, convenient, tasty, and not too expensive. The changes they've made have little to do with my advocacy for animals. A plant-based diet is just increasingly a convenient, delicious, healthy choice.

My kids—and my nieces and nephew—will grow up in a world where it might be more normal than not that a "nugget" is full of plants, not chicken; or maybe, in a not-too-distant future, made of meat grown in a lab. All my family wants, all many other families want, is good, healthy, tasty options on the shelf. We don't even need to whip out the scary factory-farming films. Plant-based options will win because they're better.

The next wave of food makers are working on exactly what this future might look like. They are motivated by two drivers. GeekWire journalist Alan Boyle writes: "One of the motivations for marketing (and eating) meat substitutes is to make a dent in the billions of animals and sea creatures that are killed every year to fuel humanity's appetite.

Another is a realization that livestock agriculture will be too inefficient to feed the estimated 9.7 billion people[1] who will be living on Earth by 2050. By one measure, it takes 40 calories of energy to produce each calorie of food output from beef."[2]

In the summer of 2016, Tyson did something[3] no one expected: they bought a 5 per cent stake in Beyond Meat, a plant-based protein company making chicken-free strips and nuggets, beef-free burgers, and more. A few months later, Tyson established a venture capital fund[4] with $150 million to invest in alternative protein startups. Protein diversification, a business strategy to include more plant-based proteins in a portfolio, had officially arrived—and it was being funded by the king of poultry. "We don't want to be disrupted," Justin Whitmore, executive vice president of corporate strategy and chief sustainability officer at Tyson Foods, said[5] at an event. "We want to be part of the disruption."[6]

The disruption he's referring to is a major revolution that is underway in the meat industry. Tyson is not the only company making big changes. Campbell's, General Mills, Nestle, and Maple Leaf Foods have also entered the alternative-protein market.

There's no question that plant-based nuggets and other products have their place in the present market. Mintel reported sales of plant-based proteins grew at least 9 per cent year over year in 2014 and 2015, with total sales in 2016 exceeding $5 billion. According to Mintel, 113 million Americans—that's one-third of the country—regularly eat protein alternatives. Those are not numbers to ignore—and they are only going to grow.

Fabulously Meat-Free

Joanna Lumley, the British icon and international star of *Absolutely Fabulous*, steps onto a brightly-lit stage in London. Every cell phone in the room is snapping a shot of her. Every ear is hanging on her every word. She is calm and effortlessly elegant, standing firm in her own truth. She is a glamorous celebrity, yes. But she's also not afraid to hold up a protest sign and shout a campaign slogan to help the pigs and lambs of this world. She's a tireless advocate for farmed animals and a decades-long patron of Compassion in World Farming (CIWF). Tonight, Joanna Lumley has taken to the stage with a different and simple proposition. Tonight she has one message: "Tempt, don't bully, darlings."

She smiles broadly and raises her eyebrows, brushing her blonde bangs to one side. The audience explodes into applause. She is adored. She throws her back and laughs a hearty laugh.

She continues: "Most anybody who criticizes vegetarians always says, 'Oh these rabbits, nibbling away at lettuce.' Well, not from what we've just seen there." She waves around the room at the tables of samples. We are in one of the most elegant and glamorous buildings in central London. All around us, tables are set up with enticing, astounding surprises to taste. People have rushed here from the day's events, afraid to miss out. The night will feature the most cutting-edge plant-based innovations in the world.

The event is being put on by CIWF as part of a wider conference raising awareness about the need to end factory farming and eat a lot fewer animal products if we are to save our planet from near-certain doom. The conference was provocatively called Extinction—because that's what is happening all around us. Elizabeth Kolbert's earth-shattering book, *The Sixth Extinction*, explains that we are in an era of mass extinction akin to that of the mass extinction of the dinosaurs.

But instead of hearing a stern lecture, the attendees are sinking their teeth into a delicious burger that bleeds, tasty deli meat, yummy chicken satay—all from plants. The great innovators of our time are gathered here in one room to stake their claim in the marketplace with one purpose: to tempt rather than bully people away from meat, dairy, and eggs.

The principle is simple. In order to succeed, plant-based products have to be unapologetically, memorably, and temptingly delicious. And they have to be as cheap or cheaper than their animal-based counterparts. Once that is achieved, no scolding is required. No sad photos of dying, tortured animals. It's just food—more specifically protein—and consumers will want it because it will win them over through flavor and cost. This approach is a relief to me. Decades of advocacy and fighting, of maneuvering and convincing, and now this: the products will be so irresistible, they'll do the advocacy on their own.

Recent innovations in plant-based food give me incredible hope for animals. Decades of effort have put the issue on the map, but bleeding veggie burgers and vegan chicken nuggets that taste close to the real thing could take plant-based eating mainstream. In other words, after years of trying to win over people's hearts and minds, it appears we'll soon be able to win them over through their stomachs.

Seth Goldman, the chairman of Beyond Meat, takes to the stage after an introduction from Joanna. Beyond Meat has reinvented the veggie burger. The company is disrupting the burger market so profoundly that major meat companies are investing in it. What was once a tiny start-up is now attracting investors like Tyson Foods and Bill Gates. It's a classic case of "If you can't beat 'em, join 'em."

"The first thing that we have to recognize is that we are entering a category where the analog has failed," Goldman says. "Veggie burgers literally have become a punchline for bad food. If we, or actually, the meat industry, was trying to design a strategy or a tool to discourage people from having plant-based diets, the veggie burger would be a very effective strategy." The crowd laughs, and Goldman goes on. "What we have seen consistently is that vegetarians eat them, but they don't cross over. People who are carnivores don't opt to have a veggie burger. So, with Beyond Meat, we said, 'Let's understand what's happening here. Let's look at it a different way.'"

For the founder of Beyond Meat, Ethan Brown, this different way was to re-create the burger from the ground up. Brown essentially did an MRI of the hamburger. The results: 70 per cent of it is water, and the next main components are proteins and amino acids, which of course you can get from peas or other legumes. Then there are lipids and fats. Those occur in coconut oil and canola oil. The rest of a burger is some trace minerals, carbohydrates, and a little bit of color and flavor. Broken down into its components, the task of replicating the burger became much less daunting.

Seth tells the audience: "We basically reassembled the burger to create a product that is close enough to meat that it is actually the first plant-based product to be carried in the meat section in the grocery store." Seth's family is vegetarian, but he points out that true vegetarians make up only 5 per cent of the market. Seth, and the founders of Beyond Meat, have their sights set much higher. They don't want to be the best-selling veggie burger. They want to transform what happens at the meat counter so that the meat counter becomes the protein counter. "Instead of hamburgers and chicken breasts," Seth says, imagining the future, "there's cow protein, chicken protein, and plant protein."

From a nutritional perspective, the Beyond Burger has half the saturated fat of a regular hamburger and no cholesterol, since cholesterol only comes from animals. This makes it healthier, which is timely. Every five years, the UN ranks the average life expectancy of every country in the world. Even though the United States is the wealthiest nation in history, and we have more knowledge of science and medicine and nutrition than any civilization has ever had, in the 2015 UN rankings, Japan was number one for life expectancy, while Italy was number two. The United States ranked only 42nd. "It's embarrassing," Seth says, "and it shouldn't happen." He believes strongly that products like Beyond Meat can improve health outcomes and save lives.

While health is a huge component of the Beyond Meat team's sales pitch, they know they won't revolutionize the meat counter on virtue alone. "No matter how good we make it," Seth says, "or how creative we are, if it doesn't satisfy the consumer, they won't come back."

Everyone in the room has just tasted the Beyond Meat burger, and Seth takes an impromptu poll. He asks if people thought the Beyond Meat burger tasted more like a bar coaster or an animal burger. The results are good—most people thought it was as good as a burger. But he's not satisfied. "We can do better," he insists. "We can keep tweaking the recipe and continue to evolve. We know the opportunity is profound."

Beyond Meat's strategy is to follow the dairy category. In the milk category, 14 per cent of the milk category is plant-based. In 2018, the global plant milk market topped $16 billion.[7] The meat category is less than 1 per cent plant-based. Seth argues that plant-based meat can get to at least 14 per cent of the total meat market, and hopefully even higher. Beyond Meat believes there is one simple way to get there: create a product that is close enough to the analog, and then package it and merchandise it in the same section of the store. In other words, make a plant-based burger that can compete with the cow-based burger, and win.

Seth closes with what he calls the tale of two Henrys. Henry Bergh created the American Society for the Prevention of Cruelty to Animals (ASPCA). As a diplomat living in

Russia, he saw how terribly horses were treated there. He came back to the United States, created the ASPCA, and worked to create standards to ensure that horses had to be given a certain amount of rest, water, and other necessities. He did a lot to improve the lives of horses.

The second Henry, the industrialist Henry Ford, once said that if he had asked his customers what they wanted, they would have said a faster horse; instead, he gave them a car. This Henry was not known as an animal-rights activist, but he also did a lot for horses. By commercializing the combustion engine and putting it inside a car, he created a new form of "horsepower" that competed with literal horsepower, and won. If you were to ask a horse, "Who did more to help your quality of life?" and the horse could answer in a way that we could understand, he might say, "Well, Henry Bergh had his heart in the right place, but Henry Ford really changed the way I lived."

Betting Against the Burger

Can a burger ever really be replaced with plants? Can plant-based products ever really threaten the shelf and menu spaces currently occupied by chicken nuggets or fish sticks? Well, some investors seem to think so.

Michael Pellman Rowland worked for Morgan Stanley in New York for 15 years, and now advises a global clientele at Alpenrose Wealth Management. He is a financial advisor helping private clients to invest their money more sustainably and responsibly. He is also a journalist for Forbes, writing about the business of food from a sustainability perspective. For him, his journey began when he met his wife Hilary.

"We went vegan together probably about three months after we met," Michael explains, "and I started learning more and more about the connection between animal welfare and our food system. That, coupled with all the things I was doing on the investing side, sort of pancaked these personal things I cared about, and my career focused on sustainability, into this one issue, which is food." I can see how passionate he is about the topic as he talks. "Food has tentacles into all the things that we care about," he says. "It's not just animal welfare, but it's the planet, it's water, it's human health, it's food security, it's reducing conflicts. I mean, a lot of wars and unrest are catalyzed by people not having enough food."

Michael tells me that there's reason to care about food sustainability purely from a security point of view. If people have enough food to eat, they're way less likely to cause unrest. They're less likely to end up being refugees, or suffering from a whole host of other problems. Food truly is a global security issue. "People can sort of stomach a lot of injustice, and a lot of suffering, but if they're worried about starving, that's when, you know, game over..."

As a financial advisor, Michael's challenge lay in finding a way to translate his concern for a more sustainable food system into a financial strategy—a way to use his money or influence to change things. So he started gathering information and analyzing balance sheets for companies, looking at their social and environmental platforms and policies. What he found was remarkable.

He began to see a pattern. It turned out that companies that had better environmental, social, and animal-welfare policies were just better-run companies all round. And that matters to investors. "I've come to learn that investing by looking at not only the companies' balance sheets, but also their scores on environmental and social governance issues, can actually help us get a better understanding of those companies," Michael explains. Corporate social responsibility can actually help investors understand which companies are more valuable than others.

Understanding corporate-governance issues basically means asking, "How is the company being run?" Investors with a focus on governance ask questions like "How diverse is your board? How do you pay? How do you treat the communities that you work in? Do you have social responsibility policies in place?" All of these questions help to determine how a company manages risk, and how they weather a storm.

Essentially, what Michael has found is that when companies respect animals and the environment, it's a good indicator that the company's governance is solid. Why? Because they are good at managing risk. Corporate social responsibility is a kind of hack into understanding if a company is a good investment. And that's music to any financier's ears.

Research has shown that more progressively governed companies tend to perform better. For example, companies that have more women on their board or in leadership roles tend to outperform those that don't, Michael explains. "If you have a board that has at least three women on it, when you go to borrow in the capital markets to raise money to expand your operations, you end up paying less on interest," he says. "The thinking goes that the brain trust* that's helping to drive the business decisions is more diverse. Women provide a perspective that men don't necessarily always have." Collective decision making is smarter, better, and ultimately less risky with a more diverse team.

That's just one example of how social and environmental data can actually be critical for understanding whether a company is being run effectively, ultimately making it more sustainable, more profitable, and more tempting to investors. This way of thinking has led to increasing interest from investors in social and environmental responsibility, to the extent that many investors now screen companies for how they manage these risks.

Seen through this lens, plant-based food companies are a tempting investment. They're less risky than animal-based food companies, and provide more room for growth. Where chicken sales, according to Mintel, were stagnating at only 1 per cent growth in 2017, plant-based alternatives sales grew

---

* Brain trust began as a term for a group of close advisors to a politician; often academics, they are prized for their expertise in particular fields. The term is most associated with the group of advisors to Franklin Roosevelt during his presidential administration.

8 per cent in the same year. With 75 per cent of people wanting to increase their protein consumption, yet 58 per cent looking to eat less meat, any smart investor would see opportunity in plant-based alternatives.

Liz Dee and Nick Garin are two of those investors. Liz is the co-president of Smarties Candy Company. She's been working at the iconic brand, which was started by her grandfather, in various ways since she was 14 years old. She worked on their first website. In college, she worked on their first Facebook page.

After years working at the company, Liz went on a yoga retreat, where she met someone who would change how she thought about business and its purpose. Like her, this acquaintance was a New Yorker working in a family business. His family was in real estate, so he did that full time, but he also had an interest in something called "impact investing."

"I had heard of the term angel investor," Liz says. She had friends who were entrepreneurs, so she'd heard them throw around terms like "Series A" and talk about start-up investing, but she'd never expected to get into the space herself. After all, Smarties was an established brand. When she heard about impact investing, however, Liz began to think about how she might use her earnings from Smarties and her position to be a force for good in the world—while also making some money. She loved working in her family business and didn't want to leave. How could she stay there, make money, and do good? "I began to see how investing in companies is another way to create the world we want to live in," she says.

Liz had been using her money to support charitable organizations. She had been investing her own time and energy at the grassroots activist level, but now she began to see a different way she could make a difference. What if she invested in businesses that were creating superior alternatives to animal products? That would help create the world she wanted—and it would make money she could then further invest or give to charitable causes.

Liz and Nick began to look for opportunities. Her first investment was something she stumbled upon because she bought their products for herself—Vaute Couture, the vegan fashion label. "That sort of opened the floodgates in our mind of what was possible," she says. "After that, we founded Baleine and Bjorn Capital (B&BC) in January 2016."

B&BC is committed to investing in companies creating superior plant-based products and other alternatives to factory farming. For example, they were one of the earliest investors in Memphis Meats, the clean-meat company which now boasts investors like Richard Branson, Bill Gates, and even Cargill, the massive food company.

Investing in plant-based products is a huge opportunity, Liz explains. With a traditional consumer, packaged-goods food company, she says, you're lucky if you triple your initial investment. "That's not the type of multiples that get people in the investment space so incredibly jazzed," Liz says. Investors in tech start-ups typically want to get back 10 times their initial investment. "With a company like Memphis Meats," Liz says, "that may very well be what we see." In the end, Liz and Nick's efforts to be a force for good through investment may also turn out to be highly lucrative as well. That's the win–win that every impact investor hopes for.

At the other end of the investment spectrum from Liz and Nick is Coller Capital, founded by Jeremy Coller and one of the world's leading investors in the private equity secondary market. Founded in 1990, the firm is headquartered in London, with offices in New York and Hong Kong, and has assets under management of approximately $17 billion. As chief investment officer of the firm, Jeremy Coller is not exactly a radical activist, and yet he is the visionary behind an organization known as FAIRR—Farm Animal Investment Risk & Return.

Rosie Wardle heads up FAIRR, which studies financial risks inherent in using animals for food. FAIRR focuses on environmental, social, and governance-based risks, including the threat of antibiotic resistance. FAIRR is interested in this because of how risky they believe livestock farming is, and, on the flip side, how lucrative alternative-protein investment is shaping up to be.

When they first started FAIRR, Rosie and her team sat down to look at what external risk factors existed for investors with regard to the current protein-production model, which is animal agriculture. Like Michael, she was shocked by what she found: the current animal protein supply chain is exposed to 28 key external risks that can damage a company's financial value.

"We've got things like animal welfare, we've got disease outbreaks, resource scarcity, worker mistreatment, climate change," Rosie says. "There's a whole slew of issues which have the potential to create financial risks for companies." These are not necessarily new ideas for investors, but FAIRR is drawing attention to their importance in a new way. "Most investors were cognizant of these issues, but they were not connecting them with the livestock industry, and were surprised about the breadth of the potential issues linked to this sector," Rosie says. "They were connecting the dots on some of these things, but they didn't realize the extent and how it all links back to this kind of livestock production. The other issue was that there was no clear guidance for what investors should do, because when you start thinking about those 28 risk factors, it seems overwhelming."

FAIRR began to mobilize around these concerns to protect investors. Investors worth a total of $5.9 trillion and growing have signed up to FAIRR's initiatives, all expressing concern about those 28 risk factors related to livestock production. FAIRR and its investors began to write to major businesses like Kroger, Walmart, and McDonald's, arguing that it is a material risk to investors to rely solely on animal proteins within their supply chains. As investors, they asked these companies what their strategies were to address this risk.

They didn't just point out the risk. "We made some suggestions around what the components of that strategy could be," Rosie says, "whether it's investing in plant-based proteins, developing own-brand products through internal R&D, or acquiring alternative protein companies and products. We are asking the companies to diversify their protein mix—thereby reducing the amount of animal proteins in the supply chain."

When a company gets a letter from a large group of global investors worth almost $6 trillion, they listen. Rosie says FAIRR got responses from nearly all the companies they contacted. "Essentially, what we're trying to do is raise awareness amongst investors about the impacts of the current supply chain," she says.

Rosie, Liz, and Michael all see the investment space going in one direction: away from animal-protein production and toward plant-protein or clean meat. While they may be guided by a similar moral compass, at the end of the day they wouldn't get very far on their path if they weren't also guided by the bottom line.

Animal activists have made huge strides over the past two decades. We've passed laws in multiple states to ban the extreme confinement of farmed animals, persuaded hundreds of food companies to improve their animal-welfare policies, exposed factory farming in the world's largest media publications, and increased awareness of vegan eating. But it hasn't been enough to tip the scales of justice.

The sad reality is that most people aren't going to change based on morality alone. For too long, animal advocates have assumed that if we just provide more information, if we can only get people to understand how bad the situation is, we will win them over. Shining a light on the problem is essential to changing a broken system, but it's not enough. It has led to some exciting progress, but making animal-free food more delicious, more convenient, and more affordable could be the key to ending factory farming. That's why I'm so inspired by business and food-science innovators asking new questions to instigate serious change.

Liz Dee started with a simple question: "How can I create the world I want and do good while still running my family business?" Rosie and Michael asked, "How can we avoid

material risk while maximizing our investments?" Seth
Goldman asked, "How can we make the most delicious
burger out there?" But it was the absolutely fabulous Joanna
Lumley who had perhaps the best advice: *tempt, don't bully.*
Make the choice irresistible, delicious, and lucrative. That
way, no one can resist.

CHAPTER FOURTEEN

Brontosaurus Burger

In spring 2017, I was in the Bay Area in California, a place of dreamers and changemakers. I had an inspiring day, where I was privileged to visit a clean-meat lab, one of only a handful of places in the country where cells are grown in a laboratory to make meat.

It seems, whatever we humans can dream up, we can make a reality. In 1931, the British politician Winston Churchill wrote in *Fifty Years Hence*: "We shall escape the absurdity of growing a whole chicken in order to eat the breast or wing, by growing these parts separately under a suitable medium. Synthetic food will ... from the outset be practically indistinguishable from natural products, and any changes will be so gradual as to escape observation."[1] Still, the idea of "growing" meat in a lab has been the stuff of dreams and science fiction—until now.

The concept is both simple and far-fetched: instead of growing an animal in a factory farm, we take just one of its cells, feed the cell nutrients, watch it multiply exponentially, and make burgers and nuggets and steaks out of the resulting material instead. There is no sentient being involved after the initial cell removal, which could be so non-invasive as to only take a skin or hair cell, so long as the cell is a stem cell, meaning it has the instructions within it to become any other cell in the body. Cells from both feathers and hairs contain this magic—which means they can be cultured.[2] Growing animal muscle or fat from a single cell clearly does not involve animal cruelty, nor does it pollute the environment or divert diminishing resources, such as land and water, to an inefficient process. The process is much more efficient and clean—hence the name "clean meat."

William van Eelen is arguably the grandfather of clean meat. Born in 1923, he had a difficult start in life. His

Dutch father ran a leprosy colony in Indonesia and as a child van Eelen witnessed starvation firsthand. Later, he fought in World War II and became a Japanese prisoner of war. In 1948, he entered medical school, where he found researchers attempting to use stem cells to grow skin for burn victims. Observing these researchers, van Eelen had an idea: could stems cells be used to grow meat as well? He set to work on what would become his life mission. In 1975, his wife died tragically early of ovarian cancer, leaving van Eelen and his young daughter, Ira. He became increasingly depressed and over the next decades buried himself in his research aim of creating meat within the confines of a laboratory. During his lifetime, he secured patents for the technology and attracted investors, but he would never see clean meat come to market. He died in 2015 at the age of 91.[3]

Secret Labs

Eitan Fischer, former director of cellular agriculture at the company JUST (formerly called Hampton Creek), did not grow up knowing that he would be directing the clean-meat program of one of only a few companies that would forge this new path for food. JUST was best known for its plant-based mayo, which took the market by storm. In just a few years, the company rose from nothing to being valued at more than $1 billion, making it a "unicorn" in the start-up world.[4] Its founders, childhood friends Josh Tetrick and Josh Balk, had done the impossible: created a mayo that was safer and cheaper, and that beat main brands in taste tests. But they weren't stopping there. Mayo was just a test case; they had their sights set on a much bigger prize.

Fischer was an unlikely character to be leading up the work at JUST in clean meat. He spent his childhood until age 13 on a kibbutz, a collective agricultural community in southern Israel. They were surrounded by similar small agricultural villages. "It was regular that we would walk by the dairy farm on the way to school," Fischer says. "It was normal that after, in the summer, we would go hang out in the pig farm. And at the time it didn't really dawn on me, the issues involved, but I was very much exposed to it when I was young."

In his early teens, Fischer's scientist father was recruited to work at university in New York. One of Fischer's high-school teachers recommended he check out Peter Singer's book *Animal Liberation*. The teacher warned him: "If you're going to read this, there's a very high chance you'll become a vegetarian." Fischer shrugged it off: "No way. I would've known about it if it was an issue. I consider myself pretty informed."

And so he read it, and two thirds of the way he thought to himself, "Obviously I need to become vegetarian." And shortly thereafter, vegan. "It was pretty much the inscrutable logic of *Animal Liberation*, as, I'm sure it's done for many," he recalls. The book changed his path—and maybe our food system—for ever.

Today, Eitan Fischer, with degrees from both Yale and Stanford, is growing meat without killing a single animal. He has left JUST to start his own clean-meat company, Mission Barns. He is a quiet talker, thoughtful and precise in his words and no doubt in his work.

"I thought with a good enough plant-based chicken, that people would switch, if it was indistinguishable," he says. But over the years, his thinking has changed. "Now, I think that it might be possible to make some products very, very similar from a plant-based perspective. And still I don't think people will switch automatically."

Fischer started thinking around the solution. He thought about the need to replicate meat precisely. Not a close approximation, but an exact duplicate. "As I learned more about it, I learned that hardly anyone in the world is working on this issue," Fischer says. He was in his early 20s when JUST co-founder Josh Balk approached him and asked him to work on cellular agriculture.

"What I don't think has been made is a super-cheap nugget that can displace chicken," Josh Balk has said.[5] "If someone would create that, I guarantee that is going to be a coup for this business." So Fischer set to work with a team of scientists in a secret lab.

A Glimpse of the Future

At the time, I had signed a nondisclosure agreement with JUST and was legally bound not to talk to anyone about what I'd seen in the clean-meat lab that day in the Bay Area. For a few hours after my visit, I sat on the edge of a pier in the Marina. The sun was warm and blinding. The air smelled of salt and seaweed. In the distance, the Golden Gate Bridge set a path across the water. Naysayers spent years trying to block the construction of that bridge,[6] but today it is impossible to imagine the Bay Area without it.

I felt certain that what I had seen was our bridge to a new food system. Watching the sailboats zip across the windy bay and the rich green water lapping up against the rocks, I couldn't have felt more hopeful about the future, more sure we will see an end to factory farming—and all the destruction it brings—in my lifetime.

That same week, on March 15, 2017, news broke from a different company, Memphis Meats.[7] Memphis Meats was also in the business of clean meat. One headline read, "A San Francisco start-up just created the world's first lab-grown chicken."[8]

I had met Uma Valeti, the founder of Memphis Meats, at a conference the year before, and his team had helped mine when we were trying to understand chicken's nutritional quality (or lack thereof). Valeti is a cardiologist by trade, but he decided he had to do something different. He was determined to drive a better way for our food system. I felt that I was witnessing a pivotal moment in history: I thought it must be like how people felt when they first learned about the lightbulb or the car. This would redirect the course of our planet. It could potentially turn us away from the path of environmental destruction.

Thomas Edison's electricity was once referred to as a "gaslight replacer." Today that seems ridiculous. One day factory-farmed meat, with all its efficiencies and cruelties, will seem as unnecessary and outdated as gaslight. The so-called replacements will outpace the very thing they are replacing.

While in San Francisco, I got a text from my husband Ben: *Ruben is having a rotten day. Will you try to talk to him? He won't talk.* I called as soon as I could. Ruben was heading to bed, refusing to talk. "Hi buddy. What's going on?" I said, trying to coax him into talking. "I don't want to talk," he grunted. "Ok. What happened?" I asked. "I don't want to talk," he grunted again.

Ruben is not a fan of school. This is a kid who just wants to look under rocks for bugs and through binoculars at wildlife and think about the chances that there's life on other planets and marvel at the unknown universe. He wants to swing from trees and vines and think about robots. Third grade, and school in general, doesn't allow for much of that. So I try to let him into my world, his future world, and share with him the secrets that lie ahead.

"Can I tell you a secret? But you really can't tell anyone, not one friend, not your teacher, absolutely no one," I said to him in a low voice.

He might not want to talk, but he was ready to listen. So I told him about a building. "It looks like any other warehouse. Even when you step inside, it just seems normal. People are working at tables, drinking coffee, having meetings. There are high ceilings in this warehouse. And in a corner that looks like any other corner, is a secret door."

I paused for effect. "What's in the door? Did you go through the door? Did you?" Now he was engaged.

"There's a sign on the door that says: No unauthorized persons allowed. Only a few very trusted people are allowed behind that door. Most people working in the warehouse aren't even allowed in. But I was allowed behind the secret door. And behind the door is the most amazing thing I have ever seen. I witnessed magic. Behind the door are four incubators growing the tissues of animals to become meat without ever hurting an animal."

"I saw it myself," I tell my son. I tell him all about the scientists working in secret, all about how we all start off as a bundle of cells and the cells have instructions and communicate to one another about which one will be the liver or the nose or the toe. Scientists have figured out how cells communicate to each other, and know how to intercept and control that communication to make the cell become almost anything we want it to become. We can do that by collecting a hair or feather or a sliver of skin because each cell, no matter where it is from, has DNA, the instructions for how to make a whole complex living being. We can take one cell and make it into a burger.

"By the time you grow up," I whisper to my son, "we'll have clean meat in the grocery store. Instead of animals on factory farms, we'll grow cells in labs and our burgers won't hurt anyone, won't pollute the land or water, or be unsafe. They can even work on growing cells from animals that we have driven nearly to the point of extinction because of our consumption of them, like the bluefin tuna. Imagine that."

There is a pause. "Do you think we could grow dinosaurs?" he asks. This kid, he makes my heart swell. "Yes! We could have brontosaurus burgers one day!" I say with a smile.

"That would be cool," he says.

We talk for a long time about the possibilities. I know he'll go to bed tonight dreaming about dinosaur burgers—and a future where kids like him save the day because they are curious about the world, have good hearts, and dream big.

The United States is a country of creative, hard-working innovators. We have been responsible for some of the world's worst innovations, such as factory farming, but we also have the capacity to create the very best—like cellular meat grown in laboratory settings; plant-based proteins that are better, cheaper, and safer than animal protein; and farming that regenerates the soil rather than sucking everything good out of it. Anything we can imagine can be possible. Anything terrible we do, we can undo. The great innovators of our nation have begun the great undoing of factory farming, working in their farms and kitchens and labs to create a better way.

Dining with Ian

Months later, there's news from Eitan Fischer. JUST had
revealed its cellular agriculture efforts to the public through
the *Wall Street Journal*.[9] A month after that news, Josh Balk,
JUST's cofounder, got in touch again. JUST had come up
with an idea. They would use the feather of the best chicken
they could find to grow a chicken nugget. That chicken was
named Ian.

Ian had a healthy waddle and comb, and enjoyed looking
for bugs and scratching in the dirt on pasture. He was raised
on Caleb Barron's Fogline Farm in northern California. At
first, Barron thought the JUST folks were downright strange,
but then he thought about it again. "In all honesty, people are
going to eat meat," he said. "And one feather from one of my
chickens could be a catalyst that feeds the world."

Ian's feather was sent to Eitan Fischer's lab, and the work
began.

The scientists first identified the exact cell within the
feather that would make the perfect starting material. Then
they had to find a food for the cell to grow in. Fischer says this
proved to be the most challenging area, because many
traditional protocols for growing animal cells use animal
blood.

"In a body, cells get a constant stream of blood, which has
all the proteins that they need," he says. "So given that we
can't use animal blood for a variety of reasons—not only
because it's the most expensive, and has contamination issues,
and has lots and lots of variability ... but mainly because, if
we use it, then what have we done?" For JUST, growing
clean meat in animal blood would undermine the whole
purpose of the experiment. "If you have to keep harvesting
blood from cow fetuses in order to feed cells to grow
hamburgers, then why do it at all?" Fischer asks.

The most difficult problem facing Fischer was how to find
a nonanimal source of protein and nutrients to feed the cells.
"As far as I know, there's one company in the world that can
actually find nonanimal ingredients that have the same
functionality as the animal ingredients that they're meant to

replace," Fischer says, "and that's a company that's invested tens of millions of dollars into a discovery platform, where it can discover those ingredients." That company was JUST itself.

JUST built a discovery platform to screen plants for qualities that could replicate what an egg does. That platform had helped them disrupt the mayo market by introducing a cheaper, safer, tastier mayo that did not contain eggs. They went on to replace egg and dairy ingredients in other products, such as liquid scramble, cookie dough, and salad dressings. And that same discovery platform turned out to be exactly what they needed to do cellular agricultural work. Robots in their lab—like Fischer's personal favorite, "Heidi"— continually screen plants to identify their functional properties.

JUST identified the cell. They identified a nutrient obtained from plants that will allow the cells to grow, and grow quickly in high density. And then, like anxious parents, they watched it grow.

"Arguably the most prized part of the chicken is something called a chicken oyster." Fischer says they asked their lead chef Thomas, "If you had to choose one cut of chicken that you had to eat, the one most delicious cut, which would it be?" Thomas's response: a piece of meat called the "chicken oyster."

The chicken oyster is a tiny piece of dark meat located near the animal's backbone. "The reason this is such a delicacy in part is because it's such a tiny, tiny piece of tissue, so you have to kill the whole chicken to get it," Fischer says. But with clean-meat technology, the possibilities are endless. "What if we can make all the chicken the most delicious part of the chicken? What if we just made all chicken oyster, and every chicken nugget, and every chicken wing, and every breast, was actually the finest, most prized part of the chicken? "

I am stunned by this idea. And it's immediately obvious how such a product could outcompete the regular chicken nugget if they can ever get close in price. Imagine, Fischer says, if every hamburger could be made from the most delicious part of the best cow in the entire world. There will be hurdles along the way, of course, but "with that kind of message, I think will sell itself," Fischer says.

The cells of Ian the chicken have been grown, they have replicated, and JUST has asked their chef Thomas Bowman to prepare a product that includes these cells. He decided to make chicken nuggets—"the best chicken nuggets ever."

"We figured out how life really works, and we don't need to cause death to create food," Bowman says. He sees clean meat not just as a culinary challenge but as an urgent mission. "We are going to have to do it if we want to continue living on this planet," he says.

On a summer day in 2017, the team sat around a picnic table and sank their teeth into Ian-cells in the form of a chicken nugget—as the actual Ian waddled around in the grass beside them. Ian is delicious. Ian is also very happily making clucking noises as he chases a bug in the grass, and has never ever been harmed throughout this entire process.[10]

Chinese Trade Deals and Mega-Meat-Makers

In August 2017, *Global Meat News* reported that JUST was in conversation with 10 global meat-and-feed companies about licensing their clean-meat technology.[11] These companies were based all over the world, from Southeast Asia to Latin America to Europe. It seemed only a matter of time before someone bit. That same month, I was due to speak to David Kay, the head of mission at Memphis Meats, when he texted me to say that he thought we should postpone our conversation until after a big announcement they were about to make. He said I would definitely be interested. I agreed, and waited on the edge of my seat.

A few days later, on August 23, 2017, Memphis Meats announced it had finished a $17-million Series A fundraising round. The company had now raised $22 million, all for developing clean meat, the largest investment to date in the new technology. Perhaps more significant was the news of *who* had invested. Richard Branson and Bill Gates seemed like the usual suspects, but no one had expected the meat-manufacturing giant Cargill to be part of the mix. For the first time in history, a meat manufacturer had invested in another doing clean meat, a business that arguably could put them out of business.

Cargill is one of the largest meat makers in the world. From Asia to Europe, North and Central America, they span the globe, providing meat. Their mission statement says they aim "to nourish the world in a safe, responsible and sustainable way." When you take a closer look at their company, a subtle shift hints at their willingness to look beyond traditional meat production to accomplish this mission. The division that used to be called Cargill Meat Solutions had changed its name to "Cargill Protein."[12] They'd positioned themselves to pivot when the opportunity arose. In summer 2017, it did.

When David Kay and I finally connected a couple of days after Memphis Meats' announcement, I could hardly get my questions in fast enough. Kay told me the first big media splash Memphis Meat made was with a beef-based meatball in February of 2016. But that one meatball didn't fulfill their mission. "We had always said, this is a technological platform that we want to develop and to be able to quickly innovate between different types of meat," Kay says. "And I think chicken and duck are very important. Chicken is, in the US, the most-consumed, and soon will be in the rest of world. And globally, duck is hugely popular." In fact, ducks are the second most consumed animal on the planet, based on the number of animals slaughtered (this is mostly in Asia, given its growing demand for protein).[13]

. Memphis Meats also understood that, in order to really be successful, convincing the meat industry to embrace the technology was critical. Uma Valeti had written to me saying he thought this was "a first step to building the coalition." I asked Kay to elaborate. "We are really interested in coming up with solutions that everybody can sign onto," he says.

This strikes me as a radical idea. They are attempting to come up with a product that a meat company, an animal activist, a concerned parent looking for the healthiest option, an environmental advocate, and perhaps even the animal itself, can agree on.

"We're out there to appeal to broad swaths of the population who eat meat because it tastes delicious and also because it's a really important part of people's cultures," Kay says. "If we can be a giant tent and we can get folks who might disagree on a bunch of other issues but can all come around and agree that this is a better way to be producing meat, we'll be in a much better place. Cargill is obviously an important part of this coalition, and by investing in us, that's a big step toward building a strong and diverse coalition."

Kay notes that, along with Cargill, they also have investors who are vegan and vegetarian, as well as folks like Bill Gates and Richard Branson, who each have their own motivations. He points out that there are many different reasons to want this innovation to succeed. "If we bring all of those motivations under one tent," he says, "then we will be a lot stronger as a movement and we will be able to have a much bigger, positive impact on the planet."

This big-tent idea sounded great in theory, but I wanted to know how they'd actually talked to a meat manufacturer like Cargill about clean meat. "This is a really compelling business opportunity, in addition to being a really great opportunity to help the planet," Kay says. "People talk a lot about the environmental inefficiencies associated with meat production, but a lot of that translates into economic inefficiencies as well." Making 1 calorie of beef takes 23 "input calories," Kay explains, in the form of grain and other feed that sustains the cow while it's growing. At scale, Memphis Meats expects to require only 3 input calories to produce 1 calorie of clean beef. "That's the reason we access a lot of these environmental benefits in terms of less water use, less land use, less greenhouse-gas emissions," Kay says. "But it's also a reason why we expect, at scale, our process to be more affordable than conventionally produced meat."

Kay describes in detail for me what production might look like in the future: big facilities with meat breweries or cultivators, where meat producers are proud of the process and consumers are proud of how their meat is made. Consumers could go tour the facilities if they want to learn more about it. There would nothing to hide.

Kay also sees a business opportunity in preventing spoilage and improving human health. "The vast majority of bacterial contamination for meat products today comes at the point of slaughter," he explains. Bacteria from feces in the animals' guts can contaminate the meat. "If we detach slaughter from the meat-production process, then what you're left with is meat that could potentially have a longer shelf life or need to be refrigerated less, and so you can get rid of some of the economic waste along the way." All kinds of diseases, from avian flu to mad cow disease, would no longer be a concern. That's a pretty solid reason for the meat industry to be interested.

David is quietly confident that clean-meat technology will succeed. It's a simple math problem. If you look at the projections for global population increase and the corresponding increase in demand for meat, we just don't have the resources to keep up with that demand. In the future, if we're not eating clean meat, a lot of us won't be eating meat at all.

From Dream to Reality

On August 11, 2017, China and Israel signed a $300 million trade agreement that would allow Chinese firms to partner with Israeli tech companies for "clean technology," with a focus on reducing greenhouse-gas emissions. With three out of the only eight worldwide clean-meat companies being based in Israel, some observers speculated that this meant China could soon be throwing its weight behind clean meat.

"It is a colossal market opportunity," says Bruce Friedrich, head of the the Good Food Institute (GFI), which supports and lobbies on behalf of meat alternative interests. "This could put [lab-made] meat onto the radar of Chinese officials who have the capacity to steer billions of dollars into this technology."[14]

The day after the deal was signed, the state-run *China Science and Technology Daily* published an article. "Imagine the future," the article observes in Chinese. "You have two identical products, one that you have to slaughter the cattle to get. The other is exactly the same, and cheaper, no greenhouse gas emissions, no animal slaughter. Which one would you choose?"[15]

With one of the world's largest meat manufacturers and the largest meat-consuming country in the world taking clean-meat technology seriously, it was no longer just a dream. At the time of writing, there are only eight companies working on this technology—but that number will continue to grow, and possibly faster than you might think. Consider that, in 1999, a flatscreen TV cost between $11,000 and $25,000.[16] Today, flatscreen TV costs have plummeted to as little as $500, and the standard type of TV everyone used for decades has all but gone extinct.

At a London press event in August 2013, Professor Mark Post of Maastricht University unveiled to the world the first lab-grown hamburger. It was a 5oz (142g) patty that cost about $325,000. Just four years after that initial launch of the clean-meat burger, scientists announced a drastic cut in the cost of production. While still expensive, recent estimates put it at less than $2,500/lb.[17] The trend seems clear. The cost will continue to go down.

The same can be seen in the car, and now the hybrid vehicle, and soon the electric. As soon as a technology is set in motion in the market, prices come down and the product becomes available to the masses. There is no reason to believe that clean meat will be any different. Just as automakers like Toyota and Lexus embraced the hybrid and electric car, meat producers will embrace clean meat. Otherwise, they risk being left behind and going the way of the horse and buggy.

The protein revolution will change the way we think about protein and where it comes from. It will also dramatically change the lives of farmed animals. Today, they're little more than widgets on an assembly line. But tomorrow they may be seen as the sentient beings they are.

The protein on the shelves, menus, and online stores in future may taste like the protein we consume today. Just as electric cars look like ordinary cars, the protein we eat in future may be shaped into familiar patties and nuggets—but it may come from an entirely new production system, one we've only begun to imagine. It is a production system that could have the power to stop the destructive force of factory farming in its tracks while still providing a safe, healthy, and delicious source of protein for the masses.

The end of slaughter

Late in 2017, I enter a large strip mall parking lot. I call David Kay and tell him I'm here. I'm near San Francisco, but this is somewhere else, somewhere grittier. It has the feeling of secret location. I'm told to stand on the corner of the Office Depot. I wait, not sure which direction David is going to come from. There are gulls flying overhead that I watch floating away into the blue skies and the setting sun. From behind me, David emerges from a glass door I had not noticed. It bears the words, "West-Gate Entrance. Fire Alarm Control Panel." There is no indication that this door leads to another world, a place where the end of slaughter begins.

I am led up what reminds me of the stairwell of a hotel. The stairs are gray, the walls are scratched up and undecorated, and fluorescent lights buzz above. We walk up above the Office Depot and down a narrow corridor, where David uses a key fob to enter a room. I am asked to sign in on an electric screen on the wall. He says I don't need to sign the NDA, because they "would never sue me," but I sign anyway. The room is silent, apart from the hum of a refrigerator. Here are stucco partitions, vertical blinds, and a blue patterned carpet. It is not a fancy place.

While David goes to find Uma Valeti, the founder of Memphis Meats, I raise to my tiptoes to peek over the partitions. But there is nothing to see. Some computers, papers, whiteboards; only a handful of people. As my eyes explore the room, I see another door, a glass window, and lab equipment to the left. Instinctively, I know this is where it happens. This is where the cells are being grown that will change our food system for ever. David comes back to find me staring at that door and says, "Uma's ready. And also, unfortunately we don't do lab tours." I nod. What I would give to be a fly on the wall of that room.

Uma greets me kindly, and remembers precisely the last time we met. We settle at a table in an atrium and dive in. I try to gauge from him how fast this change will come. As an activist working for nearly 20 years to end factory farming, how soon can I hope to see the change from animal agriculture to clean meat? I don't expect him to say what he does.

"By 2040, a majority will be a combination of plant-based and clean meat." He says without pause. "There will be traditional meat, which will be clean meat at that point in my mind. Then there will be hybrid products, these proteins in there from animals mixed with non-animal proteins. Then there will be plant based.'

According to Uma, meat from slaughter will be the minority. That phase of humanity, that brief experiment in food production, is done. "I want to make it real earlier than that.' he says. His goal is this. Within the next five years he aims to get product to market, stay on the shelf, and claim a single digit per cent of the market. He feels this is realistic.

I imagine seeking the product out, bringing it home, cooking it, and serving meat to my family for the first time in my life. All my kids will still be home, my oldest in high school and my youngest in elementary.

The main hurdles are cost, scale of production, and taste. The aim is to get cost down to close to conventional meat. That's when consumption will start to go up to double digits, Uma thinks, in the next 20 years. Then he imagines there will be an immediate jump to 30 to 50 per cent of the market being clean meat. In 30 or so years, he predicts that clean meat will make up a majority of all meat options. "If we are talking about 2040 though, then I'd say a majority of the entire meat market will be clean meat, and the rest will be plant based—algae, fungi, other synthetic proteins perhaps—and farm-raised meat."

Despite starting out in the Bay area, Uma isn't just aiming at the US market: "It's very clear there is a global appetite for this. Different countries will do that for different reasons. There's countries that have increasing demand for meat, and it's just not possible to meet that demand with conventional meat. I think those countries we'll see a really fast uptake in clean meat because clean meat will be superior on taste, texture, quality, and animal welfare. I'd look at Asia and the Middle East, where food safety and security are a really big deal."

Right now, countries are transporting millions of animals across vast distances to secure their protein. That trade depends on the relations between nations, which can be fragile. With clean meat, those dependencies and power struggles will disappear. Countries will not only be able to produce protein themselves in their own backyard, but they will do it at a fraction of cost.

In the US and Europe, Uma believes clean meat will win out on taste and health. After all, a clean chicken nugget has infinitely less opportunity to be contaminated by fecal matter and infected with E.coli than one coming from a slaughterhouse. The low-hanging fruit is that, by getting rid of slaughter, we get rid of all the possibilities of contamination that happen on the slaughter line: E.coli, Salmonella, Campylobacter, and more.

The next level is how can you tweak the nutritional profile to match the needs a consumer. Uma observes, "For clean meat you could modulate the taste and nutritional profile, which you cannot do in an animal, or if you do it, it takes seven to eight years of selective breeding. But with our cycle of innovation, we can do that every three weeks."

The last hurdle is taste. Cost, scale, and taste. These are the three hurdles to leap over. "We are putting together a puzzle that no one has ever put together before. Some of these pieces we know, and some of these pieces are unknown to us. I think as we start talking to people more and more, it will be inevitable that this will come to market.' he says.

As we are wrapping up, and I'm taking in his words, I ask him how he feels about being the man who will end the majority of slaughter for animals. Up to now he has been earnest and serious in his answers, but as I ask this question, his face transforms. A wide smile spreads across his face, and his eyes glow. "That would be a dream come true in every life, if there are more lives that I have; that would be a dream in every life I have to live." He bows his head and briefly closes his eyes, in the most humble of gestures.

After I say my goodbyes and drive away, a feeling wells up inside of me. It's one I've felt only a few times in my life. Maybe I would not experience such a feeling if I had not worked so hard for so long to end factory farming. Maybe I would not feel as I do had I not seen so much suffering of so many individuals and felt hopeless so many times about how slow the progress was, how many people didn't seem to care, how the path we had chosen was just not fast enough.

But now this. Now perhaps the light at the end of the tunnel. To hear Uma say that by 2040 the majority of slaughter could be replaced... I would still be alive then. I'd be done raising my children. I'd maybe even have a grandkid. This was not so far off. I would bear witness to both the greatest mistake of our time, factory farming, and its greatest innovation, clean meat.

I drove along the Bay with an unmistakable feeling of pure, unequivocal joy and gratitude to be living in these times.

★ ★ ★

David Bowman, the chief scientific officer of Mission Barn, stands confidently in an apron with his pale skin and floppy, jet-black hair. "I heard that more people have been to space than have tried clean meat." I am about to be one of them. I have not eaten anything like I am about to eat since I was 15.

It is June 2018 and I am back in the Bay area for the global Effective Altruism conference, where I get to nerd out on "how to do good better." It's a movement that wants to use data to choose the best strategies for solving the world's worst problems and reduce suffering. Factory farming, with its quantifiable and vast suffering, is firmly on the map as one of the world's leading causes of suffering.

Eitan is here too. He's left JUST to start Mission Barn, his own clean-meat company, and he's offered me a tour. He's decided to corner the fat market: bacon and duck are the big focus.

Mission Barn is based in Emeryville, just south of Berkeley. In the early 20th century, Emeryville was the site of meat-packing plants an other industries. A little over a mile south from where Eitan and I stand in his office lay the area known as Butchertown. It once was where farmed animals from the surrounding area were brought to be slaughtered[18]. Today, it is the site of where future clean meat will be developed.

The building is called Outermost. It has been paid for by the vegan investment fund VegInvest, which provides early stage capital and guidance for companies striving to replace animal use. It has the capacity to house 12 incubator companies like Mission Barn. Eitan's company is the first in the door, but I imagine if I return in a year it will be humming with the sounds of invention and progress.

Eitan shows us the space, with its red brick walls and 25-foot (7.6m) ceilings, a corridor with adjoining rooms and polished concrete floors. We enter a vast empty room, standing ready. This is where VegInvest will put the bioreactors and extruders they plan to purchase for the start-ups that will be based here. Extruders are machines that can cost up to a million dollars, but are essential for nugget and strip production. No start-up could afford such thing. Now 12 of them will have ready access to grow their ideas by. It is difficult to imagine how this joint-mission approach could fail. Mission driven, well resourced, gathering the most intelligent scientists and brilliant strategists under one roof: this is a certain success. The people here have degrees from Stanford and Berkeley and Harvard and none of them are a day over 30.

The blocks surrounding Outermost are buzzing with this hope. Across the street is a company called Perfect Day, arguably the most advanced company in the clean space. Perfect Day is creating dairy through clean technology. They have some 40 team members. In February 2018, they received $25 million in investment to scale up.[19] Memphis Meats has moved down the street. Earlier, we had walked over from Finless Foods, where they are using clean technology to grow bluefin tuna. Torin Yeagear, the senior tissue engineer there, told me that by 2020 they will be selling bluefin tuna to San Francisco area restaurants. He's certain of that. When I visited with Eitan a year ago, we counted eight clean meat companies. He now thinks there are as many as 24.

I had thought maybe that when this moment came, the moment I'd eat meat again, that I would hesitate. But I don't think twice. We walk into the kitchen and there stands David. A simple brown menu lays on the table reading *Tsukune Duck Sausage with garlic and white pepper.* We are here to taste the future.

The sausage is sprinkled with sesame seeds and chives, laid on a white plate. There is a brown sauce splashed next to the sausage. I pick up a fork. Someone is filming me, but I am lost in my mind. I think of what I am doing. I want to remember this moment.

My first bite of the future is of duck, which is also my past. My ducks, and their dramas in the swamps of Florida, is how my journey began. At the end of my fork lies duck, actual duck. But this duck was not slaughtered. Instead of raising the whole animal, we have grown just the cells we plan to eat. No duck had to suffer in a windowless, darkened, dirty warehouse or be killed in a cold, bloody slaughterhouse before reaching my fork.

I pause. I close my eyes. I take a breath and slip the fork into my mouth.

It is ecstasy, and not just for the deep, rich flavor, but because this is real. This moment has arrived and I am here to live it.

CHAPTER FIFTEEN

The Win–Win

"You've convinced me. Now go out and make me do it."

— *Franklin D Roosevelt*

Bruce Friedrich isn't the kind of guy you'd expect to find in a corporate boardroom. In 2001, he streaked naked in front of the first President Bush with "GoVeg.com" painted on his chest and back. He's been detained, arrested, and even spent some time in prison for civil disobedience. For a decade, he was the right-hand man of Ingrid Newkirk, founder of People for the Ethical Treatment of Animals (PETA). Bruce was known as one of the most formidable activists at PETA throughout the 1990s and 2000s, running fierce and relentless campaigns in the name of animal rights.

Now in his late 40s, he's given up streaking, put on a suit, and started working within the system instead of trying to tear it down. He's founded the Good Food Institute, an organization that supports companies creating new, innovative plant-based foods, with the sole intention of helping entrepreneurs, chefs, and food scientists do good while making money. He is a regular speaker at food technology conferences, speaking on panels with representatives from major food companies. His institute organized a conference that attracted speakers from Tyson Foods, General Mills, and Kraft Heinz. This is a man who once protested against big corporations. Now he's sitting down next to them, even giving them a platform at his own conference. What turned this radical activist into a radical corporatist?

Bruce's "ah-ha" moment came in the years following the famous McLibel case. In those days, McDonald's had a habit of suing people, a lot. In 1990, for example, McDonald's brought libel proceedings against five London Greenpeace supporters—Paul Gravett, Andrew Clarke, Jonathan O'Farrell,

Helen Steel, and David Morris—for distributing leaflets on the streets criticizing McDonald's for everything under the sun, from its treatment of animals to its environmental impact and its record on workers' rights. Between 1989 and 1991, McDonald's even hired seven private investigators to infiltrate Greenpeace meetings and activities.[1] McDonald's had also threatened to sue more than 50 organizations for libel, including Channel 4 television and several major publications. In all cases, media outlets and individuals apologized and settled out of court. McDonald's lawsuits just kept shutting down any external criticism.

Helen Steel and David Morris, however, decided they would not apologize and would not settle. The case went to court. What became known as the McLibel case ended up being one of the longest civil trials in British history. Steel and Morris were denied any access to government assistance for legal aid, despite their limited resources, and ended up having to defend themselves with some pro bono assistance.[2]

The case dragged on for 313 days, and the official court transcripts were 30,000 pages long. On June 19, 1997, the Honorable Mr Justice Rodger Bell delivered a 1,000 page verdict. About 100 of those pages were about animal protection.[3] Bell decided in favor of McDonald's on most counts, but the few points where he ruled against them proved critical in launching a major campaign to reform they way they treated the animals in their supply chain.

Bell found that McDonald's was "culpably responsible" for cruelty to animals. "His argument was that culpable responsibility came with their capacity to actually make changes," Bruce explains. He remembers this clearly 30 years later. Bell singled out a number of specific practices he described as cruel, and he found McDonald's responsible for that cruelty in cases where they had the ability to dictate their suppliers' practices.

Bruce was working at PETA at the time. He saw an opening, and sent a letter to McDonald's CEO saying, basically, "A high court judge has found that you guys are culpably responsible for cruelty to animals. Here's the half a dozen ways. You need to make changes or we are coming for you."

"Our expectation was that this would be a really good media hook. Our expectation was not that McDonald's would actually do anything," Bruce says now.

He started getting activists to lock themselves to cars by the neck, block drive-thru windows, and go into restaurants and scream "McDonald's is closed for cruelty!" McLibel co-defendants Helen Steel and David Morris launched a website called *McSpotlight,* announcing a Global Day of Action Against McDonald's for October 16, 1999.

After a few months, McDonald's began to reach out to have a conversation with PETA. This wasn't Bruce's typical approach. He was very comfortable with protest and confrontation, but talking was uncharted territory. Bruce needed help. A college friend of Bruce's, Aaron Gross, mentioned that his dad, Steve Gross, taught business negotiations. Maybe he could be useful?

For years after that, Steve did pro bono work for PETA, up to 60 hours a week. He led the conversations with McDonald's, traveling repeatedly to their headquarters in Oakbrook, Illinois. He later ran similar negotiations with other companies..

PETA ended its campaign against McDonald's in late 2000.[4] In the end, the campaign lasted 11 months, with more than 400 demonstrations in 23 countries, including high-profile celebrities and hard-hitting advertisements. Relentless activism combined with Steve's conversations proved to be a winning combination. McDonald's relented. They agreed to a comprehensive animal-welfare policy and put it into effect almost immediately. The policy made relatively marginal improvements. The company banned a couple of the most horrific practices common on chicken farms, like "forced molting," where farmers starve hens for a week or two in order to essentially restart their reproductive systems and allow spent hens to force out another laying cycle. McDonald's also required suppliers to give hens a little more space. But even these relatively minor changes were significant both because of the number of animals affected and because it provided a model for a new way to achieve change.

PETA's success with McDonald's was the first corporate campaign victory for farmed animals of its kind that Bruce can remember. Afterward, PETA launched campaigns against Burger King, Wendy's, KFC, and other fast-food companies. PETA wrote letters to all of the top fast-food chains and all of the top grocery chains, explaining McDonald's new policy and demanding these other companies follow suit. They did. The Food Marketing Institute and the National Council of Chain Restaurants also implemented their first-ever animal-welfare standards in 2000 and 2001, respectively, in response to PETA campaigns.

By today's standards, the advances these campaigns won were not nearly good enough. But these changes were the first of their kind, and they put farmed-animal welfare firmly on the map as a matter of importance for businesses. These campaigns made it clear for the first time that not caring about animal welfare could hurt your business's reputation, and therefore your bottom line.

The market shift toward higher animal-welfare standards also paved the way for legislative progress. In 2002, Florida became the first state to pass legislation banning a cruel practice for farmed animals: gestation crates for mother pigs, in which pregnant pigs are confined in crates so small they can't even turn around for virtually their entire adult lives.[5] Today, 13 states have similar laws banning the extreme confinement of farmed animals; more than 200 companies have committed to phase out cages for laying hens; 60 have committed to phase out gestation crates for mother pigs; and nearly 100 have committed to improve the lives of broiler chickens.

Bruce believes you can trace all this progress back to the McLibel case and the moment McDonald's was found "culpably responsible" for animal cruelty. It was that case, and the campaigns that followed, that put him on the path from radical activist to radical corporatist.

"Nobody thinks cramming hens in cages and pigs in gestation crates is a good idea," Bruce says. "Even the farmers don't think it is a good idea. Everybody's stomach turns when they read one of these noncompliance records from USDA about animals having to be shot through the head over and over, thousands of chickens freezing to the sides of trucks, in the back of transports in the bitter cold. Everybody recoils at that." But knowing you're on the right side of history only takes you so far. Just as Presidents John F. Kennedy and Lyndon B. Johnson wanted to do the right thing on civil rights and poverty but had to be shown the path to political action, Bruce says, when it came to companies making changes for animals, "It was a case of working with them to figure out how to help them do the right thing."

In those conversations with McDonald's and other companies, Bruce says, they'd often complain about how hard it was for them to make big changes as long as the industry was sticking to the old standards. Being the first to make a potentially expensive change puts a company at a competitive economic disadvantage. Bruce knew that if activists wanted to win, they had to take this obstacle seriously.

"The people at these corporations are not bad people," he says. "And within the context of the economic cards they've been dealt, they want to do the right thing." Where a lot of activists might see the meat industry as a monolithic beast to be destroyed, Bruce sees lots and lots of individuals trying to do their jobs. These individuals want, for the most part, to behave well, but they're constrained by economics. The key is to hack that economic formula with a solution in which everybody wins.

Bruce says he's seen a change at meat-production companies over the years he's been in dialogue with them. For example, he says of Tyson, "It's been interesting to see the transition away from sort of old-school poultry guys toward more business-minded, bottom-line leaders. All of them seem to be appropriately un-enthused about cramming chickens into filthy sheds and the entire unpleasant slaughter business."

Bruce believes the new leaders at meat-production businesses are "appropriately un-enthused" about many of their industry's practices, from both a moral and an economic perspective. Raising and slaughtering animals for food is "a tough economic space to be in," he says. That's why Bruce believes that the animal-production industry would, if we made it easy, happily transition to cheaper and more sustainable alternative proteins.

That's why Bruce wasn't surprised when the massive European chicken company PWG Group partnered with Tel-Aviv based SuperMeat, a lab-meat company,[6] or when Cargill invested in Memphis Meats, or when Tyson invested in Beyond Meat. He sees these investments as proof that the *animal* production industry is slowly transforming into a *protein* production industry. This is the transition that Bruce founded the Good Food Institute to help catalyze and support. Meat-production companies are transforming, firstly, because it makes business sense. Plant-based protein is an exciting and lucrative opportunity. But they're also changing because no one really wants to treat animals cruelly. Plant-based protein makes money and it does good. It is the win–win. It is the hack. "It's the sort of thing that smart business people and individuals with consciences would do," Bruce says.

Capitalism with a Conscience

John Mackey, author of *Conscious Capitalism* and cofounder of Whole Foods Market, has believed from the get-go that a business's mission should be to do good while making money. As the chair of the Global Animal Partnership board, I've had the privilege of getting to know him over the years, and he's become someone I rely on to help me think through how we change the market to improve life for farmed animals.

I tend to visit with John in December in Austin, Texas, when the Global Animal Partnership board meets. In 2017, the board meeting was changed, but I kept my meeting and flew in just to see him. He's one of the wisest people I've ever met and I look forward to our chats.

This particular day, it is unusually cold for Austin. That night, I would get stuck at the airport because it snowed. The airport couldn't cope; it didn't have enough equipment to de-ice the place. I'm told it has not snowed in Austin in seven years. Meanwhile, west of Texas, there are fires raging in California, driving out people and wildlife.

I've just come from Georgia, where a couple of months earlier Atlanta was hit by Hurricane Irma, the first hurricane on record to hit the state. Atlanta is full of ancient, towering trees and overland power lines. During the storm, the trees came down all around us, on our neighbor's roof, on the highways, on businesses. People drove up from Florida to escape the storm, to be safe, but even Georgia wasn't far enough. We lost power for three days. My family cooked on a camping stove and ate by candlelight. The entire contents of our refrigerator and freezer rotted or melted. Within the first hours of the power going out, we told the kids we had to eat all the ice cream, because it was otherwise definitely going to melt. I'll never forget my eldest son's determination to eat it all.

I watched the giant pecan trees around our little house toss in the gusts at the peak of the storm, praying they wouldn't fall on our house. One large branch did break and fall just inches from our back door, blocking the exit. But the storm we suffered was nothing in comparison to the scenes in Puerto Rico and the Virgin Islands. People's homes and communities were destroyed. It felt like our planet was raging back at us for what we've done.

The destructive weather, the fires, the unusual snow, the hurricanes, made my visit with John Mackey feel so much more urgent. It felt to me like Earth was reminding us that it's just a planet, and if the conditions aren't just right, we can't survive here. When I meet with Mackey this time, I want to ask him how we can make good change come faster. How can we make a business that generally exploits animals, causes them suffering, and is causing planetary destruction, do good?

Mackey is calm and measured. He's given this a lot of thought. He believes that conscious capitalism is the answer.

"If you can create ideas and systems that are good for the animals, and that are also good for the farmer—meaning they can make money doing it—those ideas are going to spread," Mackey says.

An idea that doesn't work for both animals and businesses isn't going to catch on, he says. He adds, "Goliath does not want to keep getting kicked in the shins. He would rather have peace, but he also doesn't want to die. Goliath has to feel like you're not out to destroy him." The only way to get Goliath on your side, Mackey says, is to come to the table with real solutions—win–win solutions that work both for the planet and for business.

Good Food for the Future

Those are exactly the kind of solutions that Bruce Friedrich founded the Good Food Institute to promote. We don't know what innovative new technologies are coming to disrupt the food industry, but we do know that a future-proof company would not keep animals in cages and crates, or in conditions that do not allow animals to behave naturally or acknowledge that they are sentient beings. Consumers are becoming more aware and more demanding. That trend is only going in one direction. A future-proof meat company should be transitioning away from just being about meat and toward being about protein. We don't know exactly what the future food market will look like, but we do know it will be a combination of higher-welfare meat, regeneratively farmed food, "clean" lab-grown meat, and plant-based protein. Having a hand in all these growing areas would ensure sustainability for a company as well as for the planet. That's the win–win.

Thanks to his conscious-capitalist mission, Bruce's coworkers today are no less radical than they were 30 years ago—but they are a lot more practical. Christie Lagally is one of those practical radicals. She is actively working to make it more lucrative for meat companies to transition to using plant-based protein, and to get those proteins to come to the market faster and cheaper. Her particular focus is chicken.

Christie is a vegan—and she's the only person in her entire extended family who does not have a diet-related disease. Her sister Jamie died, after two strokes and an autoimmune disease, at the age of 34. Her mother has had three strokes, her grandmother has had two. Her uncle recently had bypass surgery and her aunt died in 2017 after a second heart attack. Christie attributes all of these problems to an unhealthy diet too full of animal products.

While today Christie works with investors, patent lawyers, robots, and meat manufacturers, running her own start-up called Seattle Food Tech, her beginnings were humble. Christie grew up in a suburb of Denver in the 1980s, half rural, half urban. Her parents were divorced. Her mother, the only person in the family who worked, took care of her and her two sisters. The family received government food assistance and Christie tells me that, at least at that time in Colorado, that meant they essentially got four things: "It's white rice, block yellow cheese, bacon—tons and tons of bacon—and dry milk," she says. "We figured out how to make everything you could imagine. We had bacon, cheese, rice casserole. I don't really remember eating vegetables as a kid," Christie adds.

As she grew up, she watched the people she loved get sick around her because of what they were eating. Now she believes that, "Unless we change the world around them, they won't get better." That's why she started Seattle Food Tech, a company that aims to bring meat alternatives to price parity with meat. "I'm just convinced that we have to change the food as much as we have to change the people," Christie says. Until people with limited means can find a meat alternative that's as cheap as the chicken Walmart sells for $2.50 a pound ($1.15/kg), the system won't change.

Christie found her way out of poverty in Colorado. She left home at 17 with her dog, Max. "I found an opportunity to get out. I literally packed up everything I owned and left. I actually never went back," she says. She was escaping her old life, but she was also starting on the path that would bring her to Seattle Food Tech.

Christie moved to California, where she finished her last
year of high school. She lived in a rural area, staying for free
on a friend's farm. Legally, she qualified for a free college-
tuition program. "I was technically what was called an
independent student, because I could prove that my parents
essentially, I hate to use this word, but they couldn't care for
me," she says. Thanks to the tuition program, and to the
many odd jobs she picked up along the way, Christie was able
to go to community college.

The first year at community college, she enrolled in a
cooking program. She learned everything from traditional
French cooking to the business side of how to operate a
restaurant or a catering business. Once she got enough credits
under her belt, she transferred to Sonoma State University,
where she received a degree in organizational psychology.
But she wanted to keep going. She started taking classes in
mathematics at the community college. Eventually, after six
years of attending night classes while working full time, she
had taken enough mathematics, engineering, physics, and
chemistry courses to transfer full time to a university down in
Southern California,where she finally got an engineering
degree. She eventually landed a job at Boeing, where she
oversaw robotics and manufacturing research and
development. It's there she began to get a sense of the
importance of the manufacturing side of meat, and it's there
she began to cook up the idea for Seattle Food Tech.

Christie had been volunteering for various animal-
protection organizations, and one day she got a call from
Bruce Friedrich asking her to help with analyses of companies
they were trying to evaluate for this new nonprofit called the
Good Food Institute (GFI). Christie said, "I'm an engineer. I
can take care of that."

This was a pivotal moment. She became fascinated with
how to solve the difficult manufacturing problems involved
in developing plant-based meat alternatives—and she was
good at it. She left Boeing and starting worked for GFI. All
the while, the idea for her own company was brewing in her
head. After spending about a year helping other people work

through their manufacturing issues, she realized that some things were not going to get fixed unless she fixed them herself.

The problem Christie decided to fix was chicken. While the market was on fire with excitement about plant-based burgers, no new product had really challenged the chicken market. She looked deep into the data. Why wasn't anyone picking up the baton? Specifically, why hadn't anyone produced a cheap, plant-based "chicken" nugget?

Big-meat alternative companies like Hampton Creek and Beyond Meat were not going after the nugget, but Christie came to believe it was the lowest-hanging fruit. She approached the problem like an engineer, not a marketer. That was just the way she looked at problems, but it turned out that her different approach was just what the problem needed. So many chickens are sold every year that making any kind of dent in the market can feel like an insurmountable challenge, but Christie doesn't think that way. She tells me that if you start a company around a product, it's less likely that you're designing your company around scale. So she's laser-focused on scalability. From day one, she was thinking, "How can I make this really big, really fast, really cheap?" In other words, she's thinking just like a chicken company … except, instead of using sentient creatures, she's using plants.

"Scalability has to be designed into the product at the very beginning," Christie says. It's an engineer's approach to a market, and it's the way the food industry typically works. Even the chickens you find in today's supermarkets, Christie points out, are engineered to be mass-produced.

Most plant-based protein is made using a type of equipment called an extruder. Extruders cost $1.5 million, making scaling enormously expensive. Big meat companies can afford this kind of up-front cost, but start-ups can't. Christie saw the extruder as the single most important roadblock to overcome. She realized she'd need new and innovative equipment, new patents, new mechanisms to bring a new product to market at scale. If she can crack the extruder problem, she'll be able to compete with chicken nuggets. Christie is confident that she can solve the challenges: "I know how to do a heck of a lot of it, because that's just engineering. That's just scaling. That's just designing your entire company around not focusing on the product as much as focusing on the production."

The first place Christie looked for answers was deep inside the meat industry itself. She starting talking to meat scientists and meat manufacturers. She began to realize that, in order to really scale up, to really be successful, she had to do things the way they were doing it. She had to work with them, learn from them, and partner with them. "They were the ones with all the answers," Christie says. "Raising and killing chickens, of course, is just one portion of the supply chain of creating a chicken nugget. Everything else that they were doing becomes relevant to us."

Christie found meat manufacturers surprisingly willing to work with her. Who else could possibly have all the information that she needed to know in order to make a product at scale, just like they do? "We're certainly not going to start from scratch, because the meat industry already has a lot of the information we need," she says.

In her first round of funding for Seattle Food Tech, she raised $1 million, which is enough to get started. She has a prototype nugget, and some distribution plans. To begin with, she's aiming at schools, hospitals, prisons, and universities. Christie predicts that Seattle Food Tech will be able to initially reach about 6 per cent of the market, at $12 million a year. There's plenty of opportunity to grow. She's already thinking about what's next after the nugget: she's got her eye on chicken strips.

Christie is a committed vegan, but she's willing to look to meat manufacturers to find solutions. Bruce spent years fighting the system, and now he's working on ways to change it from the inside. Both embody the best of what conscious capitalism can be. They come to the table with a truly open heart and mind, and they focus on finding solutions. Their examples show that making money by doing good really is possible.

★ ★ ★

I am sitting in the audience of a packed room in Anaheim, California, in the late winter of 2018. It's Expo West, the largest natural-product expo in the country. I'm speaking later on, but I'm here now to listen to two cattle ranchers and someone who is maybe the opposite of a cattle rancher: Ethan Brown, the CEO and founder of Beyond Meat. Ethan is a towering, broad-shouldered, strong-looking man. His size alone is intimidating. So is his business. He sits on the end of the stage, wearing a T-shirt and jeans, coffee in hand, stretched out and relaxed. The other two look more official, and more nervous. Ethan has presence. I think he senses that they feel threatened. I could sense it from my seat.

"I have nothing against what these gentlemen are doing," Ethan says, trying to put the ranchers at ease. "I actually love farms. It's a massive market," he goes on. "People are going to eat more meat this year in the United States than ever before. There's plenty of opportunity for us to work together to serve that consumer as the consumer demands high-quality protein."

The moderator on the panel turns the discussion toward market trends. He says that a recent survey reports that 40 per cent of Americans identify themselves as having a "plant-based lifestyle," 7 per cent were vegetarian, and 26 per cent identified as flexitarian or "lessitarian"—trying to eat less meat. He turns to Ethan and asks: "What's going on here?"

"It's a really fascinating trend," Ethan replies "The US Cattlemen's Association petitioned the USDA to clarify the term 'meat,' to disallow us from using it. I thought that was really interesting. Tactically," he says, "it's not a good idea to do that, because consumers don't want to be told by the government what to call their food. Second, the consumer understands the difference and distinction between animal-based meat and plant-based meat. They are smart enough and can figure it out. But what it signifies is that there is growing momentum within the population."

Ethan holds up his iPhone. "If we look at the transition relative to this," he says, and makes a joke about nostalgia for landlines with their long cords and lack of mobility. What if telecommunication companies had argued you could not call an iPhone a phone? What if they argued that, despite delivering the same service, it could not be referred to as a phone? The audience laughs. It is, through that lens, a ridiculous suggestion.

Then Ethan takes it a step further. He wants to engage farmers, employ them in the future protein market. "I want to identify a farmer that is growing pulses and tell the story about that farmer and then tell the story of how the meat comes from those pulses," he says, referring to beans. He talks about how there is a "crisis" in rural America. He mentions the opioid epidemic. "There's an opportunity to get more money into farmers' hands," he says. "We aren't sourcing from farmers in the United States. We should be."

At this point, if I were in a cartoon, a lightbulb would have popped up above my head. *Tell a farmer's story.*

I immediately think of Craig Watts, who has 100 acres (40.5ha) of land and is no longer growing chickens. Craig is now an advocate for a better future and rural communities, and has quite a story. Could he grow pulses for Ethan Brown? Could the former chicken factory farmer become a pea farmer for one of the fastest-growing plant-based meat companies in the country?

I chase Ethan down after the talk. I possibly come off like a desperate groupie. I almost miss the set-up for my own talk because I am so focused. I tell him I heard his passion for reaching into rural America. I tell him we have to make that happen. We have to not only support the future of protein, but also the future protein farmer right here in America.

The months that followed were a whirlwind. Ethan sent me a list of the feedstocks Beyond Meat uses in their burgers. I sent the list to a contact of mine, Dr Nancy Creamer, the director of the Center for Environmental Farming Systems (CEFS). She is a professor of sustainable agriculture and community-based food systems at North Carolina State University and an all-around bad-ass. I explained that we were looking to see if these feedstocks could grow in North Carolina and the surrounding region. She quickly responded that many of the items could be grown in North Carolina. From the list Ethan sent me, yellow peas—a key component of Beyond Meat burgers—would tend to grow best.

Nancy wrote me that she had about 20 growers farming thousands of acres of yellow peas at the time. She connected us to Chris Reberg-Horton, CEFS's assistant director of collaborative research, who oversees this work. On the phone, he told Craig, Ethan, and me that he had a bunch of farmers not far from Craig growing yellow peas. He said that, in initial trials, the yield was better than expected. Their farmers were growing the peas for a new brand of grainless dog food, but it's the same yellow pea used in Beyond Meat's burgers. Chris invited Craig to visit with one of the farmers and see for himself.

In mid-April, Craig makes the trip out to meet the farmer. It's about 20 minutes south of where he lives. He drives past the Perdue slaughter plant in Dillon, South Carolina, the very one his chickens once went to.

The farmer tells Craig that planting happens in December and January. That means there's time if he wants to get going. You can get about 40 bushels (1,470kg) out of an acre, and the peas sell for $7 a bushel. She says you can't grow peas every year, but rather every other year. You have to rotate them. You need a combine, seeds, land, and a planter. The yield is good, the income steady.

Craig calls me a week after his visit. We talk through the details, the meaning of this type of farming, and the future we both want. He's got 100 acres (40ha) of land right now, so doing the math, we work out he could make $28,000 a year. But he says the farmer warned him he'd pay about half of that in costs, so he'd walk away with $14,000. Right now he's renting out his land for someone else to grow hay and making $6,500 without lifting a finger. Taking this on would mean taking on risk and hard work, all over again.

I'm keen for him to jump in, but I temper my enthusiasm. I tell him this is his life. Of course, he and Amelia have to decide what is best. They have Harrison nearing college age now, with Janie and Dalton not too far behind.

I try to think about what's stopping him. I tell him I can help him with a Kickstarter. Maybe we can subsidize his costs? Maybe we can help raise the start-up money for the transition. I'm sure the public will hear his story and want to help. People are always asking me what happened to the brave Craig Watts, and I have never stopped feeling guilty that, because he worked with me, he lost his main source of income. I know he doesn't regret it, but I can't help but feel bad. I want a different ending for Craig Watts. I want a different option for all those farmers out there who want to break free of the shackles of factory farming. I have to believe there is more to their story.

I came to realize in working with these farmers that they were not raising animals in this way because they enjoyed it. They were doing it because they had few other options to stay on the land, to lead that way of life. I thought of the misty mountains and valleys of West Virginia, the steaming swamps and meadows of North Carolina. These are beautiful, breathtaking places, places where you can let your kids run free and watch the seasons pass. These places and the people living in them are critical threads in the the quilt that is America. They are also the victims of our bad food-system choices, the bearers of the deep negative impacts that factory farming has.

But what if we turned that around? What if we offered an alternative that still allowed farmers to stay on the land, to pay their bills, send their kids to college and enjoy that way of life? What if those farmers grew plants instead to deliver protein to the masses?

This is a fundamental question we must address in order to construct the world we want. We can't just make farmers disappear; we have to build them up and prepare them for the future protein market and the world we seek. If we crack this problem and take out these foundational bricks of factory farming so that we can use them to build a new foundation, a bright future for these farmers, then the whole factory-farming system would crumble.

★ ★ ★

Sometimes the road is twisted, full of potholes, traffic lights, and construction. I tend to do very well on these roads. I like the challenge. It forces you to focus and be present. You keep going because you believe it will get better, because you need it to be better. Eventually, with some persistence, it does get better. The road turns smooth.

During these times, there is finally a moment to pause and reflect. You look around and ask, "Is this the path I am meant to be on?" Then, after a long stretch of this easier driving, you may come to an unexpected option to turn onto a different road. The view is obscured. You don't know where it leads, except you know it is connected to the road you are on. You will have to trust your gut as to whether to go for it or not.

It was a time when Compassion in World Farming (CIWF) USA had, for the second year in a row, doubled in size. Our funding was secure and the team seemingly unstoppable. As executive director, it was a time to reap the benefits of building a stable and productive organization—to watch it thrive and achieve for farmed animals. But then in July 2018, unexpectedly, I was presented with an option for my career to take a different road.

One evening, Mercy For Animals' founder Milo Runkle asked to speak to me. He put it simply: the board wanted me to lead the organization and become its president.

I had long admired Mercy For Animals, an organization I knew had endless potential. Their investigation team is one of the strongest in the world, having done more than 65 major undercover investigations since their inception. Their investigations into Walmart's and McDonald's egg suppliers had created the necessary pressure to achieve some of the most important animal-policy changes in our country's history. Their legislative team is also strong, having time and time again secured groundbreaking animal-cruelty convictions. Mercy For Animals reaches out to the public, raising awareness not just about how animals are treated on factory farms but also about the wonderful benefits of leaving animals off our plates. They have strategically built offices

where factory farming is spreading and exploding: China,
India, Brazil, Canada, the United States, and Mexico. They
have the power and resources—and the global presence—to
play a major role in ending factory farming.

I was honored to be asked to lead an organization I admired
so much, but that would also mean leaving an organization I
loved. I had started CIWF USA nearly eight years earlier
with just two days of pay and a laptop. I felt so privileged to
have been able to lead and witness its growth. But I also knew
with 100 per-cent certainty that, if I chose to walk away,
Rachel Dreskin, with whom I had been working closely over
the years, would be able to take the torch and continue the
organization's success.

The board members and I went back and forth, as I began
sifting through my questions. Then one Thursday, Milo
called and offered to go through the remaining questions in
person. By Friday afternoon I found him on my front porch.

We spent every waking hour of that weekend discussing
strategy and our hopes and dreams for the future. In the final
hours of his stay, we visited the historic Martin Luther King
Memorial. We sat in the pews of Ebenezer Church in Atlanta,
where King once gave his sermons. We stood in front of the
house where King was born, a humble home on Auburn
Avenue in downtown Atlanta. We passed through the halls of
the memorial, hearing, seeing, and reading the abuses and
hatred that were once normal in this country. We moved to
the photographs and videos of the protests, the strategies, the
sheer and unbelievable courage demonstrated not just by
King but by so many individuals who simply would not stand
down in the face of injustice. They risked their lives. They
gave everything they had to build a better world.

Each of us, to undo injustice, must push ourselves on a path
of courage and give the most we can give, be the best we can
be; we must refuse the smooth and easy road. Leading CIWF
USA had become comfortable for me. But was it my highest
use? While I loved CIWF, I knew it would continue to do
good work under its current global leadership. Mercy For
Animals, however, needed a president.

It was there, standing in the church where King gave his sermons, that I knew I would go to Mercy For Animals. It was an organization that was on the same path as CIWF, working to create a better world for farmed animals. Nonviolent leaders like King spoke of building constructive pathways to bring about justice. This means not just pointing out what is wrong, but engaging and actively building what is right.

Mercy For Animals is not just saying we need a plant-based world; they are actively building one. They had provided the seed money to start the Good Food Institute, the organization Bruce leads. They also help establish New Crop Capital, which "views conventional animal agriculture as an antiquated and inefficient food-production system with serious vulnerabilities that is ripe for innovation and large-scale disruption." They had expansive institutional corporate work in multiple countries getting schools and hospitals to increase plant-based options. They had powerful popular presence, reaching into the homes of millions to promote a plant-based world. All this alongside the work to get companies to treat farmed animals better.

Mark Twain once said: "Twenty years from now you will be more disappointed by the things that you didn't do than by the ones you did do. So throw off the bowlines. Sail away from the safe harbor. Catch the trade winds in your sails."

I knew that leaving my "safe harbor" would not be easy. To continue the theme: "A ship in the harbor is safe; but that's not what ships were built for." But I took the turn. I left my safe harbor. I would continue to work in this new capacity, building a better world for farmed animals—and for us all.

Epilogue: 2050

It's 2050. It's been more than 30 years since this book was published, depicting a wave of change in our food and farming systems. My kids are grown. Asher's got two of his own now, my grandbabies. I watched my three babies grow. I watched them struggle, overcome challenges, and triumph. I saw them formulate their dreams and become adults who thrive in the world.

I am proud that they each found their way in the world. I have deep regrets that I missed parts of their growing up because I was out working. I can't get those years back, and I will always wish I could have been everything to them. But I am now at peace; there were no bad choices. I did the best I could to raise my kids right and to show them through example how to follow your dreams, persevere, and dedicate yourself to making the world a better place. I will always be proud that I was part of a wave of change that gave them a better world than the one I brought them into.

Over the past 30 years, I have watched the world's food choices change. I watched something extraordinary and unexpected happen. Perdue and Tyson embraced what at first were seen as "alternatives"—but like electricity to gaslight, the "alternative" soon became the obvious choice. I watched the problem change. I watched our sense of "the other" change. Perceptions and loyalties shifted. We realized what unified us was our one humanity, this one planet. We expanded the conversation. There was no us against them. There was only us against a destructive, unjust system that was entirely within our capacity to change. And we set out to change it. Enemies became heroes. Opponents became collaborators.

Tyson announced it was developing its own clean-meat facilities and scaling for market at a rapid pace. Perdue licensed clean-meat technology and was also rushing to get to market.

Cargill held strong to its investment in Memphis Meats. By 2025, clean meat was on the shelves. Consumers embraced it. The dominant view was that it was indeed cleaner—made in sterile conditions, as opposed to surrounded by the host of contaminants found on factory farms.

But Tyson, Cargill, and Perdue also kept divisions in their companies that developed plant-based options, too. After all, they had the equipment already set up to produce nuggets and cutlets—all they had to do was change the main ingredient. By 2030, 25 per cent of their production was plant-based. By 2040, over half. And the majority of the meat they were producing was now clean meat.

Farm-sourced meat—what little is still produced—now only comes from regenerative organic farms. Legislation was passed that prohibited farming practices that were destructive to the soil. The regenerative farms grew, and farmers embraced their responsibility first and foremost to heal the soil. The landscapes of rural America began to change.

Companies now embraced "protein" rather than "meat" as their purpose. Perdue announced that its vision was to "feed protein to a hungry world," and its purpose was to "be the number one provider of premium protein." Not meat. Protein.

Farmers increasingly found their voice. They formed unions; they rose up. And as the alternative-protein market grew, so did the opportunities in rural America to join a more just, humane, and sustainable form of food production. Chicken sheds were turned into mushroom-growing facilities and lettuce and strawberry greenhouses, using solar energy, off grid. Corn and silage production turned to yellow-pea production for some of the largest meat companies, basing our nation's protein on regenerative, organic, plant-based sources. Very few animals were left in the fields or on the shelves.

Now, in the summer of 2050, Ben and I are driving with our grandkids through North Carolina. Our tradition of camping, escaping into the mountains, has carried on.

I remember driving through here with my own kids in 2015. I remember they pointed to the old tobacco barns used for drying tobacco and asked what there were. I told them people used to smoke a lot, but we figured out that was terrible, and the farms died along with those poor choices.

Now my grandchildren are asking me what those rusted metal longhouses are.

I pause to reflect. What were they?

They were a mistake—a brief mistake. For about 70 years, we thought it was a good idea to shove chickens wall to wall in a barn and raise them in the dark. To feed and breed them so they'd grow as fast as they could, all so we could have protein.

My grandchildren are staring at the dilapidated houses, considering them. Some of the metal has been sold, stripped, and repurposed. But the houses are a thing of the past, a relic, a reminder of a brief wrong turn. We almost burnt out the planet's lightbulb. We almost let a terrible food system destroy this beautiful planet—the only planet we have— and all the creatures on it. Thank goodness we didn't. Thank goodness we were able to turn it around before it was too late.

Craig Watts and I are old now. We both have grandkids. I visit him from time to time. We sit on his porch. He's retired. In his second career as an activist, he helped farmers find their voice. He led them out of the oppressive ways of factory farming and helped them find alternatives, where their chicken sheds were converted into more lucrative means of raising food: peas, mushroom, hemp; regenerative organic, strawberries in a greenhouse. He helped transform rural America.

A UN summit was called where 180 nations all agreed that industrial animal agriculture was the single biggest threat to the future of food security and biodiversity. Targets were set. Subsidies were ended.

In time, life started to return to the planet. Species of bees that had not seen for two decades and were thought extinct returned from the mountains where they had been hiding to the fields, and the fields filled with wildflowers. The planet would never fully recover, but it would regenerate. It would go on. Mother Nature is tough. And she forgave us for our mistake.

In 2050, Compassion in World Farming, Mercy For Animals, and other advocacy organizations shut their doors. They had grand parties across the world to celebrate; in London, Los Angeles, Tokyo, Sydney, Johannesburg, and beyond. It was the most joyous ending of a social-justice movement one can imagine. Our work was done. Factory farming had been outpaced, out-competed by new, better businesses, new food, and a better way. The work had evolved, and many who had once worked to protect farmed animals became entrepreneurs inventing the future of food. Motivated by a passion to create another world, a world we could be happy to hand off to our grandchildren, these businesses thrived.

I watched shelves and menus transform. Each year, I watched caged eggs or factory-farmed chicken or feedlot beef diminish, until they were gone altogether. The aisles in my supermarket, once laden with plastic-wrapped meats and milk and eggs with confusing and meaningless labels, now carry very few animal products.

My grown daughter orders her food digitally, and there are no bad choices for her on these virtual shelves. She clicks on bluefin tuna made from clean meat—generated from cells in a lab, innocent of destroying the seas or the cruelty of slaughter. She picks her favorite cashew yogurt and some nuggets made from pea protein.

What a relief it is for me to watch my daughter do this—to know that she does not have to worry about inadvertently buying into a system in which she doesn't believe. This generation has a bright new world that I did not have when I was growing up. My grandchildren have a world where cruelty is not an option on the shelves and menus. My children have been able to get on with living happy, fulfilled lives, fighting other urgent injustices and raising families, unburdened with any deep moral dilemmas about what to eat or not eat.

This is the world my grandchildren will grow up in: a world with only good choices on the shelf.

References

Prologue

1 https://www.nass.usda.gov/Quick_Stats/Ag_Overview/
stateOverview.php?state=GEORGIA
2 http://www.animalvisuals.org/projects/data/slaughter
3 https://www.nationalchickencouncil.org/about-the-industry/
statistics/chicken-broiler-and-other-production-head-
and-live-weight/
4 http://www.nationalchickencouncil.org/americans-to-
eat-1-3-billion-chicken-wings-for-super-bowl-50/
5 http://www.nationalchickencouncil.org/americans-to-consume-
1-25-billion-chicken-wings-super-bowl-weekend/
6 http://www.npr.org/sections/thesalt/2012/06/27/155527365/
visualizing-a-nation-of-meat-eaters
7 https://www.nationalchickencouncil.org/about-the-industry/
statistics/chicken-broiler-and-other-production-head-and-
live-weight/
8 https://www.ers.usda.gov/topics/animal-products/
9 http://www.nationalchickencouncil.org/about-the-industry/
statistics/broiler-chicken-industry-key-facts/
10 https://www.theguardian.com/environment/radical-
conservation/2016/nov/05/
birds-intelligence-tools-crows-parrots-conservation-ethics-
chickens

Chapter 1: The Determined Mother Duck

1 https://www.telegraph.co.uk/news/science/science-
news/8370301/Chickens-are-capable-of-feeling-empathy-
scientists-believe.html
2 http://journals.plos.org/plosone/article?id=10.1371/journal.
pone.0001545 Knowles et al. Leg Disorders in Broiler
Chickens: Prevalence, Risk Factors and Prevention, PLOS,
February 6, 2008.

3   Lori Marino, Thinking chickens: a review of cognition, emotion, and behavior in the domestic chicken. Received: 19 September 2015 / Revised: 30 November 2016 / Accepted: 4 December 2016 The Author(s) 2016. This article is published with open access at Springerlink.com Animal Cognition, DOI 10.1007/s10071-016-1064-4

4   Ham AD, Osorio D (2007) Colour preferences and colour vision in poultry chicks. Proc R Soc B 274: 1941–1948

5   Gleich O, Langemann U (2011) Auditory capabilities of birds in relation to the structural diversity of the basilar papilla. Hear Res 273:80–88

6   Dawkins MS (1995) How do hens view other hens—the use of lateral and binocular visual-fields in social recognition. Behaviour 132:591–606 Dawkins MS, Woodington A (1997) Distance and the presentation of visual stimuli to birds. Anim Behav 54:1019–1025

7   Rugani R, Regolin L, Vallortigara G (2008) Discrimination of small numerosities in young chicks. J Exp Psychol Anim B 34:388–399, Rugani R, Fontanari L, Simoni E, Regolin L, Vallortigara G (2009) Arithmetic in newborn chicks. Proc R Soc B 276:2451–2460 Rugani R, Regolin L, Vallortigara G (2010) Imprinted numbers: newborn chicks' sensitivity to number vs. continuous extent of objects they have been reared with. Dev Sci 13:790–797

8   Rugani R, Vallortigara G, Priftis K, Regolin L (2015) Number-space mapping in the newborn chick resembles humans' mental number line. Science 347(6221): 534–536

9   https://www.nytimes.com/2016/05/01/books/review/ are-we-smart-enough-to-know-how-smart-animals-are- and-the-genius-of-birds.html?_r=0

10 Freire R, Munro U, Rogers LJ, Sagasser S, Wiltschko R, Wiltshko W (2008) Different responses in two strains of chickens in a magnetic orientation test. Anim Cogn 11:547–552

11 Balcombe J (2007) Pleasurable kingdom: animals and the nature of feeling good. McMillan, New York

12 Mellor DJ. Updating Animal Welfare Thinking: Moving beyond the "Five Freedoms" towards "A Life Worth Living". Animals 2016, 6(3), 21; doi:10.3390/ani6030021

13 @richcampaigns and @pellio88

Chapter 2: The Belly of the Beast

1 The New Georgia Encyclopedia. http://www. georgiaencyclopedia.org/nge/Article.jsp?id=h-2120 , accessed April 17, 2017.

2 The New Georgia Encyclopedia. http://www.georgiaen cyclopedia.org/nge/Article.jsp?id=h-2120 , accessed April 17, 2017.

3 http://www.georgiaencyclopedia.org/articles/business-economy/poultry

4 https://www.ers.usda.gov/amber-waves/2003/november/ from-supply-push-to-demand-pull-agribusiness-strategies-for-today-s-consumers/ Accessed April 17, 2017

5 http://www.georgiaencyclopedia.org/articles/business-economy/poultry

6 http://www.georgiaencyclopedia.org/articles/business-economy/poultry

7 http://www.georgiaencyclopedia.org/articles/business-economy/poultry

8 http://rafiusa.org/blog/big-chicken-companies-own-and-control-everything-except-the-farm-why/

9 http://www.georgiaencyclopedia.org/articles/business-economy/gold-kist-inc

10 https://www.nass.usda.gov/Statistics_by_State/Georgia/ Publications/More_Features/GA_BragSheet2015.pdf

11 http://modernfarmer.com/2014/05/ today-eating-winners-1948-chicken-tomorrow-contest/

12 https://en.wikipedia.org/wiki/ The_Great_Atlantic_%26_Pacific_Tea_Company

13 https://en.wikipedia.org/wiki/The_Great_Atlantic_%26_ Pacific_Tea_Company

14 http://modernfarmer.com/2014/05/today-eating-winners-1948-chicken-tomorrow-contest/

15 https://www.youtube.com/watch?v=uPYYwdI0tIc
16 http://www.cobb-vantress.com/about-cobb/who-we-are/
     our-history
17 http://www.thepoultrysite.com/focus/cobb/59/
     cobb-500-the-worlds-most-efficient
18 Knowles TG, Kestin SC, Haslam SM, Brown SN, Green LE,
     et al. (2008) Leg Disorders in Broiler Chickens: Prevalence,
     Risk Factors and Prevention. PLoS ONE 3(2): e1545.
     doi:10.1371/journal.pone.0001545. http://www.plosone.
     org/article/info%3Adoi%2F10.1371%2Fjournal.pone.
     0001545
19 http://www.nationalchickencouncil.org/about-the-industry/
     statistics/u-s-broiler-performance/
20 Originally from an article published in the LEISA, April
     2002, Leah Garces, The 'Livestock Revolution' and its
     impact on smallholders
21 http://www.foodsafetynews.com/2013/01/why-we-havent-
     seen-inside-a-broiler-chicken-factory-farm-in-a-decade/#_
     ftn1
22 https://www.statista.com/statistics/237597/leading-10-
     countries-worldwide-in-poultry-meat-production-in-
     2007/
23 http://www.humanesociety.org/news/resources/research/
     stats_top_states.html?credit=web_id97753650
24 http://www.humanesociety.org/news/resources/research/
     stats_slaughter_totals.html?referrer=https://www.google.
     com/
25 https://www.agcensus.usda.gov/Publications/2012/Online_
     Resources/County_Profiles/Georgia/cp13119.pdf
26 The county of Franklin has 22,084 people and and nearly 20
     million broiler chickens at any one time.
27 https://quickstats.nass.usda.gov/results/008D4B0E-
     D8D8-3AF1-BDFE-DD95CC1B22E8
28 Food and Water Watch, Factory Farm Nation: How America
     Turned Its Livestock Farms into Factories, 2010. From the
     2007 Farm Census.
29 http://rafiusa.org/blog/big-chicken-companies-own-and-
     control-everything-except-the-farm-why/

30 http://www.opensecrets.org/lobby/indusclient.php?id=
    A09&year=2016
31 http://www.opensecrets.org/industries/indus.php?ind=A09
32 http://www.opensecrets.org/industries/indus.php?ind=
    A09
33 http://www.opensecrets.org/lobby/clientsum.php?id=
    D000042332&year=2015
34 https://www.washingtonpost.com/business/2018/10/16/
    trump-team-makes-controversial-change-allow-chicken-
    plants-operate-faster-speeds/?fbclid=IwAR2fvVkOiR2oIH1
    8F8SldCq_cHJYHVyQeVBAhF1MG9X1X-yySHq8r4
    GAh40&noredirect=on&utm_term=.ca139d2b0412
35 https://www.opensecrets.org/industries/lobbying.php?
    cycle=2016&ind=A05
36 http://www.foodandwaterwatch.org/food/farm-bill-2012/
    fair-farm-rules/

Chapter 3: No Good Choices

1 https://www.youtube.com/watch?v=EwdJAjbV-Ac
2 https://www.youtube.com/watch?v=EwdJAjbV-Ac
3 http://www.prnewswire.com/news-releases/kroger-
    introduces-simple-truth-and-simple-truth-organic-brands-
    available-exclusively-at-krogers-family-of-stores-170985811.
    html
4 http://www.care2.com/causes/chicken-poop-thanks-to-the-
    fda-its-whats-for-dinner.html

Chapter 4: The Unlikely Alliance

1 https://www.aspca.org/animal-cruelty/farm-animal-welfare/
    what-ag-gag-legislation
2 http://www.nbcnews.com/news/other/tyson-foods-dumps-
    pig-farm-after-nbc-shows-company-video-f2D11627571
3 http://cok.net/inv/pilgrims/
4 http://bizwest.com/
    pilgrims-pride-investigating-alleged-chicken-abuse-2/

5 http://www.nationalchickencouncil.org/about-the-industry/
   statistics/u-s-broiler-performance/
6 http://www.learnnc.org/lp/editions/nchist-recent/6260

Chapter 5: Crossing Enemy Lines

1 http://www.thepoultrysite.com/publications/6/diseases-of-
   poultry/196/laryngotracheitis/

Chapter 6: The Story Breaks

1 https://www.theguardian.com/environment/2013/feb/12/
   monsanto-sues-farmers-seed-patents
2 https://www.nytimes.com/2013/05/14/business/monsanto-
   victorious-in-genetic-seed-case.html
3 https://www.washingtonpost.com/news/wonk/wp/2014/
   12/08/
   the-not-so-humane-way-humanely-raised-chickens-are-
   being-raised/?utm_term=.64affdf47c2a
4 http://www.nationalchickencouncil.org/
   expert-panel-examines-video-north-carolina-broiler-farm/
5 http://www.nationalchickencouncil.org/
   expert-panel-examines-video-north-carolina-broiler-farm/

Chapter 7: Farmers Coming Out of the Woodwork

1 http://rafiusa.org/undercontractfilm/wp-content/
   uploads/2017/01/Under_Contract_Viewers-Guide_2017_
   ReducedFileSize.pdf
2 MacDonald, James. (2014). Technology, Organization, and
   Financial Performance in U.S. Broiler Production. Economic
   Information Bulletin No. (EIB-126). 53pp, June. http://bit.
   ly/2ghOj8b
3 http://interactive.fusion.net/cock-fight/
4 https://www.arktimes.com/arkansas/is-big-poultry-fair-to-
   farmers/Content?oid=4316484
5 http://www.huffingtonpost.com/2011/08/17/chicken-
   prices_n_929132.html

6 https://www.arktimes.com/arkansas/is-big-poultry-fair-to-farmers/Content?oid=4316484
7 https://www.cdc.gov/drugresistance/threat-report-2013/pdf/ar-threats-2013-508.pdf#page=41
8 http://www.fda.gov/downloads/ForIndustry/UserFees/AnimalDrugUserFeeActADUFA/UCM338170.pdf
9 http://www.foodsafetynews.com/2013/09/drug-resistant-infections/#.Wtds_i7waM9
10 https://www.cdc.gov/drugresistance/threat-report-2013/pdf/ar-threats-2013-508.pdf#page=6
11 https://www.cdc.gov/drugresistance/threat-report-2013/pdf/ar-threats-2013-508.pdf#page=6
12 McKenna, Maryn, *Big Chicken*, National Geographic, 2017. Pg. 24-25
13 http://pages.jh.edu/jhumag/0609web/farm.html

Chapter 8: How Healthy Is Chicken, Really?

1 http://www.thepoultrysite.com/publications/6/diseases-of-poultry/186/gangrenous-dermatitis/
2 http://www.thepoultrysite.com/cocciforum/issue12b/94/cover-story-solving-the-gangrenous-dermatitis-puzzle/
3 http://www.thepoultrysite.com/cocciforum/issue12b/94/cover-story-solving-the-gangrenous-dermatitis-puzzle/
4 http://www.nationalchickencouncil.org/about-the-industry/statistics/u-s-broiler-performance/
5 https://www.npr.org/sections/thesalt/2014/02/14/276976353/americans-want-antibiotic-free-chicken-and-the-industry-is-listening
6 http://www.nytimes.com/2013/10/02/business/fda-bans-three-arsenic-drugs-used-in-poultry-and-pig-feeds.html
7 https://www.foodandwaterwatch.org/sites/default/files/poisonfreepoultry.pdf
8 https://www.wsj.com/articles/pilgrims-expects-25-of-its-chicken-will-be-antibiotic-free-by-2019-1429564675
9 https://www.buzzfeed.com/venessawong/sanderson-ceo-denies-role-antibiotic-resistance?utm_term=.roELn9Lvw#.uekKZYKb9

10 https://www.fooddive.com/news/sanderson-farms-says-
the-us-has-an-oversupply-of-antibiotic-free-chicken/
514982/

11 https://www.nytimes.com/2016/04/17/opinion/sunday/
animal-cruelty-or-the-price-of-dinner.html?_r=0

12 http://www.nationalchickencouncil.org/wp-content/
uploads/2016/04/ACRP-broiler-video-04.19.16-
FINAL.pdf

13 https://www.youtube.com/watch?v=ZVfHcXUUns&feature
=youtu.be&app=desktop

14 http://feedstuffs.com/story-expert-panel-assesses-new-broiler-
farm-undercover-video-45-140309

15 Daniel, Carrie R, Amanda J Cross, Corinna Koebnick, and
Rashmi Sinha. "Trends in Meat Consumption in the USA."
Public Health Nutrition 14, no. 4 (April 2011): 575–83.
doi:10.1017/S1368980010002077

16 http://www.nationalchickencouncil.org/wp-content/
uploads/2016/04/ACRP-broiler-video-04.19.16-FINAL.
pdf

17 Havenstein, G., P. Ferket, and M. Qureshi. "Growth,
Livability, and Feed Conversion of 1957 versus 2001 Broilers
When Fed Representative 1957 and 2001 Broiler Diets."
Poultry Science 82, no. 10 (October 1, 2003): 1500–1508.
doi:10.1093/ps/82.10.1500.

18 Aviagen (2012) Ross 308 broiler performance objectives.
In-house publication, global. Aviagen Ltd.,Newbridge,
UK.

19 Bailey, Richard A., Kellie A. Watson, S. F. Bilgili, and
Santiago Avendano. "The Genetic Basis of Pectoralis Major
Myopathies in Modern Broiler Chicken Lines." Poultry
Science, October 16, 2015, pev304. doi:10.3382/ps/pev304.

20 Bailey, Richard A., Kellie A. Watson, S. F. Bilgili, and
Santiago Avendano. "The Genetic Basis of Pectoralis Major
Myopathies in Modern Broiler Chicken Lines." Poultry
Science, October 16, 2015, pev304. doi:10.3382/ps/pev304.

21 Gee, K. 2016. Poultry's tough new problem: 'Woody Breast'.
Wall Street Journal. Sect. Business and Tech, Mar 29.
CCLXVII: B1.

Chapter 9: The Radicals

1 https://www.cnbc.com/2017/03/22/egg-makers-are-freaked-out-by-the-cage-free-future.html
2 http://www.foodservicedirector.com/industry-news-opinion/news/articles/delaware-north-opting-cage-free-eggs
3 https://beta.theglobeandmail.com/report-on-business/international-business/us-business/centerplate-ceo-steps-down-after-dog-abuse-incident-in-vancouver/article20297029/?ref=http://www.theglobeandmail.com&

Chapter 10: The Year the Impossible Happened

1 https://www.agupdate.com/todaysproducer/news/livestock/process-established-for-addressing-hidden-camera-investigations/article_77796174-7365-11e1-8d6c-0019bb2963f4.html
2 https://lovemypeople.me/tag/dr-bernard-lafayette/
3 http://www.madeinalabama.com/2017/12/shaw-to-invest-184-million-in-alabama-fiber-manufacturing-facility/
4 https://waynefarms.com/wayne-farms-media/news-releases/161-wayne-farms-launches-gap-step-2-rated-products
5 David Halberstam, The Children, 1st ed. (New York: Random House, 1998), 136 – 37.; Siracusa, Anthony. Disrupting the Calculation of Violence: James M. Lawson, Jr. and the Politics of Nonviolence; Masters Thesis, May 2015. Graduate School at Vanderbilt University https://etd.library.vanderbilt.edu/available/etd-03232015-130857/unrestricted/Siracusa.pdf
6 http://www.huffingtonpost.com/entry/compass-group-aramark-animal-welfare_us_581b6704e4b0b8e11a134130
7 https://www.bloomberg.com/news/articles/2018-09-05/perdue-explores-non-meat-options-as-plant-protein-appetite-grows

Chapter 11: Business as Usual Is Not an Option

1 https://www.theguardian.com/environment/2017/aug/01/meat-industry-dead-zone-gulf-of-mexico-environment-pollution?CMP=fb_gu

2	http://www.mightyearth.org/heartlanddestruction/
3	http://www.mightyearth.org/heartlanddestruction/
4	http://markets.businessinsider.com/news/stocks/tyson-foods-sets-two-million-acre-land-stewardship-targetlargest-ever-sustainable-grain-commitment-by-a-u-s-protein-company-initiative-part-of-tyson-foods-new-sustainability-report-1020345922
5	http://www.fao.org/Newsroom/en/news/2006/1000448/index.html
6	http://www.fao.org/newsroom/en/news/2006/1000448/index.html
7	http://www.nature.com/nclimate/journal/v4/n10/full/nclimate2353.html
8	http://www.climatecentral.org/news/studies-link-red-meat-and-climate-change-20264
9	Lymbery, Philip. Deadzone. Bloomsbury, 2017.
10	https://www.buzzfeed.com/venessawong/egg-makers-are-freaked-out-by-the-cage-free-future
11	https://ourworldindata.org/meat-and-seafood-production-consumption
12	https://www.independent.co.uk/life-style/food-and-drink/white-meat-red-more-popular-uk-britain-beef-chicken-turkey-lamb-pork-a7816041.html
13	https://www.poultryworld.net/Meat/Articles/2017/7/US-chicken-consumption-at-all-time-high-but-consumers-concerned-160217E/?cmpid=NLC%7Cworldpoultry%7C2017-07-19%7CUS_chicken_consumption_at_all-time_high_but_consumers_share_concerns_
14	https://www.chicken.org.au/its-official-chicken-remains-australias-favourite-meat/
15	https://psmag.com/news/why-our-food-choices-are-determined-by-price-and-not-ethics-or-morals
16	http://www.climatecentral.org/news/studies-link-red-meat-and-climate-change-20264; http://www.wri.org/blog/2016/04/sustainable-diets-what-you-need-know-12-charts
17	https://www.telegraph.co.uk/news/earth/earthnews/3351013/Anchovies-join-cod-on-threatened-fish-list.html

18 https://www.theguardian.com/commentisfree/2017/may/16/
    meat-eaters-soil-degradation-over-grazing
19 Mintel, Plant-based Proteins, US, 2018.
20 Mintel, Poultry, US, November 2017.
21 https://www.researchandmarkets.com/research/gsv3jm/
    global_plant
22 https://www.nrdc.org/sites/default/files/less-beef-less-
    carbon-ip.pdf
23 https://www.theguardian.com/world/2016/jun/20/chinas-
    meat-consumption-climate-change
24 https://www.fastcompany.com/3068567/the-german-environment-
    ministry-makes-the-government-go-vegetarian
25 http://www.humanesociety.org/news/news/2010/01/
    compass_flexitarian.html?credit=web_id98471710
26 https://www.usnews.com/news/articles/2015/06/12/egg-
    shortage-amid-avian-flu-outbreak-scrambles-us-food-
    industries
27 http://www.foodsafetynews.com/2014/07/after-17-months-
    foster-farms-salmonella-outbreak-declared-over/
28 https://www.cdc.gov/salmonella/heidelberg-10-13/

Chapter 12: Regeneration

1 David Bronner, Regenerative Organic Panel, Expo West 2018.
   wefl
2 https://www.fastcompany.com/40541750/regenerative-
   organic-certification-wants-to-be-the-ethical-label-to-rule-
   them-all
3 Regenerative Organic Panel, Expo West 2018, Jeff Moyer.
4 in Res. Issues Relat. Strateg. Plan. U. S. Agric.Glob. Setting
   Proc. Minutes Thirty-Sixth Annu.Meet. Agric. Res. Inst. Oct.
   7-9 1987 Wash. DC(Agriculture Research Institute (U.S.) &
   Rodale, R.) (Agricultural Research Institute, 1987).
5 Rodale Institute, Regenerative Organic Agriculture and
   Climate Change. A Down-to-Earth Solution to Global
   Warming, https://rodaleinstitute.org/assets/WhitePaper.pdf
6 Patagonia, Inc. is an American clothing company that markets
   and sells sustainable outdoor clothing.

7 https://en.wikipedia.org/wiki/Rose_Marcario
8 http://fortune.com/2015/09/14/rose-marcario-patagonia/
9 http://fortune.com/2015/09/14/rose-marcario-patagonia/
10 https://www.drbronner.com/about/ourselves/
   the-dr-bronners-story/

Chapter 13: Tempt, Don't Bully, Darlings

1 http://www.un.org/en/development/desa/news/population/
   2015-report.html
2 https://www.geekwire.com/2017/can-faux-meat-deliver-
   meaty-profits-entrepreneurs-survey-food-frontier/
3 http://www.nytimes.com/2016/10/11/business/tyson-foods-a-
   meat-leader-invests-in-protein-alternatives.html
4 http://fortune.com/2016/12/05/
   tyson-foods-launches-vc-fund/
5 https://www.livekindly.co/tyson-foods-ceo-wants-to-disrupt-
   the-meat-industry-with-clean-meat/
6 https://www.livekindly.co/tyson-foods-ceo-wants-to-disrupt-
   the-meat-industry-with-clean-meat/
7 https://www.prnewswire.com/news-releases/global-plant-milk-
   market-to-top-us-16-billion-in-2018--dairy-alternative-drinks-
   are-booming-says-innova-market-insights-300472693.html

Chapter 14: Brontosaurus Burger

1 http://teachingamericanhistory.org/library/document/
   fifty-years-hence/
2 Yue, et al. Mapping stem cell activities in the feather follicle.
   Nature. 2005 Dec 15; 438(7070): 1026–1029. https://www.
   ncbi.nlm.nih.gov/pmc/articles/PMC4392896/
3 https://qz.com/1077183/
   the-idea-for-lab-grown-meat-was-born-in-a-prisoner-of-war-
   camp/
4 http://fortune.com/2017/05/01/
   hampton-creek-unicorn-management/
5 https://www.geekwire.com/2017/can-faux-meat-deliver-
   meaty-profits-entrepreneurs-survey-food-frontier/

6 http://www.history.com/topics/golden-gate-bridge
7 http://www.sfgate.com/food/article/Memphis-Meats-introduces-lab-cultured-chicken-and-11003907.php
8 http://www.businessinsider.com/memphis-meats-chicken-lab-grown-2017-3
9 https://www.wsj.com/articles/hampton-creek-aims-at-new-market-growing-meat-1498592294?mg=prod/accounts-wsj
10 https://www.eatjust.com/en-us/stories/clean-meat
11 http://www.globalmeatnews.com/Industry-Markets/Lab-grown-meat-firm-in-talks-to-license-tech
12 https://www.cargill.com/meat-poultry/cargill-meat-solutions
13 https://www.businessinsider.com.au/how-we-eat-meat-around-the-world-2014-1
14 https://qz.com/1075989/china-wants-to-import-israels-vegan-meat-technology/
15 https://qz.com/1075989/china-wants-to-import-israels-vegan-meat-technology/
16 http://articles.latimes.com/1999/feb/08/business/fi-6022
17 Dance, Amber. NATURE BIOTECHNOLOGY, VOLUME 35, NUMBER 8, AUGUST 2017
18 https://www.ci.emeryville.ca.us/659/Americans-Arrive-1840s-to-1890s
19 https://www.prnewswire.com/news-releases/perfect-day-on-its-way-to-bringing-animal-free-dairy-to-store-shelves-300604592.html

Chapter 15: The Win–Win

1 http://www.mcspotlight.org/cgi-bin/album.pl?6&show&12
2 http://www.mcspotlight.org/case/index.html
3 http://www.mcspotlight.org/case/trial/transcripts/index.html
4 http://www.ethicalcorp.com/content/kfc-and-peta
5 http://arff.org/gestation-crates
6 https://qz.com/1171500/germanys-largest-chicken-producer-wants-to-bring-vegan-meat-to-market/

Acknowledgements

To Come

Index

To Come